UNDERSTANDING
OLD TESTAMENT
THEOLOGY

UNDERSTANDING OLD TESTAMENT THEOLOGY

Mapping the Terrain
of Recent Approaches

BRITTANY KIM AND
CHARLIE TRIMM

ZONDERVAN
ACADEMIC

ZONDERVAN ACADEMIC

Understanding Old Testament Theology
Copyright © 2020 by Brittany Kim and Charlie Trimm

Requests for information should be addressed to:
Zondervan, *3900 Sparks Dr. SE, Grand Rapids, Michigan 49546*

Zondervan titles may be purchased in bulk for educational, business, fundraising, or sales promotional use. For information, please email SpecialMarkets@Zondervan.com.

ISBN 978-0-310-10647-0 (softcover)

ISBN 978-0-310-10648-7 (ebook)

Interior Design: Kait Lamphere
Cover Design: Lucas Art & Design
Cover Art: Moses with the Tablets / Public Domain

Printed in the United States of America

20 21 22 23 24 25 26 27 28 29 30 /LSC/ 15 14 13 12 11 10 9 8 7 6 5 4 3 2 1

To our fathers,
Samuel David Jones
(March 17, 1954–April 19, 2014)
and
Kenneth Lewis Trimm
(December 30, 1953–May 25, 2004),
for sharing a fervent devotion to reading great books of all kinds,
instilling in us a deep love for the Old Testament,
and modeling a passionate pursuit of truth

CONTENTS

Preface . . . . *xi*

Introduction. 1

PART 1: HISTORY

1. Old Testament Theology Grounded in Biblical (Hi)story 13
2. Historical-Critical Old Testament Theology 33

PART 2: THEME

3. Multiplex Thematic Old Testament Theology. 55
4. Old Testament Theology Focused around a Central Theme 73

PART 3: CONTEXT

5. Canonical Old Testament Theology 91
6. Jewish Biblical Theology 111
7. Postmodern Old Testament Theology 128

Conclusion. 149

Appendix: Summary of Approaches. 161
Subject Index 163
Author Index. 171
Scripture Index 175

PREFACE

This book has its origin in our Old Testament doctoral program at Wheaton College, which focused on biblical theology. We studied biblical theology in classes, talked frequently about it with fellow students and professors, and read many Old Testament theologies for our comprehensive exams. As a survey of the field, we read Hasel's *Old Testament Theology: Basic Issues in the Current Debate*. However, since the last version of that book is almost thirty years old, the idea occurred to Charlie to write an updated survey. Because of the massive number of entries in the field, he decided to recruit a coauthor. Having already cowritten an article with Brittany that analyzed a divine metaphor in the Old Testament ("YHWH the Dragon: Exploring a Neglected Biblical Metaphor for the Divine Warrior and Its Bearing on the Translation of *'Ap*," *Bible Translator* 65 [2014]: 165–84), he asked her to join the project.

The process of coauthoring a book has worked quite well for us, as it has allowed us to divide up the load of reading and writing, bounce ideas off of each other, and share the sometimes painful process of writing, editing, and even restructuring with someone who is just as emotionally invested in the project. We each wrote half of the chapters and then extensively edited each other's work to provide a consistent narrative voice. (For those who want a basis for an exercise in source and redaction criticism, Brittany wrote the biblical [hi]story chapter and Charlie wrote the historical-critical chapter.)

As we were completing this book, we came across the stained glass image of Moses descending Mount Sinai that appears on the cover. Stained glass has a long history in the church as a visual Bible, so this image evokes the legacy of centuries of Christian worship. However, this particular stained glass window is from a synagogue in Seattle—Temple De Hirsch Sinai—so it also serves as a reminder that the Hebrew Scriptures are the shared inheritance of Jews and Christians, a point we highlight in our chapter on Jewish biblical theology (chap. 6). A further point of connection is that we both grew up in the Seattle area (though we did not meet until graduate school at Wheaton College), so the provenance of this window reflects our own heritage.

More significantly, this image encapsulates the message of our book. First, stained glass windows have a way of bringing stories to life with a play of light that is always changing, making them vibrant and dynamic. The brilliance of the colors attracts our attention, invites our reflection, and beckons us to enter into the story, while also radiating the splendor of God. We hope that this book will help you see the Old Testament in a similar way—as "alive and active" (Heb. 4:12), continually drawing us into a deeper encounter with the living God, who is "clothed with splendor and majesty" and "wraps himself in light as with a garment" (Ps. 104:1–2).

Second, since we offer test cases in the book of Exodus, we highlight several perspectives on the story portrayed in this window: the covenant God makes with Israel at Mount Sinai, which is mediated through Moses. Also, as you will see in the pages that follow, our aim is to guide you in taking your own trek to the top of a mountain to encounter God. Our hope is that as you descend the mountain, you, like Moses, will be transformed. In this stained glass image, the colors of Moses' robes mirror the fiery divine appearance at the top of the mountain, signifying that Moses now reflects God's glory. In one hand he carries the tablets representing the covenant between God and his people, while his other hand stretches upward, pointing both the Israelites and us to God. May your journey up the mountain to meet with God lead you, like Moses, to reflect God's glory, embody the covenant he made with his people, and direct others to look to him.

Finally, we would like to acknowledge the many people who have helped and supported us in the process of preparing for and writing this book. We are grateful to our doctoral mentors at Wheaton College—Dan Block for Charlie, and Richard Schultz for Brittany—for their profound impact on our understanding of the Old Testament and for continued support of our scholarly careers. Ken Way and Darian Lockett have been partners in conversations about biblical theology and have read early versions of a few chapters from this book, and Sean Tosello and Meagan Bare assisted us in compiling the indexes. Charlie's Old Testament ethics and theology classes at Biola University in the fall of 2019 and spring of 2020 read early drafts of the book and offered many helpful observations. The libraries at Biola University, Roberts Wesleyan College, and Wheaton College provided access to hundreds of books and essays for this project, while the libraries at Jerusalem University College, the University of Chicago, and Loyola University Chicago also helped us with sources at key moments.

Talbot School of Theology at Biola University provided a sabbatical for Charlie in the spring of 2019, allowing him to write most of his portion of the book in Israel, Cyprus, and Ireland. Brittany's husband, Ted, enabled her to take mini sabbaticals from her full-time job of caring for their three young children so that she could do much of her writing at coffee shops and take a writing retreat at Cenacle Sisters Retreat Center in Chicago. Her mother, Cheryl Jones, also provided childcare for a crucial period of work, and several other babysitters and friends contributed as well. At Zondervan Academic, Madison Trammel worked with us at the beginning of the project to give it shape, and Katya Covrett and Brian Phipps helped us later on to bring it to fruition. Above all, we are grateful to our families, who demonstrate God's covenantal love toward us, and to God, who never fails to reveal himself to us through the Old Testament.

INTRODUCTION

THE PROMISE AND PROBLEMS OF OLD TESTAMENT THEOLOGY

Even though the Old Testament makes up almost three-fourths of the Bible, churches often give greater attention to the New Testament in their Scripture readings and teaching. When Christians do crack open the pages of the Old Testament, they generally focus on the Psalms, Proverbs, and selected stories, leaving much of its riches untouched. They also struggle to recognize how these various parts of the Old Testament relate to one another. As a result, most Christians (including even many pastors and teachers) are woefully unequipped to understand how God is speaking to them through the Old Testament.

We feel fortunate that our upbringings in the church gave us a deep appreciation for the Old Testament and familiarity with significant portions of it. But our experience of the Old Testament was like walking through a museum, gazing at two-dimensional portrayals of varied landscapes. When we began to study Old Testament theology in the early 2000s, it gave us a much different perspective, like standing on top of a high mountain. Looking in every direction, we could recognize all the landscapes we had admired in the museum, but all their depth and complexity became clear as we saw them for the first time in three dimensions. Also, instead of disconnected paintings on a wall, they appeared as parts of a single panorama, though that did not diminish their variety; we could still see mountains and valleys, deserts and plains, rivers and seas. The whole vista was astounding in its vast expanse and breathtaking in its beauty.

Whatever your experience of the Old Testament has been, we want to help you discover the breathtaking beauty of looking down from the mountaintop, by exploring Old Testament theology. But what is Old Testament theology? As we will see, the definition of Old Testament theology is hotly contested. A recent survey says that biblical theology (including both the Old and New Testaments) "has become a catchphrase, a wax nose that can mean anything from the historical-critical method applied to the Bible to a theological interpretation of Scripture that in practice appears to leave history out of the equation altogether."[1] In a similar vein, Benjamin Sommer claims that "the statement 'I am interested in biblical theology' or 'I am writing an Old Testament theology' just does not communicate anything about our intentions or methods in the way that other statements do, such as, 'I am interested in source criticism of the Pentateuch' or 'I am working on anthropological approaches to the Hebrew Bible.'"[2]

But despite all this debate, a working definition of Old Testament theology would be helpful to get us started. The phrase Old Testament theology itself suggests that it has two essential components. First, it is focused particularly on the Old Testament, in a way that differs from the focus of Christian (or systematic) theology. Whereas Christian theology seeks to organize the various doctrines of the church, often in light of questions that arise in the mind of contemporary generations, Old Testament theology usually aims to describe the theology that emerges from the Old Testament.

Second, the word theology differentiates it both from exegesis (detailed interpretation) and from an examination of Israel's history. Old Testament theology does not simply attempt to understand what the individual texts say (exegesis) or construct a history of events. Instead it seeks to provide us with a picture of YHWH and his relationship to the world as described in the Old Testament.[3] Understood in this way, Old Testament theology functions as a bridge between exegesis of the biblical text and systematic theology. It draws on the interpretation of particular Old Testament passages to build a comprehensive theology of the Old Testament that is in turn used in constructing a systematic theology. At its core, Old Testament theology seeks to reach the heart of the Old Testament. Mark Boda invites readers to join him in using "theological stethoscopes" on the Old Testament "to listen

---

1. Edward W. Klink III and Darian R. Lockett, *Understanding Biblical Theology: A Comparison of Theory and Practice* (Grand Rapids: Zondervan, 2012), 13.

2. Benjamin D. Sommer, "Dialogical Biblical Theology: A Jewish Approach to Reading Scripture Theologically," in *Biblical Theology: Introducing the Conversation*, ed. Leo G. Perdue, Robert Morgan, and Benjamin D. Sommer, Library of Biblical Theology (Nashville: Abingdon, 2009), 20.

3. YHWH (often called the tetragrammaton, meaning "four letters") is the revealed name of God in the Old Testament. Although the original Hebrew text contained only consonants, the name was probably pronounced "Yahweh." Out of a concern to avoid using the divine name irreverently, a tradition developed early in Judaism to avoid pronouncing the name altogether. Wherever YHWH is encountered in the Bible, Jews instead read *Adonai*, which means "Lord." The early Greek translation of the Old Testament (the Septuagint) therefore renders YHWH as *kurios* ("Lord"). Modern English translations also follow this custom, though they distinguish between YHWH and Adonai in the original Hebrew by using small caps for YHWH (Lord) and lowercase characters for Adonai (Lord).

carefully for the heartbeat that shows that the Scriptures are indeed 'living and active'" (Heb. 4:12).[4]

Over the past century the field of Old Testament theology has seen an explosion of growth, a trend that has only intensified in the last few decades. Not only has the number of Old Testament theologies on the market increased significantly, but also the ways scholars are doing Old Testament theology have expanded. While it is encouraging to see such a strong interest in the discipline, the wide array of options can be bewildering, especially for students, pastors, and laypeople who are trying to wade in its tumultuous waters. Even a relatively brief survey of how the phrase Old Testament theology is used reveals that scholars employ it in vastly different ways, many of which are diametrically opposed.

This diversity in Old Testament theology is caused by a series of flash points. These points will be discussed throughout this book, but it will be helpful to introduce readers to some of them now.

1. *Degree of unity.* Is the Old Testament unified in some way? Does a central theme tie the Old Testament together? Should Old Testament theology foreground the diversity of the various biblical books or texts?
2. *Connection with the New Testament.* Should we read the Old Testament as a stand-alone work or as part of the authoritative canon of the church, which also includes the New Testament? Can Jewish scholars engage in biblical theology?
3. *Significance of the interpreter's context.* Should the life context of the Old Testament theologian play a role in interpretation?
4. *Descriptive versus prescriptive.* Should Old Testament theology merely describe what ancient Israel believed, or should it seek to be prescriptive, offering authoritative guidance for the church today?
5. *Theology, history, and method.* What is the relationship between history and theology? Should Old Testament theologians employ historical criticism? What other methods should be used in constructing an Old Testament theology?
6. *Structure.* How should an Old Testament theology be organized?

If Old Testament scholars disagree so broadly on these key issues, leading to different understandings of the nature of Old Testament theology and

---

4. Mark J. Boda, *The Heartbeat of Old Testament Theology: Three Creedal Expressions*, Acadia Studies in Bible and Theology (Grand Rapids: Baker Academic, 2017), 8.

resulting in so many different kinds of Old Testament theologies, how can it be helpful for the church? There is simply too much to read! We seek to address this problem by offering a guide through the maze of publications in the field and giving you a taste of the rich banquet that Old Testament theology spreads for those who accept its invitation. We hope that sampling its delights will make you want to keep coming back for more, perhaps by reading an Old Testament theology or two but also by learning how to read the Old Testament theologically for yourself. Ultimately, we want to inspire you to spend time soaking in the views from the mountaintop so that you come to understand and love the Old Testament in a deeper way.

THE HISTORY OF OLD TESTAMENT THEOLOGY

Since the history of Old Testament theology is long and complicated, we will merely survey the highlights of that history before we spend the majority of the book looking at recent approaches.[5] In a certain sense, biblical theology has existed as long as there has been a Bible. Michael Fishbane in particular has highlighted the role of innerbiblical interpretation in the Old Testament, in which texts interpret other texts theologically within the Old Testament.[6] A good example of this is the frequent allusion to Exodus 34:6–7 throughout the Old Testament.[7] The New Testament also reads the Old Testament theologically when it sees Jesus as the fulfillment of the Old Testament.[8] In the early church, the rule of faith (the standard of belief) could be an early example of something like biblical theology.[9] A later example could be found in the Reformation, which challenged the dominant role of church

---

5. For those who want to read a more detailed history, see John H. Hayes and Frederick C. Prussner, *Old Testament Theology: Its History and Development* (Atlanta: John Knox, 1985); Gerhard F. Hasel, *Old Testament Theology: Basic Issues in the Current Debate*, 4th ed. (Grand Rapids: Eerdmans, 1991); Ben C. Ollenburger, "Old Testament Theology before 1933," in *Old Testament Theology: Flowering and Future*, ed. Ben C. Ollenburger, 2nd ed., Sources for Biblical and Theological Study 1 (Winona Lake, IN: Eisenbrauns, 2004), 3–11; Gershom M. H. Ratheiser, Mitzvoth *Ethics and the Jewish Bible: The End of Old Testament Theology*, Library of Hebrew Bible / Old Testament Studies 460 (New York: T&T Clark, 2007), 11–161.

6. Michael Fishbane, *Biblical Interpretation in Ancient Israel* (Oxford: Clarendon, 1985).

7. James K. Mead, *Biblical Theology: Issues, Methods, and Themes* (Louisville: Westminster John Knox, 2007), 15–16.

8. The literature on the use of the Old Testament in the New Testament is enormous; for a beginning point, see G. K. Beale, ed., *The Right Doctrine from the Wrong Texts? Essays on the Use of the Old Testament in the New* (Grand Rapids: Baker, 1994); G. K. Beale and D. A. Carson, eds., *Commentary on the New Testament Use of the Old Testament* (Grand Rapids: Baker Academic, 2007); Kenneth Berding and Jonathan Lunde, eds., *Three Views on the New Testament Use of the Old Testament*, Counterpoints: Bible and Theology (Grand Rapids: Zondervan, 2008).

9. For this comparison, see Daniel J. Brendsel, "Plots, Themes, and Responsibilities: The Search for a Center of Biblical Theology Reexamined," *Themelios* 35 (2010): 405–6. For further discussion of the topic of biblical theology among the church fathers, see Gerald Bray, "The Church Fathers and Biblical

tradition and brought greater focus on the biblical texts with the doctrine of *sola Scriptura* ("Scripture alone").[10]

However, the modern study of biblical theology is often considered as beginning with a lecture by Johann Gabler in 1787, in which he provided a basis for the distinction between biblical theology and dogmatic theology (or systematic theology).[11] The main distinction he draws between the two kinds of theology is the attention to context: biblical theology pays strict attention to the contexts of the biblical authors rather than to our own context, which is the concern of dogmatic theology. Therefore, according to Gabler, biblical theology should be strongly historically focused and operate as a waypoint in the journey from the Bible to dogmatic theology. Gabler contrasts the "simplicity and ease" of doing biblical theology with the "subtlety and difficulty of dogmatic theology," emphasizing that scholarly consensus can be reached only at the stage of biblical theology. However, the diversity within the discipline today has shown that this dream would not come to fruition!

This historical approach to biblical theology was paralleled by the rise of historical criticism, which sought to reconstruct the true historical world behind the biblical text and did not take the biblical claims about history at face value. With a marked focus on history and a sharp distinction between biblical and systematic theology, most biblical theologies in the 1800s and early 1900s tended to merely describe the biblical text rather than prescribe how the Old Testament functioned authoritatively for the contemporary church.[12] One of the best examples of this is found in the work of Otto Eissfeldt, who argued strongly for the division of history and religion, viewing Old Testament theology as a historical discipline.[13]

However, this characterization would change in the glory days of biblical theology from the 1930s to the 1960s, as exemplified by the work of the German scholars Walther Eichrodt and Gerhard von Rad (both of whom will be discussed later in this book). Even though their books differ dramatically

---

Theology," in *Out of Egypt: Biblical Theology and Biblical Interpretation*, ed. Craig Bartholomew et al., Scripture and Hermeneutics Series 5 (Grand Rapids: Zondervan, 2004), 23–40.

10. Walter Brueggemann, *Theology of the Old Testament: Testimony, Dispute, Advocacy* (Minneapolis: Augsburg Fortress, 1997), 1–4.

11. A copy of the lecture can be found in Johann P. Gabler, "An Oration on the Proper Distinction between Biblical and Dogmatic Theology and the Specific Objectives of Each," in *Old Testament Theology: Flowering and Future*, 498–506; John Sandys-Wunsch and Laurence Eldredge, "J. P. Gabler and the Distinction between Biblical and Dogmatic Theology: Translation, Commentary, and Discussion of His Originality," *Scottish Journal of Theology* 33 (1980): 133–58.

12. Mead, *Biblical Theology*, 27–39.

13. Otto Eissfeldt, "The History of Israelite-Jewish Religion and Old Testament Theology," in *Old Testament Theology: Flowering and Future*, 12–20.

from each other, they collectively helped to define the field of biblical theology for decades. The guiding principle for Walther Eichrodt was covenant, which he used as a central theme to organize the entire Old Testament. While he employed historical-critical principles, he tended to be optimistic about the historical reality behind the Old Testament. He also emphasized that the Old Testament could not function by itself but necessarily led to the New Testament. Eichrodt published his three-volume Old Testament theology in the years 1933–39. (The English translation in two volumes was not published until almost three decades later.[14])

Gerhard von Rad taught in German universities from 1929–71. (Teaching the Old Testament in Nazi Germany would surely have been a challenge!) He wrote his two-volume Old Testament theology (published in 1957 and 1960) from a quite different perspective than Eichrodt, vehemently denying that the Old Testament has a center.[15] Instead he organized his theology historically, tracing Israel's confessions about the great works of YHWH throughout the Old Testament. His favored interpretive method of typology allowed him to connect these historical events with the coming of Jesus in the New Testament.[16]

Paralleling these developments in the German-speaking world was the so-called biblical theology movement in the English-speaking world, which lasted from around 1940 to the early 1960s.[17] Popular particularly in the United States, it focused on YHWH's great acts in history, in some ways resembling the work of von Rad. Other characteristics of the biblical theology movement are that it highlighted the uniqueness of Israel compared with other nations in the ancient world and was marked by an optimism about the historicity (historical accuracy) of the biblical text. This optimism was supported by the "biblical archaeology" of the time (especially that practiced by William Albright), though the movement also rejected a naive "fundamentalist"

---

14. Walther Eichrodt, *Theology of the Old Testament*, trans. J. A. Baker, 2 vols., Old Testament Library (Philadelphia: Westminster, 1961–67). Eichrodt shared his focus on covenant with his contemporary Karl Barth, who led one of the major shifts in theological history during this time period. In response to many of his teachers supporting the German war cause in World War I, Barth published a commentary on Romans in 1918 that brought attention back to the theology of the biblical text and emphasized the importance of covenant. It is unknown whether there was any connection between them, but Eichrodt was Barth's Old Testament colleague at Basel. Eichrodt taught at the University of Basel from 1921–66, while Barth taught there beginning in 1935.

15. The English translation of Eichrodt's work was completed after von Rad wrote his theology, so Eichrodt was able to add an appendix responding to von Rad's critique.

16. Typology sees certain historical events (like the exodus), people (like Moses), and institutions (like the priesthood) as types that prefigure a later fulfillment in an antitype.

17. For more on this topic, see Steven J. Kraftchick, "Facing Janus: Reviewing the Biblical Theology Movement," in *Biblical Theology: Problems and Perspectives: In Honor of J. Christiaan Beker*, ed. Steven J. Kraftchick, Charles D. Myers Jr., and Ben C. Ollenburger (Nashville: Abingdon, 1995), 54–77.

reading of the text. The prime example of this trend is G. Ernest Wright's *God Who Acts*, published in 1952.[18]

Despite its vibrancy, the biblical theology movement proved to be short-lived. One of the primary critiques concerned historicity, as many scholars became disillusioned with biblical archaeology and more skeptical of the historicity of the biblical narrative. As more of the biblical text was viewed as nonhistorical, it became increasingly difficult to base an Old Testament theology on an ever-decreasing amount of history. In addition, scholars began to highlight more of the similarities between Israel and the surrounding nations rather than the contrasts.[19] In his landmark *Biblical Theology in Crisis* (published in 1970), Brevard Childs thoroughly described the weaknesses of the biblical theology movement and issued its death certificate.[20] This, however, was not to be the end of biblical theology. The decades since the 1970s have seen the resurrection of biblical theology (throwing into doubt whether it actually died!).[21] But in this resurrection, biblical theology has also splintered, resulting in multiple kinds of theologies.

MAPPING THE TERRAIN OF RECENT APPROACHES

We find ourselves today in this fractured world of biblical theology. To return to our opening metaphor, Old Testament theology does not comprise a single mountaintop from which to view the stunning landscape of the Old Testament. Instead it presents us with a whole mountain range, with each peak (approach to Old Testament theology) offering a different vantage point. Those venturing out to hike this range will soon discover a wide array of paths (individual Old Testament theologies) leading to each peak, every path having its own unique view.

For many years, the standard guide to this mountain range was Gerhard Hasel's *Old Testament Theology: Basic Issues in the Current Debate*. But the

---

18. G. Ernest Wright, *God Who Acts: Biblical Theology as Recital*, Studies in Biblical Theology 8 (London: SCM, 1952).

19. Much of this is conveniently summarized in Leo G. Perdue, *The Collapse of History: Reconstructing Old Testament Theology*, Overtures to Biblical Theology (Minneapolis: Fortress, 1994), 19–44.

20. Brevard S. Childs, *Biblical Theology in Crisis* (Philadelphia: Westminster, 1970). James Barr also played an important role in highlighting the weaknesses of the movement. For a later convenient summary of his arguments, see James Barr, *The Concept of Biblical Theology: An Old Testament Perspective* (Minneapolis: Fortress, 1999).

21. Since the biblical theology movement was primarily an American phenomenon, its death mainly affected the American context. Phyllis Bird notes that interest in Old Testament theology continued unabated in Germany (Phyllis A. Bird, "The God of the Fathers Encounters Feminism: Overture for a Feminist Old Testament Theology," in *Methods*, vol. 3 of *Feminist Interpretation of the Hebrew Bible in Retrospect*, ed. Susanne Scholz, Recent Research in Biblical Studies 9 [Sheffield: Sheffield Phoenix, 2016], 139).

latest edition of that book was completed in 1991, and much has happened in the field of Old Testament theology in the intervening years. Not only have a number of paths been forged, but even some new peaks have emerged. Edward Klink and Darian Lockett offer a more recent introduction in *Understanding Biblical Theology: A Comparison of Theory and Practice*. But while they provide an in-depth treatment of five major peaks in the biblical theology mountain range, they give more attention to New Testament theology. So they do not cover some of the peaks that are more prominent in the landscape of Old Testament theology, and they highlight only a few of the Old Testament paths.

A different approach may be found in *Old Testament Theology: Flowering and Future*, edited by Ben Ollenburger, which contains excerpts from major works and essays on Old Testament theology from around 1930 until its publication in 2004. While that volume helpfully acquaints readers with some of the prominent players in the field, it organizes them chronologically rather than by approach and so does not offer a conceptual scheme for making sense of the terrain.[22] All of these works are interesting and informative, but collectively they point to the need for a newer guide that organizes the field of Old Testament theology.

In this book, then, we aim to provide a reliable map to the mountainous terrain of recent approaches to Old Testament theology. We describe each of the peaks in the mountain range and, together with the annotated bibliography on the associated website,[23] sketch out the primary paths to each peak. We also present some snapshots of the views found along the various paths to give you a sense of the wondrous beauty that greets those who embark on the trek. Since our purpose is to map out recent approaches, we focus primarily on theologies written in the past thirty years. However, we also include a selection of older theologies that have had an enduring influence and thus are still well-trodden paths. Also, in light of our English readership, we give primary attention to theologies in English, though we discuss a handful of theologies written in other European languages. Since most of the scholars in the field of Old Testament theology have been from North America or Europe, we have also highlighted the few majority-world contributors to the discussion.

Our map divides the mountain range into three primary regions or parts. Part 1 surveys approaches to Old Testament theology that focus on history, either the biblical account of Israel's history (chap. 1) or a historical-critical

---

22. The volume also clocks in at 560 pages, which makes it a rather cumbersome read for beginning students.

23. See https://zondervanacademic.com/OTTheoBibliography.

reconstruction (chap. 2). Part 2 examines approaches that foreground theme, whether structured around a plurality of themes (chap. 3) or one central theme (chap. 4). Finally, part 3 considers approaches that highlight context, including the context of the Christian canon (chap. 5), the context of Jewish scholarship (chap. 6), and the widely divergent contexts of individual interpreters (chap. 7).

Each chapter has three main sections. First, we describe the various common features of works in the category. Second, we discuss the points of tension, showing that even scholars within the same category are far from uniform. Finally, each chapter ends with several examples of how scholars in the category deal with material from the book of Exodus. Exodus is an interesting test case because it contains significant narrative portions as well as other genres (most notably, the legal and ritual texts found in the Sinai material), and it is instructive to see which parts of the book and which genres the various approaches tend to focus on. Also, Exodus is theologically rich and multifaceted, like the stained glass window of Moses coming down from Mount Sinai on the cover of this book. Each approach, then, is like a light shining through the window from a different direction, producing beautifully distinctive patterns of reflection and refraction and illuminating a sanctuary where we can meet with God.

Returning to the mountain range metaphor, visualizing Old Testament theology as a geographical territory might lead to the conclusion that each peak and path is clearly defined and obvious to every cartographer. But the mountain range can be conceptualized in various ways. Even objective geographical regions can be described in different ways by different types of maps. For example, compare a political map, which defines national boundaries and marks major cities, with a physical map highlighting changes in elevation. Or consider how the challenge of projecting a three-dimensional world onto a two-dimensional surface always results in some distortion. The widely used Mercator projection preserves the shapes of the continents, but as a result, it misrepresents their sizes, making Greenland (836,330 square miles) appear to be roughly the size of South America (6,878,000 square miles, about eight times the size of Greenland!).[24] By contrast, the Gall-Peters projection accurately depicts the relative sizes of the continents only by manipulating their shapes. Every map is an approximation that emphasizes certain features of the terrain while downplaying or even altering others.[25]

24. See Mark Monmonier, *How to Lie with Maps*, 3rd ed. (Chicago: Univ. of Chicago Press, 2018), 15–16.

25. See Christopher J. H. Wright, "Mission as a Matrix for Hermeneutics and Biblical Theology,"

While we present a categorization of approaches to the mountainous wilderness of Old Testament theology that we think offers potential hikers the information they need to journey through it, we do not claim that it is the only way of mapping the terrain.[26] One particular difficulty for cartographers of Old Testament theology is that no matter how the categories are defined, some of the individual paths could lead to multiple mountain peaks. For example, Walter Kaiser arranges his work historically, so in our map that could lead to his placement in the biblical (hi)story chapter (chap. 1).[27] But he so strongly emphasizes the central theme of promise that we instead placed him in the central theme chapter (chap. 4).

We have tried to highlight a few of these ambiguities along the way, but we apologize to authors who feel that they would fit better in a different category (or who would like the creation of another category to fit their work more precisely!). Each of the theologies we discuss remains unique in significant ways, but we have found these categories to provide a helpful map to the complex field of Old Testament theology. Our hope is that as you get a taste for the incredible views from these mountain peaks, it will whet your appetite for more.

in *Out of Egypt*, 138–40. Wright notes how a two-dimensional representation of the earth and the map of the London Underground subway system both distort reality in order to fulfill their aims. However, he applies this metaphor to a hermeneutical framework for understanding the biblical text, rather than to a scheme for understanding the field of Old Testament theology.

26. In addition to the categories proposed by Hasel and Klink and Lockett in the surveys noted earlier, see other categorical schemes in Mead, *Biblical Theology*, 121–68; Henning Graf Reventlow, "Modern Approaches to Old Testament Theology," in *The Blackwell Companion to the Hebrew Bible*, ed. Leo G. Perdue, Blackwell Companions to Religion (Oxford: Blackwell, 2001), 221–40.

27. Walter C. Kaiser Jr., *Toward an Old Testament Theology* (Grand Rapids: Zondervan, 1978).

Part 1

HISTORY

In part 1 we cover approaches to Old Testament theology that are rooted in history. In general, these approaches highlight the diversity in the Old Testament by focusing on how Israel's faith developed over time. In chapter 1, "Old Testament Theology Grounded in Biblical (Hi)story," we examine theologies that appeal to history as it is described by the biblical text. By contrast, in chapter 2, "Historical-Critical Old Testament Theology," we consider theologies that use historical criticism to reconstruct the historical world behind the biblical text and frequently dispute the historical accounts provided in Scripture.

Chapter 1

OLD TESTAMENT THEOLOGY GROUNDED IN BIBLICAL (HI)STORY

We begin our exploration of the mountainous terrain of Old Testament theology with an approach that focuses on the progressive historical development of Israel and its faith according to the biblical presentation of Israel's history. Although this approach is associated particularly with G. Ernest Wright's classic work *God Who Acts* (1952),[1] it has also been adopted by a considerable number of recent scholars and is favored by many who desire to write an Old Testament (or biblical) theology that is accessible for the church. Since more recent scholars in this category tend to emphasize both history (the event itself) and story (the narrative of that event), we have used the term "(hi)story" in the chapter title to indicate that double focus.[2]

> DEFINITION: Old Testament theology that is grounded in biblical (hi)story focuses on retelling Old Testament history, views the Old Testament as story, understands the whole Bible as one story, and sees it as *the* story that shapes us. Points of tension among scholars who adopt this approach include how the story is outlined, how the nonnarrative literature is incorporated, and what role the New Testament plays in interpreting the Old.

---

1. G. Ernest Wright, *God Who Acts: Biblical Theology as Recital*, Studies in Biblical Theology 8 (London: SCM, 1952).

2. This category corresponds to "BT2: Biblical Theology as History of Redemption" and "BT3: Biblical Theology as Worldview-Story" in Edward W. Klink III and Darian R. Lockett, *Understanding Biblical Theology: A Comparison of Theory and Practice* (Grand Rapids: Zondervan, 2012), 59–122.

Central Texts Covered in This Chapter

T. Desmond Alexander, *From Eden to the New Jerusalem* (2008)

Craig G. Bartholomew and Michael W. Goheen, *The Drama of Scripture* (2004; 2nd ed.: 2014)

Tim Chester, *From Creation to New Creation* (2003; 2nd ed.: 2010)

Matthew Y. Emerson, *The Story of Scripture* (2017)

Peter J. Gentry and Stephen J. Wellum, *Kingdom through Covenant* (2012; 2nd ed.: 2018)

John Goldingay, *Israel's Gospel* (vol. 1 of his *Old Testament Theology*, 2003)

Graeme Goldsworthy, *According to Plan* (1991)

Jeong Koo Jeon, *Biblical Theology* (2017)

Michael Lawrence, *Biblical Theology in the Life of the Church* (2010)

Jeffrey J. Niehaus, *Biblical Theology* (2014–17)

C. Marvin Pate, J. Scott Duvall, J. Daniel Hays, E. Randolph Richards, W. Dennis Tucker Jr., and Preben Vang, *The Story of Israel* (2004)

Sandra Richter, *The Epic of Eden* (2008)

Nick Roark and Robert Cline, *Biblical Theology* (2018)

Vaughan Roberts, *God's Big Picture* (2002)

Geerhardus Vos, *Biblical Theology* (1948)

Michael D. Williams, *Far as the Curse Is Found* (2005)

G. Ernest Wright, *God Who Acts* (1952)

Roy B. Zuck, ed., *A Biblical Theology of the Old Testament* (1991)

COMMON FEATURES

Focus on Retelling Old Testament History

The key distinguishing feature of Old Testament theologies that fall into this category is that they seek to retell Israel's history. Since they often focus on God's acts of redemption, they sometimes refer to it as redemptive history (or adopt the German term *Heilsgeschichte*).[3] Observing that it is primarily through history that God has chosen to reveal himself, scholars who take this approach see that history as inherently theological. While theological abstractions about God's nature may be a necessary next step—often understood as falling within the purview of systematic theology—they argue that a truly *Old Testament* theology will mirror the historical development found within the

---

3. See, e.g., Jeong Koo Jeon, *Biblical Theology: Covenants and the Kingdom of God in Redemptive History* (Eugene, OR: Wipf and Stock, 2017), xiii–xv; Jeffrey J. Niehaus, *The Common Grace Covenants*, vol. 1 of *Biblical Theology* (Wooster, OH: Weaver, 2014), 33; Wright, *God Who Acts*, 60.

biblical text.[4] Wright contends that only with this approach can we capture the "living, active and warm Presence" of God, which does not emanate from dogmatic statements about God's nature.[5]

This approach recognizes the historical-cultural rootedness of God's revelation to Israel, acknowledging that God acted on behalf of a particular people in particular historical moments, and that the Old Testament text bears that historical-cultural stamp.[6] It also provides a framework for acknowledging the considerable diversity within the biblical witness. John Goldingay declares that "our theological statements tend to be more univocal than Scripture, and thus less true. Even God (especially God) cannot make truth less complex than it is."[7] Whereas a propositional theology that focuses on never-changing universal statements about God may be likened to isolating the major themes of a symphony, a historical theology attempts to discern how those themes fit in the context of the whole piece and interact with other, minor themes.[8]

The history that forms the basis for theologies in this category is the history of Israel as it is recounted in the Old Testament, not as it is reconstructed by historical criticism. Most scholars who take this approach offer little to no engagement with historical-critical views. Many do not even raise the issue.[9] Jeong Koo Jeon, however, issues a clear indictment of historical-critical methods, contending that "the evangelical church has to put to death the historical critical reading of the Bible, which has been one of the major sources of intellectual and spiritual poisons in the church."[10] Jeffrey Niehaus simply dismisses historical-critical conclusions as "flawed at their foundations," arguing that archaeological discoveries "have shown us how the ancients actually wrote."[11]

---

4. Geerhardus Vos contends that "the Bible is not a dogmatic handbook but a historical book full of dramatic interest" (Geerhardus Vos, *Biblical Theology: Old and New Testaments* [Grand Rapids: Eerdmans, 1948], 26). See also Peter J. Gentry and Stephen J. Wellum, *Kingdom through Covenant: A Biblical-Theological Understanding of the Covenants*, 2nd ed. (Wheaton, IL: Crossway, 2018), 45–46.

5. Wright, *God Who Acts*, 110.

6. See Jeannine K. Brown, "Is the Future of Biblical Theology Story-Shaped?" *Horizons in Biblical Theology* 37 (2015): 26.

7. John Goldingay, *Israel's Gospel*, vol. 1 of *Old Testament Theology* (Downers Grove, IL: InterVarsity, 2003), 40–41; see also Brown, "Is the Future of Biblical Theology Story-Shaped?" 19–20.

8. As Jeannine Brown observes, however, not all theologies that take this approach "provide a sustained narrative reading of the biblical text with attention to its 'blessed messiness'" ("Is the Future of Biblical Theology Story-Shaped?" 28, quoting Beverly Roberts Gaventa, "Reading for the Subject: The Paradox of Power in Romans 14:1–15:6," *Journal of Theological Interpretation* 5 [2011]: 3).

9. E.g., Nick Roark and Robert Cline, *Biblical Theology: How the Church Faithfully Teaches the Gospel*, 9Marks (Wheaton, IL: Crossway, 2018); Michael D. Williams, *Far as the Curse Is Found: The Covenant Story of Redemption* (Phillipsburg, NJ: P&R, 2005); Vaughan Roberts, *God's Big Picture: Tracing the Storyline of the Bible* (Downers Grove, IL: InterVarsity, 2002).

10. Jeon, *Biblical Theology*, xix. Similarly, Gentry and Wellum reject a historical-critical approach because it "stands in antithesis to historic Christian theological convictions" (*Kingdom through Covenant*, 44).

11. Niehaus, *Common Grace Covenants*, 23.

In his view, these discoveries undercut the criteria historical-critical scholars have used, for example, to separate out the various sources of the biblical writings. Wright and Goldingay, on the other hand, are more accepting of a moderate use of historical criticism,[12] yet they still base their Old Testament theologies on the biblical portrait of Israel's history.

For works in this category, it is crucial that God has acted on behalf of his people in real space and time as the Bible describes. As Wright puts it, "Now in Biblical faith everything depends upon whether the central events actually occurred."[13] Israel's faith was grounded in the belief that God had delivered his people in the past and would continue to do so in the future. Therefore the theology of the Old Testament is integrally tied to the historicity of God's acts of redemption.[14] Focusing particularly on the patriarchs, Geerhardus Vos extends Wright's insight to speak of the importance of historicity for the church: "If Abraham was the father of the faithful, the nucleus of the Church, then the denial of [the patriarchs'] historicity makes them useless from our point of view."[15]

The Old Testament as Story

A second common feature is that theologies in this category view the Old Testament not just as history but also as story.[16] While earlier interpreters tended to focus more on the events of history themselves,[17] they still recognized that revelation cannot consist solely of events; as Wright puts it, "Events need interpretation."[18] Wright even uses the language of story: "This two-

---

12. See Wright, *God Who Acts*, 127; John Goldingay, "What Are the Characteristics of Evangelical Study of the Old Testament?" *Evangelical Quarterly* 73 (2001): 109–12.

13. Wright contends further that historical and archaeological research has served to affirm "the basic reliability of Biblical history" (*God Who Acts*, 126–27). Although archaeology has raised some significant questions for biblical history since the time of Wright, scholars in this category would still tend toward harmonizing the archaeological record with the biblical portrait.

14. See Goldingay, "What Are the Characteristics of Evangelical Study of the Old Testament?" 110; Williams, *Far as the Curse Is Found*, 16–18. Another stream of narrative theology describes the biblical narratives as "history-like" and locates meaning entirely within the narrative rather than seeing meaning in any reference to events or realities behind the text (see, e.g., Hans W. Frei, *The Eclipse of Biblical Narrative: A Study in Eighteenth and Nineteenth Century Hermeneutics* [New Haven, CT: Yale Univ. Press, 1974]; for a summary of this approach, see Leo G. Perdue, *The Collapse of History: Reconstructing Old Testament Theology*, Overtures to Biblical Theology [Minneapolis: Fortress, 1994], 231–62). However, this approach has not been widely applied to biblical theology.

15. Vos, *Biblical Theology*, 80; see also Craig G. Bartholomew and Michael W. Goheen, "Story and Biblical Theology," in *Out of Egypt: Biblical Theology and Biblical Interpretation*, ed. Craig Bartholomew et al., Scripture and Hermeneutics Series 5 (Grand Rapids: Zondervan, 2004), 164–65.

16. See Bartholomew and Goheen, "Story and Biblical Theology," 156–57.

17. For example, Wright contends that "the primary means by which God communicates with man is by his *acts*, which are the *events* of history" (*God Who Acts*, 107, italics ours). Similarly, Vos defines biblical theology as "the study of the actual self-disclosures of God in time and space which lie back of even the first committal to writing of any Biblical document" (*Biblical Theology*, 13).

18. Wright, *God Who Acts*, 107; this idea is natural for Vos in light of his focus on revelation, which he describes as "the interpretation of redemption" (*Biblical Theology*, 14).

sided relation between God and man is not developed as doctrine, but rather is set forth as happening in a story."[19] More recent theologies place considerable emphasis on the storied nature of the Old Testament text. They therefore give attention to the narrative shaping of events by the biblical authors, who do not just report the brute facts of history but carefully sculpt their presentations with narrative artistry, selecting and arranging their material to make theological points. By attending to this narrative artistry, theologies in this category often make keen observations about how the details of the narrative portrayal communicate the authors' points.

For example, Peter Gentry and Stephen Wellum point out that Genesis records three named sons of Adam and Eve and also concludes the genealogies in chapters 5 and 11 with three named sons. They contend that "This parallel is a literary technique inviting the reader to compare Abram with Noah and Adam."[20] Goldingay observes that the exodus account skims over the Israelites' journey to the Red Sea but describes the plagues and repeated hardening of Pharaoh's heart in some detail. This emphasis serves to offer a substantial narrative treatment of a complex topic: "the interrelationship between divine sovereignty and human free will."[21]

The Story of Israel notes that Genesis describes Cain, the people who build the Tower of Babel, and Lot as all moving eastward, mirroring Adam and Eve's expulsion from the garden of Eden and similarly symbolizing a movement away from the presence of God.[22] In its discussion of the David account, *The Story of Israel* highlights the narrative's characterization, noting that Saul serves "as a foil for David," who "is everything that Saul is not—valiant, courageous and obedient to Yahweh."[23] However, after David commits adultery with Bathsheba, his "kingdom and his private life begin to unravel."[24] When his son Absalom seizes his throne, "in shame, David is driven out of Jerusalem, the city he once conquered. Adding to the insult, along the road a man pelts him with rocks (2 Sam 16), contrasting with his earlier spectacular victory with rocks over Goliath."[25]

Analyzing the account of Elijah fleeing from Jezebel after YHWH's contest with Baal, Niehaus notes that the messenger Jezebel sends Elijah with

---

19. Wright, *God Who Acts*, 90.

20. Gentry and Wellum, *Kingdom through Covenant*, 260. They also cite further connections between Genesis 1–3 and 12, which indicate that "we should view Abram as a new Adam" (pp. 260–64).

21. Goldingay, *Israel's Gospel*, 39.

22. C. Marvin Pate et al., *The Story of Israel: A Biblical Theology* (Downers Grove, IL: InterVarsity, 2004), 34, 37–38.

23. Ibid., 61–62.

24. Ibid., 63.

25. Ibid.

a threat to kill him (1 Kings 19:2) is described with the same Hebrew word used for the angel who offers food to restore his life (v. 5, both *mal'ak*).[26] He therefore suggests that the passage draws a deliberate comparison, which "shows a conflict between two kingdoms: the kingdom of Israel and the kingdom of Yahweh. The two ought to be in concert—Israel ought to be an extension of the heavenly kingdom—but because Israel's monarchy is false, they are opposed."[27] Later, when he discusses Elisha's request to receive a double portion of Elijah's spirit (2 Kings 2:9), Niehaus points out that in ancient Israel a double portion of the inheritance would go to the oldest son. He then observes that the books of Kings record twice as many prophecies and miracles for Elisha as for Elijah.[28] Acknowledging that these figures undoubtedly gave more prophecies and performed more miracles than are recounted, Niehaus contends that "when the composer of the Elijah/Elisha accounts wrote his history, one purpose he apparently had was to show that Elisha did receive *twice as much* of the Spirit as Elijah had received."[29]

An emphasis on story also highlights the unity of the Old Testament. Even though the Old Testament is a collection of books written by different authors and redactors (editors) over a period of hundreds of years, these books together tell a single overarching narrative.[30] For scholars who take this approach, the various parts of Scripture are held together not by the accidents of history but by the purpose of a divine author, who carefully crafts his story to move it toward its climax. Each story and character, then, serves its function within the plan of the larger narrative and should be interpreted not in isolation but in relation to that broader context.[31] Tim Chester goes so far as to say that "understanding the story is the only way to understand the Bible and its theology."[32]

The Whole Bible as One Story

A third common feature of theologies grounded in biblical history is that they see the story of the Old Testament as continuing into the New

---

26. Jeffrey J. Niehaus, *The Special Grace Covenants: Old Testament*, vol. 2 of *Biblical Theology* (Bellingham, WA: Lexham, 2017), 356.

27. Ibid., 357.

28. He cites the following statistics: Elijah—4 prophecies, 7 miracles; Elisha—8 prophecies, 14 miracles (ibid., 407–8).

29. Ibid., 408, italics original.

30. See Graeme Goldsworthy, *According to Plan: The Unfolding Revelation of God in the Bible* (Downers Grove, IL: InterVarsity, 1991), 56; Williams, *Far as the Curse Is Found*, x.

31. See Matthew Y. Emerson, *The Story of Scripture: An Introduction to Biblical Theology* (Nashville: B&H Academic, 2017), 85; Roark and Cline, *Biblical Theology*, 26.

32. Tim Chester, *From Creation to New Creation: Making Sense of the Whole Bible Story*, 2nd ed. (Charlotte: Good Book, 2010), 8.

Testament; they view the whole Bible as one story. Vaughan Roberts argues that reading either testament by itself is like cutting a mystery novel in half and reading only one part; the first part is incomplete (who committed the crime?), and the second does not make sense without the first (what crime was committed?).[33] Therefore this category draws a strong connection between the testaments, and in fact most theologies span the whole Bible.[34] As they tell the biblical story, they highlight how the Old Testament points to the story's climax in Christ.

For example, Michael Lawrence highlights the dimensions of sacrifice in the Old Testament that anticipate and illuminate Jesus' work on the cross: "Abel's sacrifice was about thanksgiving. Noah's sacrifice was about thanksgiving and assuaging the Lord. Abraham and Isaac's episode included all this, but also the ideas of utter devotion and a substitute. The Passover sacrifice introduced the ideas of a spotless lamb, the representative role of the firstborn Son, and the distinguishing of a people. Then the Levitical sacrifices emphasized atonement for sin."[35] After describing how these aspects are fulfilled in Christ, Lawrence cites Hebrews 9–10 to argue that "the whole sacrificial system had only been a picture, a teaching aid, designed, as Paul says in Galatians, to lead us to Christ, and to recognize him when he appeared."[36]

Urging pastors to draw connections to Christ when they preach the Old Testament, Nick Roark and Robert Cline caution against a moralistic preaching of David's victory over Goliath with a message like, "David was really brave; so therefore we need to work hard at being brave like David."[37] Instead they counsel readers to recognize that the narrative points toward Jesus as David's son and "the One who is the ultimate champion of God's people."[38] In *Biblical Theology of the Old Testament*, Robert Chisholm examines the Servant Songs of Isaiah in some depth (42:1–9; 49:1–13; 50:4–11; 52:13–53:12). Although he sees the language of the final song about the servant's suffering as rather ambiguous, he points out that ultimately Jesus appears as the servant

---

33. Roberts, *God's Big Picture*, 20. See also Sandra Richter, *The Epic of Eden: A Christian Entry into the Old Testament* (Downers Grove, IL: IVP Academic, 2008), 17. Richter contends that lack of familiarity with the Old Testament "renders much of the wealth of the New Testament inaccessible."

34. Only the following are purely Old Testament theologies: Goldingay, *Israel's Gospel*; Wright, *God Who Acts*; Roy B. Zuck, ed., *A Biblical Theology of the Old Testament* (Chicago: Moody, 1991), though see his companion volume on the New Testament: idem, *A Biblical Theology of the New Testament* (Chicago: Moody, 1994). Richter's primary focus in *The Epic of Eden* is to help Christians understand the Old Testament. However, because she places the Old Testament in the framework of the larger biblical story, she also gives attention to Jesus and the new creation in Revelation.

35. Michael Lawrence, *Biblical Theology in the Life of the Church: A Guide for Ministry*, 9Marks (Wheaton, IL: Crossway, 2010), 158.

36. Ibid., 162.

37. Roark and Cline, *Biblical Theology*, 82.

38. Ibid.

par excellence, fulfilling these prophetic texts through his miraculous healings and vicarious death.[39]

Sandra Richter situates the Old Testament within the larger story of redemptive history by observing how it leads toward "God's Final Intent" in Revelation 21–22.[40] She also highlights various ways in which the biblical portrayal of Jesus builds on Old Testament themes. For example, noting that for ancient Israelites, "the sea evoked a mixture of myth and theology, fear and wonder," she describes how God restrains the sea at creation, delivers Noah from the sea during the flood, and parts both the Red Sea and the Jordan River to allow the Israelites to cross.[41] Therefore when Jesus calms the Sea of Galilee during a turbulent storm (Matt. 8:23–27), he is clearly depicted as God. Richter explains, "It is Yahweh who said at the dawn of creation: 'thus far you [sea] shall come, but no farther' [Job 38:11]; and it is only Yahweh the Son who could stand and remind the Sea of Galilee of the same."[42]

The Bible as *the* Story That Shapes Us

A final common feature of theologies in this category is that they see the Old Testament as *the* story—the one true story of the world—which therefore should shape how we as Christians live today. The rise of postmodernism has drawn attention to the power of stories to form communities by providing a framework for understanding life and instilling certain values. In a postmodern perspective, every culture or religion has its own story with its own perspective on reality. While these stories may vie for dominance, none can truly profess to describe the world as it really is.[43] Postmodernism is frequently defined, in the words of French philosopher Jean-François Lyotard, as "incredulity toward *metanarratives*,"[44] where a metanarrative is understood as a narrative that explains and governs all of life and thus claims to offer absolute truth.[45]

---

39. Robert B. Chisholm Jr., "A Theology of Isaiah," in *Biblical Theology of the Old Testament*, 328–33.

40. Richter, *Epic of Eden*, 127–36.

41. Ibid., 146.

42. Ibid., 146–47.

43. See chap. 7.

44. Jean-François Lyotard, *The Postmodern Condition: A Report on Knowledge*, trans. Geoff Bennington and Brian Massumi, Theory and History of Literature 10 (Minneapolis: Univ. of Minnesota Press, 1984), xxiv, italics ours.

45. According to James K. A. Smith, however, "Lyotard very specifically defines metanarratives as universal discourses of legitimation that mask their own particularity" (James K. A. Smith, *Who's Afraid of Postmodernism? Taking Derrida, Lyotard, and Foucault to Church*, The Church and Postmodern Culture [Grand Rapids: Baker Academic, 2006], 69). What Lyotard was critiquing was not "any grand story with a global scope" (p. 62) but discourses like modern science that claim to legitimate themselves through universal reason without realizing that they are grounded in their own particular narratives (see pp. 65–68).

Theologies that are grounded in biblical history respond to postmodernism on the one hand by countering its relativistic viewpoint. T. Desmond Alexander expresses clearly what is broadly assumed—that the Bible offers "a meta-story that claims to communicate absolute truth that cannot be discovered by any other means."[46] Likewise, according to Craig Bartholomew and Michael Goheen, the church believes "that there is *one* true story: the story told in the Bible. . . . Only in this one narrative can we discover the meaning of human history."[47]

Yet on the other hand, these scholars recognize the significance of giving attention to the stories that form us. Acknowledging that all people live out of some kind of story that guides their perspective, Bartholomew and Goheen express the concern that "if we neglect the biblical story, . . . the fragments of the Bible that we *do* preserve are in danger of being absorbed piecemeal into the dominant stories of our own cultures. . . . Thus instead of allowing the Bible to shape us, we may in fact be allowing our culture to shape the Bible for us."[48] They use an analogy of the biblical story as a play, and Christians as actors who are called to improvise their parts in it in a way that is consistent with the rest of the drama.[49] To play our parts appropriately, "we need to know the biblical story well, to feel it in our bones."[50]

Quoting Michael Goldberg, Goldingay suggests that "being a Christian or a Jew is not so much a matter of subscribing to one['s] community's core doctrine[s] as of affirming its core story."[51] Similarly, Lawrence claims that in the Bible "we discover a story that challenges our tendencies to reduce Christianity to a limited set of doctrinal propositions and instead claims the totality of our lives under the Lordship of the King."[52] However, as Richter points out, much of the church is unfamiliar with the roots of its story in the Old Testament. She compares this to Alzheimer's disease, saying, "The church does not know who she is, because she does not know who she was."[53]

Some theologies suggest particular ways that the Old Testament shapes

---

46. T. Desmond Alexander, *From Eden to the New Jerusalem: An Introduction to Biblical Theology* (Grand Rapids: Kregel Academic, 2008), 9.

47. Craig G. Bartholomew and Michael W. Goheen, *The Drama of Scripture: Finding Our Place in the Biblical Story*, 2nd ed. (Grand Rapids: Baker Academic, 2014), 20, italics original; see also Lawrence, *Biblical Theology in the Life of the Church*, 31.

48. Bartholomew and Goheen, *Drama of Scripture*, 213, italics original; see idem, "Story and Biblical Theology," 152, 155–57.

49. Bartholomew and Goheen, *Drama of Scripture*, 214, following N. T. Wright, "How Can the Bible Be Authoritative?" *Vox Evangelica* 21 (1991): 7–32.

50. Bartholomew and Goheen, *Drama of Scripture*, 213.

51. Goldingay, *Israel's Gospel*, 31, quoting Michael Goldberg, *Jews and Christians: Getting Our Stories Straight; The Exodus and the Passion-Resurrection* (Nashville: Abingdon, 1985), 15.

52. Lawrence, *Biblical Theology in the Life of the Church*, 31.

53. Richter, *Epic of Eden*, 17.

Christian life today. In his discussion of Genesis 1:26, Roberts declares that God's original design for humanity to rule over the created world places a responsibility on people today: "That is certainly not a charter for abuse. God is a loving ruler and, as his image-bearers, we are called to rule in a loving way. We are God's stewards, entrusted with the care of his precious creation."[54] Roberts also suggests that the prophetic pronouncements of judgment "should warn us against being complacent," recognizing that we too will face a final judgment.[55]

Graeme Goldsworthy concludes his book with a couple of biblical theology case studies. The first addresses the issue of finding guidance from God for both everyday questions and major life decisions. He suggests studying biblical texts to ask, "How does God guide people towards his ultimate goal for them at each level of redemptive revelation?"[56] For example, in the narratives of the patriarchs, he contends that "guidance is related to the covenant and its operation for the salvation of God's chosen people."[57] When the Israelites enter the promised land, God gives guidance about possessing the land and about Israel's leaders, but "there is no evidence of God guiding ordinary people in the specific decisions of their private lives."[58] Ultimately, he concludes that God gives us freedom to make wise decisions between good alternatives, rather than leading us toward specific decisions in every area of our lives.[59]

Goldingay observes that Exodus does not "describe Yhwh's rescue of Israel as an act of liberation" but instead portrays the Israelites as transferring their service from Pharaoh to YHWH. He then declares, "The way Exodus talks of freedom—or rather, fails to do so—confronts the Western preoccupation with freedom. Freedom in Scripture is the freedom to serve Yhwh."[60] Later he draws a parallel between the contemporary church and different stages of Israel's history: "The church in Europe lives in exile [in a post-Christian society]; . . . The church in the United States lives in the time of Josiah, assimilated to the culture around it. The question is whether it will turn or whether it must follow the church in Europe into exile."[61]

Finally, Alexander considers Habakkuk 2:5–14—which condemns Babylon for gaining wealth through oppression—together with the portrait of Babylon in Revelation 17–18. He contends that "history witnesses to the

---

54. Roberts, *God's Big Picture*, 31.
55. Ibid., 98.
56. Goldsworthy, *According to Plan*, 238.
57. Ibid.
58. Ibid.
59. Ibid., 239.
60. Goldingay, *Israel's Gospel*, 323.
61. Ibid., 695.

ongoing existence of Babylon, as one nation after another has used its power to grow rich at the expense of others."[62] He then addresses "the seductiveness of wealth" and "affluenza" that plague contemporary Western society, leading to "overconsumption, 'luxury fever,' consumer debt, overwork, waste, and harm to the environment," as well as psychological problems and self-medication.[63] In Alexander's view, we are living in Babylon now and must heed Habakkuk's warning that woe comes to those who follow Babylon's ways.

POINTS OF TENSION

How the Story Is Outlined

A primary point of tension for theologies in this category concerns how the Old Testament story is outlined. The most common way of organizing the biblical narrative is with a linear structure that progresses from beginning to end, but the proposals for this structure are surprisingly varied. (See table 1.1 on p. 26.) Vos divides his section on the Old Testament into two parts. "The Mosaic Epoch of Revelation" examines how God reveals himself from creation through the time of Moses, primarily in the form of theophanies (divine appearances), dreams, the angel of YHWH, and YHWH's name and face. The rise of Israel's monarchy leads to "the Prophetic Epoch of Revelation," in which God speaks to the kings and people through prophetic mediators. A final section covers New Testament revelation.[64] Given Vos's focus on God's self-revelation, he gives little space to events like the wilderness wanderings and conquest.

A few works follow the four-part structure that has become standard in systematic theology.

- creation
- fall
- redemption
- consummation / new creation[65]

---

62. Alexander, *From Eden to the New Jerusalem*, 182.

63. Ibid., 184–85.

64. It should be noted here that Vos draws a distinction between biblical history, which focuses on the history of redemption, and biblical theology, which traces the history of revelation. As noted earlier, he sees revelation as "the interpretation of redemption" (*Biblical Theology*, 14), so these two disciplines overlap. Nevertheless, his aim is to identify not what God has done in history but how he has disclosed himself (p. 24). Goldsworthy similarly identifies two primary stages of redemptive history in the Old Testament—the history of Israel from creation/Abraham to Solomon and prophetic eschatology—with a third stage comprising fulfillment in Christ (Graeme Goldsworthy, *Christ-Centered Biblical Theology: Hermeneutical Foundations and Principles* [Downers Grove, IL: InterVarsity, 2012], 24–27).

65. Emerson, *Story of Scripture*, 11; Roark and Cline, *Biblical Theology*, 93; Williams, *Far as the Curse*

These theologies give significant attention to Genesis 1–3 and emphasize how the rest of the Old Testament describes God's plan to redeem humanity and all of creation through Israel—a plan that is ultimately fulfilled in Christ.

Covenant is also a prominent theme or structuring device. Richter describes covenant as the "general law" that she uses "to give order to the whole."[66] After arguing for a covenantal understanding of God's relationship with Adam and Eve in Eden, she centers her discussion of the rest of the Old Testament narrative on the series of five covenants—the Noahic, Abrahamic, Mosaic, Davidic, and new covenants—which constitute God's "great rescue plan" to bring "humanity back to Eden."[67] Others combine the themes of covenant and kingdom of God. Korean American scholar Jeon argues that "exploring and understanding God's covenants are key to understanding redemptive history,"[68] and he explains that the covenants are God's means of establishing his kingly rule.[69] Similarly, Gentry and Wellum focus on how "God's *saving* kingdom comes to this world *through* the covenants," which they see as "the backbone of Scripture's metanarrative," while Niehaus contends that "the whole Bible is a product of the covenantal relationships" that the Divine King has made with people.[70]

However, Jeon presents the Reformed view that God's original covenant with Adam was a "covenant of works" and that God instituted a "covenant of grace" in Genesis 3:15 after the fall. Therefore "the proper historical order . . . is law and [then] grace."[71] By contrast, Niehaus and Gentry and Wellum deny such a distinction. In Niehaus's view, all of God's covenants entail some degree of conditionality, so "in that sense, one may say that all God's covenants are 'covenants of works.'"[72] Yet he also argues that "God graciously initiates every human-divine covenant, and all of those covenants are therefore acts of his grace."[73] In addition, he points out that the covenants are restored by God's grace when humans fail to uphold them.

Bartholomew and Goheen see "covenant (Old Testament) and kingdom

---

Is Found, xi; see also the use of these terms in the outline by Bartholomew and Goheen, *Drama of Scripture*, 22–23, as well as by Jeon, *Biblical Theology*, xv; Gentry and Wellum, *Kingdom through Covenant*, 792.

66. Richter, *Epic of Eden*, 69.

67. Ibid., 103–4, 130–31; see also Williams, *Far as the Curse Is Found*, xii.

68. Jeon, *Biblical Theology*, xxiii.

69. Ibid., xv.

70. Gentry and Wellum, *Kingdom through Covenant*, 31, 34, italics original; Niehaus, *Common Grace Covenants*, 2, 4–8; Goldsworthy highlights "the linked themes of the covenant and the new creation as a unifying element in the biblical message," while also focusing on how these relate to the kingdom of God (*According to Plan*, 76–77).

71. Jeon, *Biblical Theology*, 32; see also Williams, *Far as the Curse Is Found*, 71–75.

72. Niehaus, *Common Grace Covenants*, 77.

73. Ibid.; see also Gentry and Wellum, *Kingdom through Covenant*, 36; Williams, *Far as the Curse Is Found*, 73–74.

(New Testament)" as "the most comprehensive images found in Scripture."[74] While their narrative retelling of the Old Testament highlights the covenants, they structure the biblical story as a drama in six acts, which are all centered on God's kingdom.

- "Act 1: God Establishes His Kingdom: Creation"
- "Act 2: Rebellion in the Kingdom: Fall"
- "Act 3: The King Chooses Israel: Redemption Initiated"
- "Interlude: A Kingdom Story Waiting for an Ending: The Intertestamental Period"
- "Act 4: The Coming of the King: Redemption Accomplished"
- "Act 5: Spreading the News of the King: The Mission of the Church"
- "Act 6: The Return of the King: Redemption Completed"[75]

Goldingay foregoes a center or traditional theological scheme, instead following Wright's emphasis on God's acts and dividing the Old Testament into nine periods with titles indicating a characteristic action of God during each period.

- "God Began" (creation)
- "God Started Over" (rebellion, flood, and Tower of Babel)
- "God Promised" (patriarchal narratives)
- "God Delivered" (exodus)
- "God Sealed" (Sinai)
- "God Gave" (wilderness wanderings and conquest of the land)
- "God Accommodated" (judges and beginning of the monarchy)
- "God Wrestled" (kingdom split to the exile)
- "God Preserved" (exile and return from exile)[76]

He includes a final chapter dealing with the New Testament, which focuses on how "God Sent" Jesus. Goldingay's structure emphasizes that the Old Testament is primarily a narrative about God working to initiate and fulfill his purposes in the world, though he is careful to point out that "humanity has a key role to play" in the story as well.[77]

---

74. Bartholomew and Goheen, *Drama of Scripture*, 22.
75. Ibid., 22–23; see also Roberts's eight-part outline of the biblical narrative, centered on the theme of kingdom (*God's Big Picture*, 23), as well as Chester's seven-part outline: creation and fall, Abraham, Israel, Israel's decline and prophecy, Jesus, the church, new creation (*From Creation to New Creation*, 18).
76. Goldingay, *Israel's Gospel*, 5–8.
77. Ibid., 36.

TABLE 1.1: Proposals for the Narrative Structure of the Bible

Revelation (Vos)	Four-Stage (Emerson, Roark/Cline, Williams)	Covenant (Richter, Jeon, Gentry/Wellum, Niehaus)	Six-Act (Bartholomew/ Goheen)	God's Acts (Goldingay)
	Creation	Creational	Creation	Began
	Fall	Noahic	Fall	Started Over
Mosaic	Redemption	Abrahamic	Israel	Promised
		Mosaic		Delivered
				Sealed
				Gave (the Land)
		Davidic		Accommodated
Prophetic				Wrestled
				Preserved
		New	Jesus	Sent (Jesus)
NT			Church	
	New Creation		New Creation	

By contrast, Alexander and Lawrence both offer multiple readings of the biblical narrative, which parallel each other and draw out different aspects of the story. Alexander's retellings highlight God's presence with his people, his rule as king, the defeat of Satan, redemption through sacrifice, the holiness and wholeness of God's people, and the contrast between the corrupt kingdoms of this earth and the coming kingdom of God.[78] Lawrence, on the other hand, narrates the stories of creation, fall, love, sacrifice, and promise, which he sees as interwoven throughout the Bible.[79] *The Story of Israel* also differs from most theologies in this category by describing the biblical narrative as having a cyclical structure with a repeating "pattern of sin–exile–restoration."[80] Creation is treated as the backdrop to the story, describing the blessings of order, "dominion and fertility," and God's presence that are continually threatened by the sin of God's people.[81]

---

78. Alexander, *From Eden to the New Jerusalem.*
79. Lawrence, *Biblical Theology in the Life of the Church,* 113–76. To some degree, this approach amounts to an analysis of major themes, so these two works could go in the multiplex chapter (chap. 3). But since they emphasize story so strongly, we have placed them here.
80. Pate et al., *Story of Israel,* 18–27, esp. p. 22.
81. Ibid., 29–30.

Incorporation of Nonnarrative Literature

While this approach fits quite naturally with the Old Testament historical books (Genesis–Esther), incorporating nonnarrative literature has proven something of a challenge. Jeannine Brown sees the nonnarrative portions of Scripture as "assuming stories"—they build on foundational narratives, such as the stories about God's covenants with his people.[82] However, that is clearest in the case of the law, which is embedded into the covenant at Mount Sinai, and the prophetic books and some of the more historically oriented psalms, which are often incorporated into the narrative of Israel's monarchy, exile, and return to the land.[83] The nonhistorical psalms and wisdom books offer fewer connections to the biblical narrative, so scholars who ground their theology in Israel's history have difficulty fitting them into their work.

Some scholars respond to the problem by not discussing these parts of the Old Testament, perhaps with the understanding that they are not as central to grasping the theology of the Old Testament or simply because addressing them was beyond the scope of their book.[84] Others note the biblical association of the Psalms with David and the wisdom literature with Solomon and therefore cover these books in conjunction with their reigns.[85] A third strategy is taken by the multiauthored *Story of Israel* and *Biblical Theology of the Old Testament*. They both roughly follow the canonical sequence of the Old Testament, which allows them to give significant attention to the Psalms and the wisdom books, though they adopt different strategies for connecting them with their narrative focus.[86] *The Story of Israel* relates its discussion of the wisdom literature to the sin-exile-restoration paradigm that it traces throughout the biblical narrative. It focuses on how the wisdom books engage with the assumptions that obedience leads to blessing and disobedience leads to curse, contending that "the sages wrestle with whether such a notion aptly represents Israel's history—and reality in general."[87]

---

82. Brown, "Is the Future of Biblical Theology Story-Shaped?" 17; see also Bartholomew and Goheen, "Story and Biblical Theology," 160.

83. See, e.g., Goldingay, *Israel's Gospel*, 378–85, 465–75, 668–95; Bartholomew and Goheen, *Drama of Scripture*, 68–70, 108–10; Goldsworthy, *According to Plan*, 142–43, 167–68, 187–200.

84. See Richter, *Epic of Eden*; Williams, *Far as the Curse Is Found*; Vos, *Biblical Theology*; Jeon, *Biblical Theology*; Niehaus, *Special Grace Covenants: Old Testament*. Gentry and Wellum describe these books as "commentary on the historical/narrative section" and mention them in connection with covenantal instruction in Deuteronomy, but they do not offer any substantial discussion of them (*Kingdom through Covenant*, 169, 404).

85. See Bartholomew and Goheen, *Drama of Scripture*, 99–100; idem, "Story and Biblical Theology," 160; Roberts, *God's Big Picture*, 88; Roark and Cline, *Biblical Theology*, 46–47. See also Goldsworthy, *According to Plan*, 168–79. Goldsworthy discusses these books in a chapter that immediately follows his treatment of David and Solomon.

86. *Story of Israel* treats these books in one chapter (chap. 4), while *Biblical Theology of the Old Testament* gives separate chapters to the wisdom books and Song of Songs (chap. 6) and to the Psalms (chap. 7).

87. Pate et al., *Story of Israel*, 71. Note, however, that this book does not give significant attention to the nonhistorical psalms.

Roy Zuck's discussion of the wisdom literature in *Biblical Theology of the Old Testament* highlights how these books connect to the Old Testament narrative by means of

- the fear of YHWH,
- overlap with the law,
- creation theology.[88]

He then offers a theology of each wisdom book, using systematic categories to describe the book's views on God and man. Robert Chisholm's chapter on the Psalms in the same volume departs from the historical emphasis of the volume by presenting the theological message of the Psalms, which he sees as focused on God's universal kingship.[89]

Role of the New Testament in Interpreting the Old

As noted earlier, theologies in this category read the whole Bible as one story.[90] However, they disagree about whether we should read the story only forward (from the Old Testament to the New) or also backward (interpreting the Old Testament in light of the New). On one end of the spectrum, Bartholomew and Goheen tell the Old Testament story with hardly any reference to the New Testament.[91] It is only when they narrate the story of the New Testament that they emphasize how it fulfills the Old.[92]

Similarly, John Goldingay expresses a concern to describe the theology of the Old Testament "without looking at it through . . . New Testament lenses."[93] For example, concerning the snake in the garden of Eden, Goldingay observes that the New Testament draws a connection to Satan, but he cautions that "we should not go about relating them too quickly or too unequivocally, or we will miss the point Genesis . . . was making."[94] He points out that the snake is described as one of "the wild animals the LORD God had made" (Gen. 3:1) and that Genesis 1:21 portrays even the "sea monsters" *(tanninim)*

---

88. Roy B. Zuck, "A Theology of the Wisdom Books and the Song of Songs," in *Biblical Theology of the Old Testament*, 214–19.

89. Robert B. Chisholm Jr., "A Theology of the Psalms," in *Biblical Theology of the Old Testament*, 258.

90. See pp. 18–20.

91. Bartholomew and Goheen, *Drama of Scripture*, 25–117.

92. See, e.g., ibid., 138–39, 143, 163–64.

93. Goldingay, *Israel's Gospel*, 20. However, he occasionally notes connections with the New Testament. For example, he draws a parallel between God's appearances in Genesis and "Jesus' unthreatening coming as a human being," and he relates the fiery Sinai theophany to Hebrews' description of God as "a consuming fire" (12:29; p. 391).

94. Ibid., 134.

as God's creations, "not embodiments of dynamic power resistant to God."[95] Therefore he argues that "if anything, Genesis thus downplays supernatural involvement in humanity's downfall."[96] With regard to God's promise that Eve's offspring will crush the snake's head (Gen. 3:15), he contends that reading this verse as "'the first gospel' (protoevangelium) in the sense of a first messianic promise is a reinterpretation of it in light of the coming of Jesus, which reads a new meaning into the text."[97] Instead he argues that "offspring" should be understood as a collective noun referring to all of Eve's offspring and suggesting a continual battle with the offspring of the snake.[98]

On the other end of the spectrum, Michael Williams adopts the idea of "*sensus plenior* (the fuller sense)" to argue that because the Old Testament is divinely authored, certain texts can have "a fuller meaning" than the human author recognized.[99] In his view, this concept "derives from the fact that Christ is the center of the progressively unfolding biblical drama, Old Testament as well as New," which should lead us to ask, "What additional levels of significance does [this passage] take on in light of Christ?"[100] With regard to Genesis 3:15, he suggests that even though the human author was not aware that it was a promise of Jesus' victory over Satan, that is nevertheless an appropriate *sensus plenior* reading.[101] Jeon also sees Genesis 3:15 as an announcement of the gospel, and he understands God making garments of animal skins for Adam and Eve in verse 21 as "clothing them 'in the righteousness of Jesus Christ.'"[102] Therefore he takes that verse as "the first indirect revelation that God declares sinners as righteous with the imputation of the righteousness of Jesus Christ."[103]

Goldsworthy takes a similar approach, arguing that "in doing biblical theology as Christians, we do not start at Genesis 1 and work our way forward until we discover where it is all leading. Rather we first come to Christ, and he directs us to study the Old Testament in the light of the gospel. The gospel will interpret the Old Testament by showing us its goal and meaning."[104] Therefore he begins his retelling of the biblical narrative with Christ before

---

95. Ibid. The NIV translates *tanninim* as "the great creatures of the sea."

96. Ibid.

97. Ibid., 141.

98. Ibid.

99. Williams, *Far as the Curse Is Found*, 78.

100. Ibid., 79. See also Chester, *From Creation to New Creation*, 7. Chester declares that "Christ is the key that unlocks the meaning of the Scriptures. . . . We can only understand the Old Testament when we see how it points to Jesus."

101. Williams, *Far as the Curse Is Found*, 78.

102. Jeon, *Biblical Theology*, 26, quoting Edward J. Young, *Genesis 3: A Devotional and Expository Study* (Edinburgh: Banner of Truth Trust, 1966), 148.

103. Jeon, *Biblical Theology*, 26.

104. Goldsworthy, *According to Plan*, 55.

backtracking to creation.[105] Highlighting the themes of grace, election, and faith in his discussion of Abraham, he notes that these themes ultimately "find fulfillment in the gospel event" and declares that "it is the later fulfillment which must interpret the real significance of the earlier expressions."[106]

Niehaus's tendency to interpret the Old Testament in light of the New is demonstrated by his reading of the creation account in Genesis 1. He observes a parallel between Genesis 1:2, where "the Spirit of God was hovering over the waters," and Matthew 3:16, where Jesus "saw the Spirit of God descending like a dove." He also notes that John 1:1–3 describes Jesus as the Word through whom "all things were made." He then suggests that the New Testament picture of the Spirit working through Jesus to bring about God's kingdom through miraculous works parallels creation. This parallel allows us to see that "the Father caused the Spirit to work through the preincarnate Word to produce the kingdom that then was—namely, the visible creation."[107]

Alexander falls somewhere in the middle. Contending that "a good denouement [conclusion] sheds light on the entire story," he takes his point of departure from Revelation 20–22, noting how it connects back to Genesis 1–3.[108] For example, in his first chapter, he begins with the declaration in Revelation 21:3, "Look! God's dwelling place is now among the people."[109] However, he then proceeds to trace the story of God's presence from the beginning of the biblical narrative to its end, without allowing the New Testament to significantly reinterpret the Old. He observes that although God designs Eden as a "temple-garden," where "divinity and humanity enjoy each other's presence,"[110] Adam and Eve are exiled because of their sin. When God establishes his relationship with Israel, he dwells with them in the tabernacle and later the Jerusalem temple. Yet because Israel continually fails to uphold "the standards of holiness necessary to live in the presence of God," God removes his presence from Jerusalem (Ezekiel 9–10).[111] Nevertheless, the prophets envision a future restored temple (Ezekiel 40–48), which is fulfilled in Jesus and the church as a new temple, climaxing in Revelation's portrait of the New Jerusalem.[112]

---

105. Ibid., 81–89; see also Williams, *Far as the Curse Is Found*, 1–19.

106. Goldsworthy, *According to Plan*, 123.

107. Niehaus, *Common Grace Covenants*, 11. He also examines Ephesians 5:22–33 in connection with the institution of marriage in Genesis 2, saying that "what is later revealed illuminates what is primordial [at the beginning]" (p. 86). For another Trinitarian reading of creation, see Jeon, *Biblical Theology*, 4–7.

108. Alexander, *From Eden to the New Jerusalem*, 10.

109. Ibid., 13.

110. Ibid., 25.

111. Ibid., 49, 56.

112. Ibid., 57–73.

TEST CASE: EXODUS

Theologies that are grounded in biblical (hi)story tend to feature the exodus event prominently.[113] As Richter puts it, the exodus "is the single most important event in all Israelite history."[114] It explains *"why* Israel should serve Yahweh" and expresses "how Yahweh has chosen to be known"—as "the God who rescues slaves from their bondage and claims them as his own."[115] Williams discusses the nature of the exodus as a type, or pattern, saying, "God's delivering Israel through the Red Sea sets the pattern of redemption and blessing by which his people would forever recognize God's mighty action, most centrally in Jesus Christ."[116] Its central importance to the biblical narrative leads him to cover the exodus before creation, noting that it reveals God's desire to enter into intimate relationship with his people, requiring their obedient response.[117]

Alexander observes that at the beginning of Exodus, the Israelites are fulfilling God's creational command to "be fruitful" and "fill the earth" (Gen. 1:28). He contends that "implicit in this is the possibility that they will establish God's temple-city on the earth. However, the new king of Egypt feels threatened by them and sets them to work building cities for his own benefit."[118] Therefore Alexander describes the exodus as a story "about moving from one kingdom to another; it is about escaping corrupt human kingship and experiencing loving, divine kingship; it is about becoming priest-kings and entering into God's sanctuary where he reigns forever."[119]

Goldingay discusses the signs God performs through Moses to demonstrate his sovereignty over both the political and natural spheres. He observes that when Aaron throws down his staff and it turns into a snake—a feat matched by Pharaoh's magicians—the word used for "snake" is *tannin*. He then notes that *tannin* can also refer to a sea serpent, which serves as "a symbol for the powers that threaten to consume God's people and God's purpose. Egypt itself becomes a figure for such powers: it threatens to consume God's people and God's purpose (cf., e.g., Ps 74:13; Is 51:9). . . . But Aaron's cane swallows the Egyptians', and in due course the thrusting of an Israelite cane will lead to the swallowing up of the Egyptians themselves [at the Red Sea]

---

113. A notable exception is Pate et al., *Story of Israel*, 38–39, perhaps because the exodus does not fit clearly into its pattern of sin-exile-restoration.

114. Richter, *Epic of Eden*, 174.

115. Ibid., italics original.

116. Williams, *Far as the Curse Is Found*, 24.

117. Ibid., 36–39.

118. Alexander, *From Eden to the New Jerusalem*, 85.

119. Ibid., 85–86.

(Ex 14:16; 15:12)."[120] The final sign, the death of all the firstborn sons of Egypt, is a punishment both for Pharaoh's steadfast refusal to return God's firstborn son, Israel (Ex. 4:22–23), and for his edict that all the newborn sons of the Israelites should be drowned. Through these signs, not only Israel but also Egypt ultimately comes to recognize YHWH's power.[121]

Bartholomew and Goheen observe literary connections to creation in Israel's victory hymn after the defeat of the Egyptians at the Red Sea. Concerning Exodus 15:17, which declares, "You will bring [your people] in and plant them on the mountain of your inheritance—the place, LORD, you made for your dwelling, the sanctuary, Lord, your hands established," they contend, "All these phrases indicate that the land is like a second Eden, a place in which the Lord will dwell among his people. In the ancient Near East, the gods were traditionally thought of as living on mountains. Here, however, the whole land is pictured as the Lord's mountain, his dwelling, his sanctuary. God's planting of the Israelites in the land will be a major step on the way toward the recovery and restoration of the creation."[122]

Fewer authors dwell on the law. However, Roberts observes that "the exodus from Egypt is not the climax of the book" but prepares for the giving of the law and culminates in the building of the tabernacle.[123] Chester compares our modern tendency to view law as restrictive with the ancient Israelite perspective on God's law as life-giving in the context of the exodus. Contrasting the oppressive rule of Pharaoh with the rule of God, expressed in the law, he observes that under Pharaoh "vulnerable workers are exploited and overworked," whereas God's rule provides "rest for all with protection for vulnerable workers."[124] Likewise, while Pharaoh rules with violence, ordering that all the baby boys of the Hebrews be killed, God demands that human life be respected. Finally, although the Hebrew slaves have no legal recourse in Egypt, God requires the "integrity and impartiality of [the] judicial system" for the protection of society's vulnerable members.[125]

---

120. Goldingay, *Israel's Gospel*, 315, 317.
121. Ibid., 320–21.
122. Bartholomew and Goheen, *Drama of Scripture*, 64.
123. Roberts, *God's Big Picture*, 68.
124. Chester, *From Creation to New Creation*, 107.
125. Ibid.

Chapter 2

HISTORICAL-CRITICAL OLD TESTAMENT THEOLOGY

The previous chapter focused on theologies that are grounded in the historical accounts found within the biblical text. The scholars in this chapter also employ history, but they adopt a version of history that is reconstructed using the tools of historical criticism. A historical-critical reading of the Old Testament text does not simply accept the text at face value but seeks to read between the lines of the biblical text to discover the true history of events, in conversation with archaeology and other historical sources. For those readers unfamiliar with historical criticism, the basics of the historical-critical method will be summarized in the first section.[1] The use of historical criticism is not unique to this category, but the scholars discussed in this chapter employ historically reconstructed data as the foundation of their Old Testament theology.[2]

> DEFINITION: Historical-critical Old Testament theologies employ historical-critical reconstructions as the foundation for their Old Testament theology and read the Old Testament descriptively. Points of tension include debate about whether to call their work Old Testament theology or history of Israelite religion, which historical-critical reconstructions they use and the degree of historicity they see in the text, and the role of the New Testament in their work.

---

1. For a short introduction to Old Testament historical criticism, see Mark S. Gignilliat, *A Brief History of Old Testament Criticism: From Benedict Spinoza to Brevard Childs* (Grand Rapids: Zondervan, 2012).

2. This category corresponds to "BT1: Biblical Theology as Historical Description" in Edward W. Klink III and Darian R. Lockett, *Understanding Biblical Theology: A Comparison of Theory and Practice* (Grand Rapids: Zondervan, 2012), 29–56.

> ## Central Texts Covered in This Chapter
>
> Rainer Albertz, *A History of Israelite Religion in the Old Testament Period*
>   (German: 1992; English: 1994)
> James Barr, *The Concept of Biblical Theology* (1999)
> John Barton, "Biblical Theology" (2006)
> John J. Collins, "Is a Critical Biblical Theology Possible?" (1990)
> Erhard S. Gerstenberger, *Theologies in the Old Testament* (German: 2001;
>   English: 2002)
> Hartmut Gese, *Essays on Biblical Theology* (German: 1977; English: 1981)
> Antonius H. J. Gunneweg, *Biblische Theologie des Alten Testaments* (1993)
> Wolfram Herrmann, *Theologie des Alten Testaments* (2004)
> Jörg Jeremias, *Theologie des Alten Testaments* (2015)
> Niels Peter Lemche, *The Old Testament between Theology and History* (2008)
> Roland Murphy, "Reflections on a Critical Biblical Theology" (1997)
> Gerhard von Rad, *Old Testament Theology* (German: 1957–60; English:
>   1962–65)
> Konrad Schmid, *A Historical Theology of the Hebrew Bible* (German: 2018;
>   English: 2019)

COMMON FEATURES

Historical-Critical Reconstruction as the Foundation of Old Testament Theology

The rationale for scholars in this category to use historical-critical methods is that it is the only intellectually responsible way to study the Old Testament.[3] In the strong words of James Barr, "A relation to critical study is proper to biblical theology, and . . . no serious biblical theology has arisen where the truly conservative anti-critical principles have prevailed."[4] Jörg Jeremias rejects a historical account based on the biblical sequence of events, which would place creation at the beginning of the story,[5] arguing that "such a retelling is ultimately unhistorical because the Old Testament texts only at a relatively late stage took up the origin of the theme of creation: the time of the exile."[6]

---

3. This section will discuss the necessity of practicing historical criticism, while the point of tension "Historical-Critical Reconstructions and Degree of Historicity" that follows will address specific types of historical criticism.

4. James Barr, *The Concept of Biblical Theology: An Old Testament Perspective* (Minneapolis: Fortress, 1999), 83.

5. See the theologies discussed in chap. 1.

6. Jörg Jeremias, *Theologie des Alten Testaments*, Grundrisse zum Alten Testament 6 (Göttingen: Vandenhoeck and Ruprecht, 2015), 4–5, translation ours.

Even more bluntly, Roland Murphy argues that most biblical theologians would agree with the following statement: "historical criticism is not only basically compatible with biblical theology, but indeed indispensable to it."[7]

Rather than simply accepting traditional understandings of the biblical text, historical criticism seeks to reconstruct the true historical world behind the text. To some degree, virtually all Old Testament scholars follow such principles. For example, although it has traditionally been believed that Moses wrote all of the Torah, scholars today agree that Deuteronomy 34 was not written by Moses, because it records his death. Likewise, the history of the Hebrew language shows that the text of the Old Testament—including quotations by characters in the stories—has been updated over time. Also, later explanatory comments have been added (e.g., Deut. 3:11), and place names have at times been revised. Genesis 14:14 refers to the city of Dan long before the events of Judges 18, which records the conquest of that city by the tribe of Dan, giving the city its name.[8]

However, the common use of the phrase historical criticism suggests much more extensive revision of traditional understandings. Historical-critical methods affect two areas of research. First, they pass judgment on the historicity of the text—whether the events described in the biblical text happened as described. Some historical critics adopt an antisupernaturalist viewpoint, leading them to reject the historicity of miraculous accounts recorded in the biblical text. In other cases, skepticism about the historicity of certain biblical narratives derives from a reconstruction of history based on other historical sources or a particular reading of the biblical texts. One example is the "finding" of the book of the law in the temple during the reforms of the Judean king Josiah late in the divided monarchy (2 Kings 22:8), which many historical critics understand not as the recovery of an ancient book but rather as code for the initial writing of the book. It is often described as a "pious fraud" because in this understanding Josiah had the book composed with the appearance of an ancient document (technically, a fraud) for the purpose of consolidating worship of YHWH (hence, a pious aim).

Second, historical criticism theorizes about the composition of the text—who wrote what texts during which time period. In the example just cited, the book of the law is typically identified with Deuteronomy, so historical

---

7. Roland E. Murphy, "Reflections on a Critical Biblical Theology," in *Problems in Biblical Theology: Essays in Honor of Rolf Knierim*, ed. Henry T. C. Sun and Keith L. Eades (Grand Rapids: Eerdmans, 1997), 269.

8. For a discussion of this kind of textual updating from an evangelical viewpoint, see Michael A. Grisanti, "Inspiration, Inerrancy, and the OT Canon: The Place of Textual Updating in an Inerrant View of Scripture," *Journal of the Evangelical Theological Society* 44 (2001): 577–98.

critics argue that Deuteronomy was written by Josiah's officials in the seventh century BCE. The prophetic books have also come under scrutiny. Historical critics have challenged traditional views of prophetic authorship, which were based on superscriptions at the beginning of a book, identifying the prophet (e.g., Isa. 1:1), or references to the prophet within a book (e.g., Dan. 7:1). Critics who follow an antisupernaturalist principle deny the possibility of true predictive prophecy. Therefore texts that exhibit knowledge of supposedly later events are considered prophecy *ex eventu*—written "after the event." However, others argue merely that the historical context leads us to expect prophecy to be relevant to its time period. Hence they contend that Isaiah 40–55, which speaks to the situation of the Babylonian exiles, should be dated to the sixth century BCE rather than to the eighth-century preexilic context of the prophet Isaiah.[9] Also, whereas time markers within the book of Daniel suggest a sixth-century time frame, historical critics often date Daniel 7–12 to the second century BCE. They observe that these chapters seem to refer to events in the Maccabean period, and they see this dating as supported by Greek influences on the book. In sum, historical criticism does not take the historical descriptions in the text at face value but views the text as a window that allows glimpses into the actual historical events and history of composition.

The first work we will study in this category is a classic: Gerhard von Rad's *Old Testament Theology*. Arguing against those who ground their Old Testament theology in the categories of systematic theology, he says that "a theology which attempts to grasp the content of the Old Testament under the heading of various doctrines [the doctrine of God, the doctrine of man, etc.] cannot do justice to these creedal statements which are completely tied up with history."[10] However, his view of history is filtered through historical criticism; he does not necessarily believe that an event included in Israel's confession happened exactly as it is recorded in Scripture.[11] His indebtedness to historical criticism is seen most clearly in his organization of the postconquest material (Judges–Kings), where he begins with the monarchy and only later discusses the judges, arguing that the tradition of the judges was joined to the tradition of the monarchy later in Israel's history.[12]

The influence of historical criticism remains widespread among Old

---

9. Many scholars see Isaiah 56–66 as deriving from the postexilic period.

10. Gerhard von Rad, *Old Testament Theology*, trans. D. M. G. Stalker, 2 vols. (Edinburgh: Oliver and Boyd, 1962–65; repr. Peabody, MA: Prince, 2005), 1:vi.

11. See the point of tension "Historical-Critical Reconstructions and Degree of Historicity" on pp. 44–47.

12. Von Rad, *Old Testament Theology*, 1:308.

Testament theologies. To offer just one example, Konrad Schmid arranges a significant part of his theology according to historical reconstructions, by looking at the effect on Old Testament theology of events like the destruction of the Northern Kingdom (722 BCE), the salvation of Jerusalem from the Assyrian king Sennacherib (701 BCE), the later destruction of Jerusalem by the Babylonians (587/586 BCE), and the fall of Persia (333–331 BCE). He then discusses the texts associated with each event as determined by historical criticism.[13] Even when he looks at themes running throughout the Old Testament, he structures his discussion of each theme around its historical development, following his historical-critical reconstruction.[14]

Primarily Descriptive

In general, scholars who take a historical-critical approach tend to emphasize the descriptive nature of their reading of the Old Testament rather than viewing it prescriptively. John J. Collins argues that biblical theology is not prescriptive at all, because biblical theologians should not be judging the merits of worldviews but rather be helping to clarify the content and function of worldviews.[15] He goes so far as to say that historical criticism is not compatible with any kind of confessional theology that holds to definite positions.[16] In a later article, he argues that biblical theology has lost much of its prestige because its proponents have engaged in apologetics that essentially amount to lying for God. Instead biblical theologians should read the Old Testament critically, accepting the good and rejecting the evil.[17]

In a similar fashion, John Barton argues for the necessity of a more secular biblical theology that is less indebted to religion and will therefore provide clearer data.[18] Erhard Gerstenberger opposes seeing religious texts as authoritative and rejects any kind of exclusivity: "Because in our deeply pluralistic world claims to absoluteness of any kind which seek to impose themselves on others have simply no chance of survival, and are also impossible for scholarly

---

13. Konrad Schmid, *A Historical Theology of the Hebrew Bible*, trans. Peter Altmann (Grand Rapids: Eerdmans, 2019), 203–58. Jeremias sets up his work in a similar fashion.

14. Ibid., 259–445.

15. John J. Collins, "Is a Critical Biblical Theology Possible?" in *The Hebrew Bible and Its Interpreters*, ed. William Henry Propp, Baruch Halpern, and David Noel Freedman, Biblical and Judaic Studies 1 (Winona Lake, IN: Eisenbrauns, 1990), 14.

16. Ibid.

17. John J. Collins, "Biblical Theology between Apologetics and Criticism," in *Beyond Biblical Theologies*, ed. Heinrich Assel, Stefan Beyerle, and Christfried Böttrich, Wissenschaftliche Untersuchungen zum Neuen Testament 295 (Tübingen: Mohr Siebeck, 2012), 238–41.

18. John Barton, "Biblical Theology: An Old Testament Perspective," in *The Nature of New Testament Theology: Essays in Honour of Robert Morgan*, ed. Christopher Rowland and Christopher Tuckett (Oxford: Blackwell, 2006), 18–30.

discussion, we must learn to think again."[19] Othmar Keel passionately condemns the intolerance of Christianity and argues that texts like Deuteronomy 13—in which the person who spreads apostasy is sentenced to death—cannot be authoritative today.[20] A descriptive approach is particularly prominent in histories of Israelite religion.[21] Rainer Albertz says that a "history of Israelite religion must have a consistent historical construction and may not secretly or openly reintroduce dogmatic [systematic] principles of division and selection."[22]

However, the distinction between descriptive and prescriptive is not airtight, as even Albertz is willing to grant some measure of prescriptive status to the Old Testament if done correctly. Starting from contemporary problems, scholars could make "thematic cross-sections through the history of the religion of Israel and early Christianity in order to describe what insights or patterns of behaviour" might be helpful in considering those contemporary issues.[23] However, he also says that "this would be a different kind of 'Old Testament theology' from what has been customary so far."[24]

This tension can be found in many of the works in this category. They are unwilling to view the Old Testament as a uniquely inspired work that can be read in a prescriptive way for life today, but they are also unwilling to simply disregard its relevance.[25] However, their method is generally the same as that of historians who seek to learn from history in general. Gerstenberger illustrates this principle well when he says that it is impossible to derive ethical norms from ancient civilizations. However, what they thought about religion should help us enter into conversation with our own cultural expressions about God and religion.[26] For example, after condemning ancient Israel for their violence, he claims that "we can also learn theologically and ethically from a critical discussion of the old tribal traditions of Israel" because they model how an oppressed minority can survive.[27]

Schmid emphasizes his descriptive stance by adding the term historical

---

19. Erhard S. Gerstenberger, *Theologies in the Old Testament*, trans. John Bowden (London: T&T Clark, 2002), 207; see also p. 272 for a similar sentiment.

20. O. Keel, "Religionsgeschichte Israels oder Theologie des Alten Testaments?" in *Wieviel Systematik erlaubt die Schrift? Auf der Suche nach einer gesamtbiblischen Theologie*, ed. Frank-Lothar Hossfeld, Quaestiones Disputatae 185 (Freiburg: Herder, 2001), 97.

21. For the definition of this genre, see pp. 39–44.

22. Rainer Albertz, *A History of Israelite Religion in the Old Testament Period*, trans. John Bowden, 2 vols., Old Testament Library (Louisville: Westminster John Knox, 1994), 1:11.

23. Ibid., 1:17.

24. Ibid.

25. Barton claims that biblical theologians who employ historical criticism view the Bible reverently (John Barton, "[Pan-]Biblical Theology in the German- and English-Speaking Worlds: A Comparison," in *Beyond Biblical Theologies*, 256).

26. Gerstenberger, *Theologies in the Old Testament*, 2, 12.

27. Ibid., 156.

to the title of his book in its English translation because "'Theologie' is a less loaded term in German than 'theology' in English and may very well denote a historical approach without a kerygmatic [preaching] perspective."[28] Later in the book he contends that the Bible cannot play a prescriptive role because the Bible itself offers diverse views on many topics.[29] He also argues that "no one must maintain the truth of certain statements against their better judgment . . . simply because they are in the Bible."[30] However, he concedes that prescriptive readings can be legitimate, though "the inquiry into the validity of biblical texts cannot take place solely within the text; it must rather be considered in relation to the corresponding interpretive community."[31]

POINTS OF TENSION

Old Testament Theology versus History of Israelite Religion

One point of tension among scholars in this category is whether to describe their work as Old Testament theology or history of Israelite religion. Given that this is a book about Old Testament theology, it may not seem like an obvious choice to include a discussion of the history of Israelite religion. However, it is important because some scholars label the type of work that is normally included in the category of Old Testament theology as history of Israelite religion. The difficulty is that the relationship between the fields is often debated.[32]

The definition of the history of Israelite religion is generally agreed upon. (See the first column in table 2.1 on p. 42.) First, it employs a large database, including both nonbiblical texts and the findings from other disciplines, such as archaeology and sociology. Second, it is purely descriptive. Third, it is diachronic, as it focuses on the development of religious perspectives over time. Fourth, it tends to ignore connections with the New Testament. Finally, a history of Israelite religion focuses just as much on popular religion, the religion actually practiced by the people, as on official religion.

Given this understanding of the history of Israelite religion, many scholars see Old Testament theology and the history of Israelite religion as entirely

---

28. Schmid, *Historical Theology of the Hebrew Bible*, xvi–xvii.

29. Ibid., 125.

30. Ibid., 114.

31. Ibid., 127. Albert de Pury and Ernst Knauf argue that the work of the biblical scholar must be descriptive and not be confused with the work of a preacher, which is creative and prescriptive. However, they end their article with a plea that scholars and preachers sometimes put away their own way of speaking in order to listen to each other (Albert de Pury and Ernst Axel Knauf, "La théologie de l'Ancien Testament: Kérygmatique ou descriptive?" *Etudes théologiques et religieuses* 70 [1995]: 323–34).

32. For a helpful overview of this debate, see Barr, *Concept of Biblical Theology*, 100–139; Leo G. Perdue, *Reconstructing Old Testament Theology: After the Collapse of History*, Overtures to Biblical Theology (Minneapolis: Fortress, 2005), 25–75.

different enterprises. For example, Isaac Kalimi says, "There is nothing vague in the difference between 'Old Testament theology' and the 'history of Israelite religion.' These are two distinct legitimate demarcations. Deep differences exist between them, differences that can never overlap."[33] Albertz argues passionately not only for a clear division between them but also for the superiority of the history of Israelite religion over Old Testament theology. Since published Old Testament theologies frequently disagree with each other, he believes that the field is too diverse to be helpful. Also, in his view, Old Testament theology

- tends to downplay various parts of the Old Testament that do not fit its argument,
- has trouble integrating history and theology,
- too often includes anti-Semitic attitudes,
- discusses the ancient Near Eastern context only in an adversarial tone,
- ignores the religious life of the Israelites.

On the other hand, the history of Israelite religion

- boasts a clearer historical method,
- offers more external data to control subjectivity,
- better accounts for differences within the Old Testament,
- more productively compares the Old Testament with the ancient Near East.[34]

Thomas Thompson goes even farther by rejecting both the history of Israelite religion and Old Testament theology. He believes that all material and textual remains of the ancient Israelites are from the elite, so we can know nothing of

---

33. Isaac Kalimi, "History of Israelite Religion or Hebrew Bible / Old Testament Theology? Jewish Interest in Biblical Theology," in *Early Jewish Exegesis and Theological Controversy: Studies in Scriptures in the Shadow of Internal and External Controversies*, Jewish and Christian Heritage 2 (Assen: Van Gorcum, 2002), 114.

34. Rainer Albertz, "Religionsgeschichte Israels statt Theologie des Alten Testaments! Plädoyer für eine forschungsgeschichtliche Umorientierung," *Jahrbuch für Biblische Theologie* 10 (1995): 3–24. Albertz blames the First World War for the death of the genre of history of Israelite religion and writes his two-volume book as an attempt to revive it in the face of the overwhelming popularity of Old Testament theology (*History of Israelite Religion in the Old Testament Period*, 1:2–12). Gerstenberger does not use the phrase history of Israelite religion, but his employment of the plural in his title (*Theologies in the Old Testament*) effectively puts him in this category. He critiques those who write a "theology of the Old Testament," because such theologies arbitrarily emphasize certain parts of the Old Testament and downplay other parts: "But the Old Testament cannot of itself offer any unitary theological or ethical view, since it is a conglomerate of experiences of faith from very different historical and social contexts" (*Theologies in the Old Testament*, 1).

popular religion. As part of the Copenhagen school—who take a so-called minimalist approach to Old Testament history—he sees the entire Old Testament as written during the Persian or Greek period after the exile and as containing very little real history. Because Old Testament Israel did not exist in reality, he suggests that "we are dealing more with a history of ideas than a history of religion."[35] Niels Peter Lemche offers a similar argument in his provocatively titled article "Why the Theology of the Old Testament Is a Mistake."[36]

However, upon closer analysis, those scholars who reject the connection between the two fields employ a narrow definition of Old Testament theology—what we might call a stereotypical view—which can be defined in opposition to the history of Israelite religion. (See the first two columns in table 2.1 on p. 42.) In this understanding, Old Testament theology first focuses on the Old Testament as a discrete text, with less attention paid toward ancient Near Eastern material. Second, it tends to view the Old Testament prescriptively and authoritatively. Third, it reads the Old Testament synchronically by downplaying changes over time and seeking to make universal and timeless statements. Fourth, it often looks forward to the New Testament. Finally, because of its desire to be prescriptive, it focuses only on official religion in ancient Israel—on what God called the people of Israel to do, not necessarily what they did.

The difference between the history of Israelite religion and this definition of Old Testament theology can be illustrated by their respective approaches to stories of Israelites who were opposed to YHWH. As Barr phrases it, "No one has proposed to write a 'theology' based upon the views of Ahab and Jezebel, or upon those of Aaron when he made the Golden Calf."[37] An Old Testament

---

35. Thomas L. Thompson, "Das Alte Testament als theologische Disziplin," *Jahrbuch für Biblische Theologie* 10 (1995): 173, translation ours. Some scholars have questioned whether the Old Testament even contains any theology at all. Given how often the Old Testament speaks of YHWH, this might be a surprising claim. However, these scholars define the term theology more narrowly. According to Schmid, the Old Testament does not have "theology in the didactic sense or as a systematically explicit entity" (Konrad Schmid, *Is There Theology in the Hebrew Bible?* trans. Peter Altmann, Critical Studies in the Hebrew Bible 4 [Winona Lake, IN: Eisenbrauns, 2015], 116). However, he concedes that the Old Testament "is shown from a number of angles to be a collection of books that, while they do not formulate explicit theologies, because of their implicit theological character can count in a broader sense as theological writings" (p. 115). For a similar argument, see Roland E. Murphy, "A Response to 'The Task of Old Testament Theology,'" *Horizons in Biblical Theology* 6 (1984): 67; Barr, *Concept of Biblical Theology*, 606.

36. Niels Peter Lemche, "Warum die Theologie des Alten Testaments einen Irrweg darstellt," *Jahrbuch für Biblische Theologie* 10 (1995): 79–92, translation ours. For more on the status of Old Testament theology for those who deny much of the historicity of the Old Testament, see Brent A. Strawn, "What Would (or Should) Old Testament Theology Look Like If Recent Reconstructions of Israelite Religion Were True?" in *Between Israelite Religion and Old Testament Theology: Essays on Archaeology, History, and Hermeneutics*, ed. Robert D. Miller II, Contributions to Biblical Exegesis and Theology 80 (Leuven: Peeters, 2016), 129–66.

37. Barr, *Concept of Biblical Theology*, 133.

theology would refer to these events only as popular religion and would contrast such behavior with official religion prescribed by YHWH. However, a history of Israelite religion would consider these accounts as just as important as official theology and might even refer to them as parallel theologies.

In contrast to the view that these two fields are opposites, a significant number of historical critics see them more similarly. They reach this conclusion partly by defining Old Testament theology in a way that corresponds in many aspects to the history of Israelite religion. In particular, like the history of Israelite religion, they see Old Testament theology as descriptive, diachronic, and separate from the New Testament. However, they understand Old Testament theology as focusing more on the Old Testament text than on other sources and as describing official religion.

TABLE 2.1: History of Israelite Religion versus Old Testament Theology

History of Israelite Religion	Stereotypical Old Testament Theology	Historical-Critical Old Testament Theology
Focused on ancient Israel more broadly	Focused on Old Testament as a text	Focused on Old Testament as a text
Descriptive readings	Prescriptive readings	Descriptive readings
Diachronic	Synchronic	Diachronic
Tends to ignore New Testament	Tends to connect more with New Testament	Tends to ignore New Testament
Official and popular religion	Only official religion	Primarily official religion

Collins offers an example of this perspective, describing biblical theology as a subcategory of the history of religion, which "deals with the portrayal of God in one specific corpus of texts," the Bible.[38] Other scholars see Old

---

38. Collins, "Is a Critical Biblical Theology Possible?" 9. This view of Old Testament biblical theology as a subcategory of the history of Israelite religion is shared by Benjamin D. Sommer ("Dialogical Biblical Theology: A Jewish Approach to Reading Scripture Theologically," in *Biblical Theology: Introducing the Conversation*, ed. Leo G. Perdue, Robert Morgan, and Benjamin D. Sommer, Library of Biblical Theology [Nashville: Abingdon, 2009], 15–20). Barr rejects all of the distinctions between the two except that, first, they focus on different material—Old Testament theology on the mainstream biblical message, and the history of Israelite religion on a much broader basis. Second, they have different attitudes toward asking truth questions. Old Testament theology structures its work in a way that facilitates asking truth questions, while the history of Israelite religion shies away from them (*Concept of Biblical Theology*, 133–37). Barton suggests that according to his historical and nonprescriptive definition, Old Testament theology and the history of Israelite religion are very similar (John Barton, "Covenant in Old Testament Theology," in *The Old Testament: Canon, Literature, and Theology: Collected Essays of John Barton*, Society for Old Testament Studies Monograph Series [Burlington, VT: Ashgate, 2007], 276–77). He sees a special place for Old Testament theology in connection to reception history: "Biblical theology as I am defining it is

Testament theology as building upon the foundation of the history of Israelite religion.[39] Similar to a history of Israelite religion, Wolfram Herrmann structures his Old Testament theology around four parts arranged by time period. However, at the end of each section, he shifts more toward an Old Testament theology by discussing the characteristics of YHWH during that time.[40] In Jörg Jeremias's view the history of religion is "pointed at the origin and historical development of Old Testament faith," and Old Testament theology at "the central content of the Old Testament testimonies of God."[41]

Antonius Gunneweg views the two as similar enough that he puts them both in the title of his book: *Biblical Theology of the Old Testament: A History of Israelite Religion in Biblical-Theological Perspective.*[42] His book is arranged like a traditional history of religion, tracing the changes in Israel's religion over time. However, he offers more discussion of the Old Testament's theological connection with the New Testament than many scholars in this category.[43] Joachim Schaper argues that the distinction between the two genres is minimal, highlighting how even Albertz desires some level of modern relevance.[44] Keel contends that Albertz's work is "more a history of theology" than a history of religion and should have included more about Israelite religious *practice* as well as data from areas like iconography (the study of images) and archaeology.[45] He concludes that "for a 'history of Israelite religion' the practice of the religion is just as important as the ideas and opinions united with this practice."[46]

---

a critical analysis of the reception history of biblical texts, but one which compares that history carefully both with the original meaning of the texts and with the theological doctrine that has both resulted from and been read back into the texts in question" (idem, "The Messiah in Old Testament Theology," in *King and Messiah in Israel and the Ancient Near East: Proceedings of the Oxford Old Testament Seminar,* ed. John Day, Journal for the Study of the Old Testament: Supplement Series 270 [Sheffield: Sheffield Academic, 1998], 371); see also idem, "Alttestamentliche Theologie nach Albertz?" *Jahrbuch für Biblische Theologie* 10 (1995): 25–34.

39. Theo Sundermeier, "Religionswissenschaft versus Theologie? Zur Verhältnisbestimmung von Religionswissenschaft und Theologie aus religionswissenschaftlicher Sicht," *Jahrbuch für Biblische Theologie* 10 (1995): 206.

40. Wolfram Herrmann, *Theologie des Alten Testaments: Geschichte und Bedeutung des israelitisch-jüdischen Glaubens* (Stuttgart: Kohlhammer, 2004), 21.

41. Jeremias, *Theologie des Alten Testaments*, 20, translation ours. He further describes the history of Israelite religion as employing a broader set of data by incorporating texts and images from outside the Bible to reach a picture of Israel's faith that generally corresponds to the early stage of its faith. Old Testament theology then tends to focus on how that early form shifted to later forms (pp. 20–21).

42. Antonius H. J. Gunneweg, *Biblische Theologie des Alten Testaments: Eine Religionsgeschichte Israels in biblisch-theologischer Sicht* (Stuttgart: Kohlhammer, 1993), translation ours.

43. See pp. 48–50.

44. Joachim Schaper, "Problems and Prospects of a 'History of the Religion of Israel,'" in *The Twentieth Century—From Modernism to Post-Modernism,* part 2 of vol. 3 of *Hebrew Bible / Old Testament: The History of Its Interpretation,* ed. Magne Saebø (Göttingen: Vandenhoeck and Ruprecht, 2015), 638–39.

45. Keel, "Religionsgeschichte Israels," 103, translation ours.

46. Ibid., 107, translation ours.

In sum, it is difficult to make dogmatic statements about the differences between the two fields, because scholars employ the phrase Old Testament theology in such dramatically different ways. If the more synchronic and prescriptive definition of Old Testament theology is used, then the differences between the two fields remain significant. However, if Old Testament theology is viewed as diachronic and descriptive (as most historical critics understand it), then the differences between the fields are minimal and the choice of genre title is dependent on the preference of the scholar.

Historical-Critical Reconstructions and Degree of Historicity

While all scholars in this category employ historical-critical methods, the specifics of their historical-critical reconstructions and the degree of historicity they see in the Old Testament vary greatly. In the early years of the twentieth century, the reigning historical-critical method was source criticism, which was popularized in the late nineteenth century by Julius Wellhausen. The focus of source criticism is on discovering the original sources of various biblical texts. In the Hexateuch (Genesis–Joshua), Wellhausen identified four interwoven sources, which were symbolized by the letters JEDP.[47] The J and E sources are distinguished by their choice of divine name: J (the Yahwist) uses YHWH,[48] while E (the Elohist) uses *Elohim*, the Hebrew word for "God." D (the Deuteronomist) is naturally connected primarily with Deuteronomy, while P (the priestly source) focuses on the cultic life of ancient Israel.[49]

Source criticism still plays an important role in Old Testament theology, but other methods have grown up alongside it, as illustrated by the classic work of Gerhard von Rad. Following Wellhausen, von Rad suggests a background of the early monarchy for the Yahwist (J), a later Northern Kingdom (Israel) background for the Elohist (E), Levitical preaching in the Northern Kingdom during the late monarchy for the Deuteronomist (D), and a postexilic Southern Kingdom (Judah) background for the priestly source (P). However, in addition to identifying these sources, von Rad also highlights the role of the redactor (editor) who combined the various sources. Whereas source critics had tended to view the redactor merely as a collector of earlier sources,

---

47. The English translation of his work is Julius Wellhausen, *Prolegomena to the History of Ancient Israel: With a Reprint of the Article* Israel *from the "Encyclopaedia Britannica"* (Edinburgh: Adam and Charles Black, 1885; repr. New York: Meridian, 1957).

48. While it appears to English speakers that the source should be called Y, the divine name YHWH is spelled with a J in German.

49. This source-critical understanding of the Hexateuch (or Pentateuch: Genesis–Deuteronomy) is known as the Documentary Hypothesis. Although it has undergone substantial revision since the time of Wellhausen, many historical-critical scholars still hold to some version of it.

for von Rad the redactor becomes a true author, using those sources to create a coherent document. Examining the activity of the redactor in combining and editing the sources is known as redaction criticism. Von Rad also combines the results of source and redaction criticism to trace the whole development of Israel's traditions and their relationship to each other, an enterprise that is often called tradition-historical criticism. His aim is to identify how historical traditions grew from historical kernels, and in his view the earliest core of Israel's faith can be found in Deuteronomy 26:5–9.[50]

Rather than seeking to outline Israel's history, von Rad focuses on Israel's confession (its *account* of its history), which he sees as related to Israel's actual history in varying degrees. On the one hand, he believes that Israel's confessions need to reflect some historical realities: "If we divorced Israel's confessional utterances from the divine acts in history which they so passionately embrace, what a bloodless ghost we would be left with!"[51] Therefore, while he sees the order and details of the events as uncertain, he is still optimistic about some degree of historical truth in the patriarchal and exodus events. For example, he is confident about the historical reality that the nation of Israel developed from an amphictyony (a league of tribes), declaring, "The assumption that the Israelite clans' worship of Jahweh is to be understood on the analogy of the sacral cultic leagues of ancient Greece and Rome is not a new one, but it has only recently been developed systematically and raised to such a degree of certainty as is attainable in this field."[52]

On the other hand, his historical-critical methods ultimately lead him to doubt the historicity of many biblical accounts: "What lies at the back of the picture offered in the Hexateuch is still far from being the actual historical course of events, but is once again only certain interpretations and conceptions of older traditions."[53] As one specific example, he says that the concept of a unified people of Israel already present in Egypt and Sinai is simply importing a later reality into an earlier time period.[54]

However, although von Rad maintains that the history told in the Old Testament is often inaccurate, he wants to retain the label of history. He attempts to explain this claim in relation to the conquest, in which he argues that in historical fact the tribes entered the land of Canaan individually, not as

---

50. Von Rad, *Old Testament Theology*, 1:129–35.

51. Ibid., 1:112.

52. Ibid., 1:16–17. In retrospect this is an ironic statement, since not only do very few scholars hold to the idea of an amphictyony today, but it was one of the first parts of his historical reconstruction to be challenged.

53. Ibid., 1:3–4.

54. Ibid., 1:6.

"all Israel" as described in Joshua. Yet in spite of this, he does not see Joshua as nonhistorical: "Unlike any ordinary historical document, it does not have its centre in itself; it is intended to tell the beholder about Jahweh, that is, how Jahweh led his people and got himself glory. In Jawheh's eyes Israel is always a unity: his control of history was no improvisation made up of disconnected events: in the saving history he always deals with *all Israel*. . . . Faith had so mastered the material that the history could be seen from within, from the angle of faith."[55] He explains historical discrepancies by appealing to his view of the text's openness to the future (his suggested typological reading):[56] "This knowledge of the future occasionally asserted itself so strongly when the material was being shaped that the event is described as having a glory which far transcends the actual historical experience, as for example in the description of the entry of the whole of Israel into Canaan."[57]

Other older works are also based on these "assured results" of earlier historical criticism. One of the more ambitious projects is that of Peter Ellis, who writes a theology of just the Yahwist (J) rather than of the Hexateuch or the Old Testament as a whole.[58] However, this older historical-critical view has fallen into disfavor, especially with regard to its dating of the various sources. This is exemplified by Georg Fischer's critique of von Rad: "He did not consider the possibility of later origins of the biblical books; nowadays we assume that most of them came into being in their final redaction only in postexilic times. In addition to that, archaeological evidence has dramatically altered our understanding of Israel's history."[59] Dating these sources to the postexilic period is frequently supported by matching events in this time period to emphases of various texts in the Hexateuch.[60] In addition, the identity and character of the sources have been questioned, as most scholars today reject both the existence of the E source and the historicity of the narrative in the J source. The shifting nature of the field is well illustrated

---

55. Ibid., 1:302, italics ours. Von Rad provides another example in the accounts of David, since he sees 1 Samuel 16:1–13 as a late addition: "Historically, the pious story is therefore in error. But on the other hand, it is the one which most strongly emphasises the element of the completely unexpected and incomprehensible in this new action of God" (1:309).

56. See p. 48.

57. Von Rad, *Old Testament Theology*, 2:423. Barton suggests that von Rad creates such problems for himself in his attempt to focus on both the confession of Israel and historical-critical reconstructions that the only way out would have been to "eschew historical concerns, altogether, and practice a consistent canonical criticism" ("Messiah in Old Testament Theology," 369).

58. Peter F. Ellis, *The Yahwist: The Bible's First Theologian* (Notre Dame, IN: Fides, 1968).

59. Georg Fischer, "Biblical Theology in Transition: An Overview of Recent Works, and a Look Ahead at How to Proceed," in *Biblical Theology: Past, Present, and Future*, ed. Carey Walsh and Mark W. Elliott (Eugene, OR: Cascade, 2016), 79.

60. Even for those who reject a late dating of the Hexateuch, these links are a gold mine of innerbiblical connections.

by comparing two collections of essays with the same title: *A Farewell to the Yahwist.* In one the title ends with a question mark, suggesting that the issue is still in doubt, while the other offers a more definitive statement about the Yahwist's demise.[61]

In general, more recent historical critics have also become even less optimistic about the historicity of biblical events, especially events that fall before Israel's monarchy. Gerstenberger represents the majority of historical critics today when he expresses his skepticism about the historicity of the exodus: "The biblical tradition of the exodus from Egypt is virtually unusable for reconstructing the history of Israel."[62] This opinion is shared by the members of the Copenhagen School, such as Lemche: "The conclusion must be that the exodus is most likely legendary, constructed by Old Testament historiographers in order to create a 'national' foundation myth for the Jewish people."[63]

Schmid also expresses skepticism about the historicity of the Old Testament, declaring that "virtually no one today holds that the account of Genesis–2 Kings simply records the historical events."[64] He also demonstrates how source-critical results have changed over time. His view of the exodus as an entirely separate block of tradition from the patriarchal narratives, which is becoming more widespread, marks a radical departure from Wellhausen's understanding of the JEDP sources as interwoven throughout the patriarchal and exodus narratives. According to Schmid's reconstruction, the patriarchal and exodus traditions were first connected in the priestly source (P), but only after P were they fully joined together in texts like Joshua 24:2–13— the speech of Joshua, which incorporates both traditions into one history.[65] However, despite its growing popularity, this view does not dominate the field. Scholars today continue to employ historical-critical methods in different ways, leading to diverse results, which in turn produce varied understandings of Old Testament theology.

---

61. Thomas B. Dozeman and Konrad Schmid, eds., *A Farewell to the Yahwist? The Composition of the Pentateuch in Recent European Interpretation*, Society of Biblical Literature Symposium Series 34 (Atlanta: Society of Biblical Literature, 2006); Jan Christian Gertz, Konrad Schmid, and Markus Witte, eds., *Abschied vom Jahwisten: Die Komposition des Hexateuch in der jüngsten Diskussion*, Beihefte zur Zeitschrift für die alttestamentliche Wissenschaft 315 (Berlin: de Gruyter, 2002).

62. Gerstenberger, *Theologies in the Old Testament*, 112. For a survey of recent work on the historicity of the exodus, see Megan Bishop Moore and Brad E. Kelle, *Biblical History and Israel's Past: The Changing Study of the Bible and History* (Grand Rapids: Eerdmans, 2011), 77–144.

63. Niels Peter Lemche, *The Old Testament between Theology and History: A Critical Survey* (Louisville: Westminster John Knox, 2008), 131.

64. Konrad Schmid, *Genesis and the Moses Story: Israel's Dual Origins in the Hebrew Bible*, trans. James D. Nogalski, Siphrut 3 (Winona Lake, IN: Eisenbrauns, 2010), 2.

65. See ibid.

Role of the New Testament

The third point of tension among scholars in this category involves the role of the New Testament in their theological work. Some scholars, most prominently von Rad, see a tighter connection between Old Testament theology and the New Testament.[66] Although he rejects an overly tidy view of salvation history,[67] von Rad desires to draw the two testaments together with his view that Old Testament texts have a "radical openness for the future" and expect to be reinterpreted.[68] This leads to his understanding that "the Old Testament can only be read as a book of ever increasing anticipation."[69] Therefore the New Testament treatment of the Old Testament follows a practice of typological reinterpreting that had begun already within the Old Testament itself and that the texts expected from the beginning.[70]

This typological hermeneutic fits with von Rad's historical viewpoint: "No special hermeneutic method is necessary to see the whole diversified movement of the Old Testament saving events, made up of God's promises and their temporary fulfilments, as pointing to their future fulfilment in Jesus Christ."[71] Hence he argues that any historical critic should be able to see how the Old Testament finds its end in the New Testament, without resorting to theological exegesis. He even declares that "the coming of Jesus Christ as a historical reality leaves the exegete no choice at all: he must interpret the Old Testament as pointing to Christ."[72] For von Rad, connecting the Old Testament with the New Testament is so important that he claims that Old Testament theology can properly be called biblical theology only if it seeks to do that. If it does not, then it is merely a "history of the religion of the Old Testament."[73]

Hartmut Gese adopts von Rad's focus on tradition history and extends it farther by incorporating the New Testament more firmly into that tradition history.[74] Like most historical-critical scholars, he understands Isaiah 40–55

---

66. Since von Rad taught in an anti-Semitic context in Nazi Germany, it was important for him to connect the Old Testament to the New as a way to preserve the Old Testament for Christians. For a study of von Rad in his historical context, see Bernard M. Levinson, "Reading the Bible in Nazi Germany: Gerhard von Rad's Attempt to Reclaim the Old Testament for the Church," *Interpretation* 62 (2008): 238–54.

67. For example, note von Rad's statement, "We find it impossible to see in all of this an 'organic evolution of salvation,' with all its parts co-ordinated and, indeed, with the end already 'given along with' the beginning" (*Old Testament Theology*, 2:362).

68. Ibid., 2:361.

69. Ibid., 2:319.

70. Ibid., 2:361.

71. Ibid., 2:374.

72. Ibid.

73. Ibid., 2:428–29.

74. Hartmut Gese, *Essays on Biblical Theology*, trans. Keith Crim (Minneapolis: Augsburg Fortress, 1981), 1–33; idem, "Tradition History," in *Old Testament Theology: Flowering and Future*, ed. Ben C. Ollenburger, Sources for Biblical and Theological Study 1 (Winona Lake, IN: Eisenbrauns, 2004), 382–98.

(Second Isaiah) as the product of a later time than the Isaiah of Jerusalem who is connected with much of Isaiah 1–39 (First Isaiah). However, he also believes that Second Isaiah was added deliberately as a faithful continuation of the tradition of First Isaiah. Therefore he contends that "when the New Testament identifies the author of a passage in Second Isaiah as 'Isaiah the Prophet,' this is completely in keeping with the data of tradition history and true to the material involved."[75]

To some extent, Jeremias also follows von Rad by adopting his typological hermeneutic, though he rarely cites the New Testament.[76] Likewise, Gunneweg understands the Old Testament as linked to the New Testament in important ways because of the Christian canon, and he observes that the church has selectively chosen various portions of the Old Testament to emphasize, such as monotheism (the belief in only one God).[77] Several of his chapters end by discussing references to the topics under consideration (such as the divine name) in the New Testament.[78] However, he does not view the Old Testament as a preliminary stage for the New Testament, and he rejects the traditional ways of connecting the Old and New Testaments, such as through allegory or typology.[79]

Most recent scholars in this category see even greater distance between the testaments. For example, Barr desires to see more "intrinsic separateness" between them, contending that "real Old Testament theology can be, and probably should be, reached and expressed on the terms of the Old Testament itself . . . the New Testament neither assists in this process nor can be adequately connected with the Old as a result of this process."[80] Gerstenberger argues that we should actively seek to remove the New Testament from our mind when reading the Old Testament.[81] Likewise, Schmid sees a divide between Old Testament theology and the New Testament: "In this respect it is neither a Christian nor a Jewish, but rather a Hebrew Bible undertaking."[82] At the conclusion of his tome, he compares both Jewish and Christian interpretations of the Old Testament to "architectural structures that integrated earlier buildings—like, for example, the cathedral of Syracuse on Sicily, which originated as a Greek temple, was then converted into a basilica, served as a

---

75. Gese, *Essays on Biblical Theology*, 22.

76. Jeremias's Scripture index includes only the Old Testament.

77. Gunneweg, *Biblische Theologie des Alten Testaments*, 34–36.

78. Ibid., 83–84.

79. Ibid., 34–36.

80. Barr, *Concept of Biblical Theology*, 187–88. Herrmann illustrates this approach, as the Scripture index of his work reveals that he cites only four texts from the New Testament.

81. Gerstenberger, *Theologies in the Old Testament*, 284.

82. Schmid, *Historical Theology of the Hebrew Bible*, xvii.

mosque in the time of the Moors, and in the baroque period was furnished with a new façade."[83] Later readings of the Old Testament, such as those found in the New Testament, stand as objects of study in their own right but are not necessarily reflective of the original meaning of the texts.

TEST CASE: EXODUS

The exodus plays an important role for von Rad, for obvious reasons: it is one of the most prominent divine acts in the Old Testament and is frequently repeated in the confessions of ancient Israel. Citing Psalm 74:2, he shows how the theological importance of the event can scarcely be overstated: "In the deliverance from Egypt Israel saw the guarantee for all the future, the absolute surety for Jahweh's will to save, something like a warrant to which faith could appeal in times of trial."[84] However, other portions of Exodus also receive close attention. Concerning the revelation of the divine name (Exodus 3), he declares, "Thus the name Jahweh, in which, one might almost say, Jahweh has given himself away, was committed in trust to Israel alone."[85] He also spends almost a hundred pages on the revelation at Sinai in the latter chapters of Exodus, though he views the Sinai texts as late additions because of their absence in such historical overviews as Deuteronomy 26:5–9 and Joshua 24:2–13. The core of the Sinai traditions for von Rad is that "at Sinai Jahweh revealed to his people binding ordinances, on the basis of which life with its God was made possible."[86]

Responding to criticism of his decision to begin his history of Israelite religion with the exodus, Albertz argues that the ideals of the exodus, including the rejection of imperialism and oppression, permeate the rest of Old Testament religion.[87] He contends,

> In contrast to the state religions of the ancient Near East, which derive themselves from earliest mythical times, Yahweh religion has a historical foundation and did not from the beginning have the function of legitimating rule and stabilizing the existing social order. Rather, as the symbolic world of a social outsider group fighting for its right to life, it serves to provide internal solidarity for this group and to detach it from a

---

83. Ibid., 446.
84. Von Rad, *Old Testament Theology*, 1:176.
85. Ibid., 1:182.
86. Ibid., 1:188.
87. Rainer Albertz, "Hat die Theologie des Alten Testaments doch noch eine Chance?" *Jahrbuch für Biblische Theologie* 10 (1995): 185–87.

social order which was felt to be unjust, in the direction of a future social integration which makes possible a freer and more equitable social life.[88]

Even though Gerstenberger does not think that the exodus happened,[89] he argues that the story of the exodus is still important. As he puts it, "The narrative passages already mentioned, especially in the books of Genesis and Exodus, do not so much have historical and documentary value as give examples of right behavior, the practice of faith and courage to confess the faith."[90] For example, he suggests that the model of YHWH communicating with the Israelites in the book of Exodus teaches the people about what to expect in their own communication with YHWH.

Herrmann sees the exodus as playing an important role in the origin of YHWH faith early in Israelite history, demonstrating "help and salvation" for those who follow him.[91] In contrast, Schmid sees the exodus account playing a role later in Israel's history, arguing that it is dependent upon Assyrian models of a sovereign god in control of the entire world. However, he contends that Exodus turns these motifs around against Assyria when he suggests that "the Moses-exodus narrative emerges as the first clearly anti-imperial literary document in Israel."[92] Because YHWH is sovereign over the world, Assyria and other empires have no power over Israel. Israel's task is absolute trust in YHWH.

Jeremias provides an example of the benefit of working with ancient Near Eastern material, when he recognizes the parallels between the birth of Moses (Ex. 2:1–10) and the Sargon Birth Legend from Mesopotamia. In that legend Sargon is conceived by a priestess, who places him in a river to keep him safe. He is later rescued and eventually becomes king. However, Jeremias also notes the differences between the stories and highlights their significance for the exodus account, referring to Moses as a "kind of anti-king" who never ruled any territory nor became a king but instead functioned as the representative of YHWH before the oppressive Pharaoh.[93] Jeremias concludes that "at the level of the narrative, Moses represents the counter-model to Pharaoh."[94]

---

88. Albertz, *History of Israelite Religion in the Old Testament Period*, 1:47.
89. See p. 47.
90. Gerstenberger, *Theologies in the Old Testament*, 211.
91. Herrmann, *Theologie des Alten Testaments*, 72, translation ours.
92. Schmid, *Historical Theology of the Hebrew Bible*, 164.
93. Jeremias, *Theologie des Alten Testaments*, 102, translation ours.
94. Ibid., translation ours.

Part 2

THEME

In part 2 we examine approaches to Old Testament theology that focus on theme(s). Chapter 3, "Multiplex Thematic Old Testament Theology," surveys theologies that emphasize the diversity of the Old Testament by discussing a variety of themes. By contrast, chapter 4, "Old Testament Theology Focused around a Central Theme," covers theologies that highlight the unity of the Old Testament by proposing a central theme around which the entire Old Testament is organized.

MULTIPLEX THEMATIC OLD TESTAMENT THEOLOGY

Like the categories examined in part 1, the approach covered in this chapter is also concerned to preserve the diversity found within the Old Testament. However, rather than viewing that diversity primarily in terms of historical progression, a multiplex thematic approach focuses on the variety of topics found in the Old Testament, structuring its theological reflection around a number of key themes.[1]

DEFINITION: Old Testament theologies that adopt a multiplex thematic approach are structured around multiple themes, draw connections to the New Testament, and reflect a concern for the church. Points of tension for multiplex thematic theologies include the source of the themes, which themes are emphasized, and which interpretive methods are used.

Central Texts Covered in This Chapter

Leslie C. Allen, *A Theological Approach to the Old Testament* (2014)

Bryan C. Babcock, James Spencer, and Russell L. Meek, *Trajectories* (2018)

Michaela Bauks, *Theologie des Alten Testaments* (2019)

Reinhard Feldmeier and Hermann Spieckermann, *God of the Living* (German: 2011; English: 2011)

John Goldingay, *Biblical Theology* (2016)

John Goldingay, *Israel's Faith* (vol. 2 of his *Old Testament Theology*) (2006)

John Goldingay, *Israel's Life* (vol. 3 of his *Old Testament Theology*) (2009)

Scott J. Hafemann, *The God of Promise and the Life of Faith* (2001)

B. Donald Keyser and H. Wayne Ballard, *From Jerusalem to Gaza* (2002)

▶

---

1. The term "multiplex" seems to have been coined by Gerhard Hasel, who favors a "multiplex canonical approach" (Gerhard F. Hasel, *Old Testament Theology: Basic Issues in the Current Debate*, 4th ed. [Grand Rapids: Eerdmans, 1991], 111–14).

Dennis F. Kinlaw with John N. Oswalt, *Lectures in Old Testament Theology* (2010)

Ludwig Köhler, *Old Testament Theology* (German: 1935; English: 1957)[2]

Iain Provan, *Seriously Dangerous Religion* (2014)

Robin Routledge, *Old Testament Theology* (2008)

Ralph L. Smith, *Old Testament Theology* (1993)

John H. Walton, *Old Testament Theology for Christians* (2017)

Ronald Youngblood, *The Heart of the Old Testament* (1971; 2nd ed.: 1998)

Walther Zimmerli, *Old Testament Theology in Outline* (German: 1972; English: 1978)

COMMON FEATURES

Structured around Multiple Themes

In contrast to the scholars we will be examining in the next chapter, those who follow a multiplex thematic approach argue that no one central theme is sufficient to do justice to the rich variety of the Old Testament. After all, if there were a central theme in the Old Testament, would we not expect to see some agreement about what that center is? As Gerhard Hasel puts it, the "smorgasbord of centers" that have been suggested "seems to demonstrate its own inherent limitation. The centers as organizing or systematizing criteria are rooted in the OT *and* in the OT theologian's choice, but hardly in the former alone."[3] Therefore theologies in this category instead examine several key themes, which together provide an overview of Old Testament theology.[4]

The historical arrangement of the theologies outlined in part 1 can make

---

2. The English version was translated from the third German edition, published in 1953.

3. Hasel, *Old Testament Theology*, 167–68, italics original; see also Ralph L. Smith, *Old Testament Theology: Its History, Method, and Message* (Nashville: Broadman and Holman, 1993), 92.

4. A few scholars identify some kind of overarching theme but do not focus their thematic arrangements around it. For example, John Walton describes "the establishment of God's presence among his people" as "the primary theme that progresses throughout the Old Testament, and indeed throughout the entire Bible" (John H. Walton, *Old Testament Theology for Christians: From Ancient Context to Enduring Belief* [Downers Grove, IL: IVP Academic, 2017], 26), though he purposefully avoids the terminology of *center* (p. 7). Similarly, Leslie Allen identifies "God in relationships" as a "generic center," but he contrasts that with a "thematic" center, which is unable to capture the rich breadth of the Old Testament (Leslie C. Allen, *A Theological Approach to the Old Testament: Major Themes and New Testament Connections* [Eugene, OR: Cascade, 2014], 10). Ludwig Köhler sees "*God is the ruling Lord*" as "*the one fundamental statement in the theology of the Old Testament*," though he organizes his theology around systematic categories (Ludwig Köhler, *Old Testament Theology*, trans. A. S. Todd [Philadelphia: Westminster, 1957], 30, italics original). Finally, the subtitle of the coauthored *Trajectories* volume suggests that gospel is a primary theme, but the chapters do not consistently connect the theme in view with the gospel (Bryan C. Babcock, James Spencer, and Russell L. Meek, *Trajectories: A Gospel-Centered Introduction to Old Testament Theology* [Eugene, OR: Pickwick, 2018], chaps. 4, 7, and 8).

it difficult to grasp the whole testimony of the Old Testament concerning a particular topic, since references to that topic may be scattered over the various periods of Israel's history. By contrast, the thematic structure of theologies in this category allows them to treat the wide variety of Old Testament passages that bear on a topic together in one place. For example, Leslie Allen surveys worship in the sacrificial system and the Psalms, while also highlighting the prophetic critique of worship practices that were not accompanied by devoted hearts and acts of social justice.[5]

Robin Routledge marshals texts from each part of the Old Testament to describe God's nature and characteristics, portraying him as:

- "a personal being" who walks in the garden of Eden (Gen. 3:8) and exhibits anger (Num. 11:10; Ps. 78:21) and grief (1 Sam. 15:11);[6]
- righteous, which means that he demonstrates "right behaviour within the context of a particular relationship," such as executing justice (Deut. 32:4) and bringing deliverance (Ps. 24:5);[7]
- "compassionate and gracious" (Ex. 34:6), showing faithful love (khesed) toward his people (Hos. 2:19; Neh. 1:5);
- a God who exhibits wrath toward both Israel (Deut. 6:13–15; Amos 2:4–16) and the nations (Isa. 10:12–19; Zeph. 3:8) when they engage in sinful behavior, but whose anger "is temporary and limited" (Isa. 26:20; Ezek. 16:42).[8]

Reinhard Feldmeier and Hermann Spieckermann examine how blessing and praise function throughout the Old Testament, declaring that "blessing creates a comprehensive reality signifying God's benevolent proximity."[9] They observe that in the first creation account, God blesses animals, humanity, and the seventh day (Gen. 1:22, 28; 2:3), but humanity's attempts to be like God lead to curse (3:14–19; 4:11–16). Later the blessing promised through Abraham for "all peoples on earth ('adamah)" (12:3) echoes and overturns the curse on the "ground" ('adamah) in Genesis 3:17, as well as the first curse enacted against a person, Cain (4:11).[10] The priests are empowered to bless

---

5. Allen, *Theological Approach to the Old Testament*, 92–101.

6. Robin Routledge, *Old Testament Theology: A Thematic Approach* (Downers Grove, IL: InterVarsity, 2008), 102.

7. Ibid., 106–7.

8. Ibid., 108–12.

9. Reinhard Feldmeier and Hermann Spieckermann, *God of the Living: A Biblical Theology*, trans. Mark E. Biddle (Waco, TX: Baylor Univ. Press, 2011), 271.

10. Ibid., 274.

people with YHWH's name, which signifies his presence (Num. 6:22–27; 1 Chron. 23:13), and the priestly blessings are linked in part to the acts of sacrifice and prayer (Ex. 20:24). "Praising" *(barak)* God is the standard response to God's "blessing" *(barak,* see, e.g., Ps. 115:12–18), yet Job continues to "praise" *(barak,* Job 1:21) even when God turns "blessing" *(barak,* 1:10) into curse. Finally, they note that blessing plays a role in prophetic promises of end-time restoration (Isa. 65:23; Zech. 8:13; Mal. 3:10).[11]

Connection to the New Testament

A second common feature of works surveyed in this chapter is that they seek to draw connections with the New Testament, although their degree of interaction with the New Testament varies. On one end of the spectrum lie the whole-Bible theologies, which balance attention to both testaments in their discussion of each theme.[12] For example, after outlining humanity's purpose to rule over creation in a way that reflects God's glory (Gen. 1:26–28), Scott Hafemann quotes Romans 1:21 to identify "the root of sin" in "the fact that 'although [people] knew God they did not honor him as God or give thanks to him,'" which led to idolatry (see vv. 22–23).[13] He then turns to Psalm 115:3–8 to explain that idolatry "is the tragically pathetic attempt to squeeze life out of lifeless forms that cannot help us meet our real needs," and he notes Paul's description of coveting as idolatry (Col. 3:5; Eph. 5:5).[14]

Some of the purely Old Testament theologies also emphasize connections to the New Testament. For example, the coauthored *Trajectories* speaks of "a reciprocal theological 'loop' in which the New Testament reinforces and expands upon the theology of the Old Testament even as the Old Testament informs and provides a crucial framework for the New Testament."[15] Therefore "respecting and studying the discrete witness of the Old Testament cannot be separated from the canonical task of describing the Triune God as he is presented in both the Old and New Testaments."[16] This perspective is demonstrated in the chapter on creation, which considers the New Testament's testimony that

---

11. Ibid., 274–81.
12. John Goldingay, *Biblical Theology: The God of Christian Scriptures* (Downers Grove, IL: IVP Academic, 2016); Scott J. Hafemann, *The God of Promise and the Life of Faith: Understanding the Heart of the Bible* (Wheaton, IL: Crossway, 2001); Feldmeier and Spieckermann, *God of the Living.*
13. Hafemann, *God of Promise and the Life of Faith,* 27, 35.
14. Ibid., 35, 37.
15. James Spencer, "Introduction," in *Trajectories,* xvii.
16. Ibid. See also Allen, *Theological Approach to the Old Testament,* 152–74. Allen is concerned to exegete the Old Testament in its historical context but also speaks of "a process of what one may call reverse exegesis," which involves reading the Old Testament in light of Christ (p. 159).

- everything was created through Jesus (John 1:1–3),
- creation is suffering under the weight of human sin (Rom. 8:19–23),
- Jesus' redemption encompasses not just humanity but all of creation (Revelation 21).[17]

Other theologies trace only certain theological themes into the New Testament. For example, Ralph Smith observes that humanity's creation "in God's likeness" grounds James's warning against cursing people (James 3:9–10).[18] Elsewhere the New Testament describes Christ as God's image (2 Cor. 4:4; Col. 1:15) or speaks of Christians being made into Christ's image (Rom. 8:29; 1 Cor. 15:49).[19] John Walton points out that Jesus is portrayed as a tabernacle (John 1:14). Then, after explaining that the tent of meeting was the room in the tabernacle outside the holy of holies, where priests could encounter God, he declares that through his death Jesus tears the curtain in the tent of meeting (Matt. 27:51), "allowing unimpeded access to the presence of God (Heb 10:20) and removing the hazard posed to sinful people by the presence of God."[20]

However, Walton also critiques attempts to interpret the Old Testament christologically (in light of Christ), saying that it puts us "at great risk of implying . . . that the authority of the Old Testament derives solely from whatever christological interpretations can be identified."[21] His concern to read the Old Testament on its own terms sometimes leads him to emphasize areas of discontinuity between the testaments. For example, he argues that in the Old Testament, salvation is always temporal, not eschatological—it is accomplished within history rather than at the end of time. Sometimes it involves liberation from sociopolitical oppression, such as slavery in Egypt or Babylonian exile. At other times, salvation is from "disorder in covenant relationship" and is accomplished through the Torah and its sacrificial rites, which function to restore covenant order.[22] Since the Old Testament is focused on maintaining covenant relationship, not on dealing with "human sin as a whole," Walton contends that "it would be misguided to talk about salvation from sins in the Old Testament."[23] Instead he sees that idea as a development that happens only in the New Testament.[24]

---

17. Russell L. Meek, "Creation," in *Trajectories*, 10–13.
18. Smith, *Old Testament Theology*, 245.
19. Ibid.
20. Walton, *Old Testament Theology for Christians*, 123.
21. Ibid., 10.
22. Ibid., 227.
23. Ibid., 228–29.
24. Walton lists nine other points of discontinuity between the testaments, saying that the Old Testament has (1) no recognition of God's nature as a Trinity, (2) no understanding of a final judgment leading to

At the far end of the spectrum lie Walther Zimmerli and Ludwig Köhler, who make few references to the New Testament. Nevertheless, even Zimmerli connects the view that Zion (Jerusalem) is secure from enemy attack (Psalms 46; 48) with Jesus' statement that "the gates of Hades will not overcome" the church (Matt. 16:18).[25] Köhler cites Galatians 4:26–28 in connection with his view of Israel as a spiritual reality and quotes Romans 3:1 when discussing Israel's election vis-à-vis the nations.[26]

Concern for the Church

Finally, theologies in this category tend to reflect a concern for how Old Testament theology may be used in the life of the church.[27] Some scholars aim to produce a theology that informs the church but do not offer practical contemporary applications of Old Testament theology themselves. For example, in the hope that her work would be useful for "church practice" *(kirchlichen Praxis)*, Michaela Bauks includes an appendix collating the sections of her theology that correspond to the readings in the lectionary for the United Evangelical Lutheran Church of Germany.[28]

Routledge identifies a four-step process in reading the Old Testament.

1. Interpreting individual passages
2. Identifying "the underlying theological principles"
3. Bridging the context to our contemporary situation
4. Seeking "to work those principles out in practice"[29]

His theology gives primary attention to the second of these, providing a basis for later application.[30] Feldmeier and Spieckermann suggest that the biblical text is by nature transformative, declaring that the biblical texts "bear witness to the experience of God's liberating, life-giving act," producing "a normative [prescriptive] tradition."[31] In their view, "the knowledge of God sets slaves

---

eternal reward or punishment, (3) no doctrine of original sin, (4) no understanding of "Satan as the devil," (5) no recognition of the Holy Spirit as an indwelling presence, (6) the temple—rather than his people—as the place where God's presence dwells, (7) no mission to evangelize, (8) God's people identified with a particular nation (marked by circumcision), and (9) no understanding of "God as spirit" (ibid., 286–91).

25. Walther Zimmerli, *Old Testament Theology in Outline*, trans. David E. Green (Louisville: John Knox, 1978), 77, 134, 220, 226.

26. Köhler, *Old Testament Theology*, 65, 81.

27. Only the older theologies of Zimmerli and Köhler lack this concern.

28. Michaela Bauks, *Theologie des Alten Testaments: Religionsgeschichtliche und bibelhermeneutische Perspektiven* (Göttingen: Vandenhoeck and Ruprecht, 2019), 305, 419–37. The appendix was prepared by Jochen Wagner.

29. Routledge, *Old Testament Theology*, 78–79.

30. Ibid., 80.

31. Feldmeier and Spieckermann, *God of the Living*, 2.

free," and they contend that "scholarly exegesis must adhere to this intention of the biblical documents if it wants to take seriously the true objective of the texts beyond the circumstances in which the texts originated."[32]

Other scholars sprinkle prescriptive comments throughout their work. For example, in *Israel's Faith*, John Goldingay warns that "when great world powers [like Britain and the United States] . . . see themselves as heirs to Israel's position in God's purpose, their posturing becomes demonic."[33] Instead, he suggests that they should seek "self-understanding" in the Old Testament's perspective on "the nations in general."[34] Elsewhere Goldingay declares that the Sabbath "confronts the 24/7 mentality" of Western culture.[35] He also considers how the sabbatical principle in Deuteronomy 15 challenges modern economic practice, contending that the Western tendency to prize "scientific progress, economic growth and technical advance . . . looks like the worship of a false god."[36] Similarly, Ronald Youngblood relates the first commandment of the Decalogue (Ten Commandments), which prohibits the worship of other gods, to Jesus' words, "You cannot serve both God and money" (Matt. 6:24). He then suggests that "many of us at times tend to ensconce material wealth in the uppermost throne room of our hearts."[37]

Iain Provan offers contemporary responses to the problem of evil. In his view, the Old Testament nowhere suggests that all suffering is the result of sin, which leads him to distinguish between "'intrinsic suffering' (the suffering that is intrinsic to life in creation) and 'extrinsic suffering' (the suffering that arises from embracing evil)."[38] Natural disasters like earthquakes he sees as "simply an aspect of the created order, just as wind and lightning are" (1 Kings 19:11–12; Psalm 148).[39] He suggests—based on the Old Testament perspective on humans as one of God's many creatures but also as created in God's image—two approaches to intrinsic suffering. At times the Old Testament may lead us to "intervene in and change aspects of creation as we find it, especially when it causes suffering," and at other times to "respect and accept creation as we find it, *even when* it causes suffering."[40] Wisdom is required to determine which path is better in a particular situation.

---

32. Ibid.
33. John Goldingay, *Israel's Faith*, vol. 2 of *Old Testament Theology* (Downers Grove, IL: InterVarsity, 2006), 732.
34. Ibid.
35. Idem, *Israel's Life*, vol. 3 of *Old Testament Theology* (Downers Grove, IL: InterVarsity, 2009), 332.
36. Ibid., 438.
37. Ronald Youngblood, *The Heart of the Old Testament: A Survey of Key Theological Themes*, 2nd ed. (Grand Rapids: Baker Academic, 1998), 73–74.
38. Iain Provan, *Seriously Dangerous Religion: What the Old Testament Really Says and Why It Matters* (Waco, TX: Baylor Univ. Press, 2014), 107.
39. Ibid., 109.
40. Ibid., 242, italics original.

With regard to extrinsic suffering, Provan outlines five responses we might take from the Old Testament. First, it calls us to resist evil and choose what is good (Deut. 30:15; Mic. 6:8). Second, it illustrates "the path of patient endurance" (Ps. 37:7, 34).[41] Third, it encourages prayer that calls on God to deliver his people (Ps. 7:1; 69:1–4). Fourth, it advocates the act of reflecting God's compassion by showing compassion to those who are suffering (Ex. 22:25–27). Finally, it inspires us to hope "that what is bad in the world can somehow be turned to good" (Mic. 4:3; Isa. 11:9).[42] In a similar vein, Russell Meek encourages Christians who are not experiencing God's presence to follow the example of Job and the psalmists and "continue to pray, pouring out those feelings to God in honest, open communication," while reminding themselves of the truth that God dwells in them.[43]

Finally, Dennis Kinlaw's pastoral concern is evident throughout his work. From the beginning, he declares that theological study should lead to divine encounter: "If it does not bring me to Him as a living Person, I have only found a substitute for Him."[44] For Kinlaw, if we truly encounter the living God in our study, then it will drive us to worship and produce a transformed life, marked by God's concern to care for the vulnerable, as exemplified by the story of William Wilberforce.[45] Kinlaw also challenges pastors who seek their "portion" (see Ps. 16:5) in ministerial success or in anything else other than God, and he advocates trusting in God to fulfill his promises, rather than attempting to "pull strings or play politics" (see Genesis 13).[46]

POINTS OF TENSION

Source of the Themes

A primary point of tension between theologies in this category concerns the source of the chosen themes. Should they be taken from the categories of systematic theology, from questions that modern people are asking, or from the Old Testament itself? Köhler states that "the Old Testament itself does not offer any scheme for that compilation we call its theology. One must therefore borrow it from elsewhere and take good care that it does not distort

---

41. Ibid., 148–49.

42. Ibid., 152.

43. Russell L. Meek, "'God with Us,'" in *Trajectories*, 151.

44. Dennis F. Kinlaw with John N. Oswalt, *Lectures in Old Testament Theology* (Wilmore, KY: Francis Asbury, 2010), 15.

45. Ibid., 16, 37–38. Kinlaw concludes his series of lectures by suggesting that the business of academic study of the Bible should be to engender the kind of passion and transformation experienced by a convicted murderer who found forgiveness in Jesus (p. 462).

46. Ibid., 67–69, 156.

the facts."[47] Following an approach more common among much older Old Testament theologies, he takes the standard categories of systematic theology (God, man, salvation) as his framework. However, he notes that he found it difficult to determine where Israel's cult (religious system) should fit, ultimately including it in his discussion of man.[48]

Both Provan and Hafemann structure their work around a series of questions that modern people are asking. Provan's questions are derived from the realm of philosophical and religious inquiry, such as "What is the world?" "Who is God?" "Who are man and woman?" "Why do evil and suffering mark the world?" and "How am I to relate to my neighbor?" These questions provide a foundation for him to compare the Old Testament metanarrative with alternate philosophical and religious metanarratives.[49] Ultimately, he seeks to demonstrate that the Old Testament provides a plausible account of the world that is not dangerous in the way that some modern critics suppose.[50] However, while philosophical categories provide his starting point, they do not govern his interpretation of the text.

Hafemann's categories exhibit some overlap with Provan's (e.g., "Why Do We Exist?" and "Why Is There So Much Pain and Evil in the World?"), but they are more specifically Christian (for example, "What Does It Mean to Know God?" "Why Can We Trust God, No Matter What Happens?" and "Why Do God's People Obey Him?").[51] For the most part, his discussion remains firmly rooted in the biblical text itself. However, when considering the problem of suffering, he engages with modern theological responses (from Arminianism, open theism, and process theology) before offering his own Reformed perspective.[52]

Other theologies are more concerned to avoid imposing alien categories on the Old Testament. Therefore they derive their themes from within the Old

---

47. Köhler, *Old Testament Theology*, 9.

48. Köhler explains this decision by arguing that it is "the essential dialectic of the Old Testament cult that man tries to save himself by his works" (ibid.), a claim that many Old Testament theologians today would dispute.

49. Provan, *Seriously Dangerous Religion*, 11–13. Smith also includes a couple of categories that seem to be derived from philosophical inquiry—"What Is Mankind?" and "The Good Life"—and he discusses various theological perspectives on the fall (*Old Testament Theology*, 234–72, 290–92, 337–72). Feldmeier and Spieckermann consider the philosophical category of "Eternity and Time," interacting with ancient Greek thought on the subject (*God of the Living*, 403–23).

50. Provan, *Seriously Dangerous Religion*, 17.

51. Hafemann, *God of Promise and the Life of Faith*. Elsewhere he contends that "biblical theology should develop its theological categories inductively from the biblical text, not from a predetermined systematic framework" (idem, "What's the Point of Biblical Theology? Reflections Prompted by Brevard Childs," in *Biblical Theology: Past, Present, and Future*, ed. Carey Walsh and Mark W. Elliott [Eugene, OR: Cascade, 2016], 119).

52. Hafemann, *God of Promise and the Life of Faith*, 129–48.

Testament itself rather than using systematic categories or modern questions. As Routledge puts it, a systematic approach "may focus on issues of interest to us, but not necessarily of concern to the Bible writers."[53] He also expresses the fear that such an approach may lead to the Old Testament being "treated as little more than a source of proof texts, with little regard for it as authoritative revelation in its own right."[54]

In his *Biblical Theology*, Goldingay expresses his aim "to avoid reading into the Scriptures the categories and convictions of postbiblical Christian theology."[55] This objective affects not only his choice of governing themes but also how he reads the biblical text. For example, although he subscribes to the Christian doctrine of the Trinity, he sees it as "a set of inferences from the Scriptures" developed in later philosophical categories.[56] Therefore he contends that the fully formed doctrine is not found within the biblical text. He also argues that a scriptural understanding of God begins not from systematic categories like divine omnipotence (that God is all-powerful) but from "the biblical portrait of Yahweh as the one God and as the God who has a name, which reflects his being not an idea but a person."[57]

In contrast to many systematic portrayals of God, Goldingay maintains that the Old Testament presents YHWH as having deep feelings and genuinely interacting with people in a way that demonstrates flexibility, though not inconsistency. YHWH's character and purposes remain firm, though his actions may change in response to human choices. For example, as YHWH declares in Jeremiah 18:1–12, if a nation repents after he pronounces judgment against it, then he will relent from his judgment (and vice versa!).[58] Elsewhere Goldingay illustrates YHWH's flexibility by pointing to Ezekiel's unfulfilled prophecy that Tyre would fall at the hands of Babylon (chaps. 26–28): "When Tyre declines to lie down and die because that is what Yhwh intends for them to do, . . . Yhwh's response is not to overwhelm it by a literal hurricane or a tidal wave of the kind that Ezekiel poetically describes and Yhwh could certainly send, if Nebuchadnezzar's army is not enough. It is rather to rework the plan."[59]

Zimmerli also avoids reading Genesis 3 in light of the categories of systematic theology. He notes that the passage has traditionally been understood

---

53. Routledge, *Old Testament Theology*, 28.

54. Ibid.; see also Bauks, *Theologie des Alten Testaments*, 19.

55. Goldingay, *Biblical Theology*, 17.

56. Ibid.

57. Ibid., 33, see also 42–58; cf. idem, *Israel's Faith*, 18, 59, 64–65, 89, 132–33; similarly, Walton, *Old Testament Theology for Christians*, 49.

58. Goldingay, *Biblical Theology*, 30–33.

59. Idem, *Israel's Faith*, 84, see also 88–92.

as portraying a "doctrine of the fall of man," but he contends that its connection with the idea of "original sin" (that humanity inherits Adam's sin "almost biologically") stems from Augustine's "misinterpretation" of Romans 5:12.[60] Zimmerli argues that "the Old Testament (apart from distant echoes in Ecclesiastes) never speaks of such a 'doctrine.'"[61] Nevertheless, he does see Adam's sin as being in some sense paradigmatic, as indicated in part by his name (which means "man"), and he points out how Genesis 3–11 highlights the continual increase of evil.[62]

Themes Emphasized

Multiplex thematic Old Testament theologies also reflect substantial diversity in their choice of themes and organization.[63] While many first examine the God of the Old Testament, their focus varies. Youngblood highlights monotheism,[64] Kinlaw underscores personal knowledge and experience of God (with a focus on the Psalms),[65] Goldingay and Feldmeier and Spieckermann outline God's nature and character,[66] Bauks, Köhler, and Zimmerli emphasize God's self-revelation in his name and deeds,[67] and Routledge and Walton examine God in relation to other so-called gods and supernatural beings.[68] Donald Keyser and Wayne Ballard, on the other hand, begin with humanity, considering God only after a chapter titled "God's Chosen: Israelites and Gentiles," whereas Provan, Hafemann, Allen, and the coauthors of *Trajectories* open with creation, highlighting both God as creator and the nature of the created world.[69]

---

60. Zimmerli, *Old Testament Theology in Outline*, 168; see also Walton, *Old Testament Theology for Christians*, 214.

61. Zimmerli, *Old Testament Theology in Outline*, 168.

62. Ibid., 168–69; see also Allen, *Theological Approach to the Old Testament*, 25–26.

63. Although Hasel never wrote an Old Testament theology, because of his untimely death in a car accident, he advocated a structure that differs from the other works in this category, with a focus on examining the theologies of each biblical book or group of books before analyzing "longitudinal themes" that emerge from that study (*Old Testament Theology*, 113–14). Also, Goldingay's *Israel's Life* is not discussed in this section, because it is more limited in scope than the other works in this category. Its study of how Israel was called to live is divided into three parts: "Living with God," "Living with One Another," and "Living with Ourselves."

64. Youngblood, *Heart of the Old Testament*, 9–18.

65. Kinlaw and Oswalt, *Lectures in Old Testament Theology*, 11–114.

66. Goldingay, *Israel's Faith*, 21–172; idem, *Biblical Theology*, 19–81; Feldmeier and Spieckermann, *God of the Living*, 17–247. Feldmeier and Spieckermann also give significant attention to God's names.

67. Bauks, *Theologie des Alten Testaments*, 35–236; Köhler, *Old Testament Theology*, 17–126; Zimmerli, *Old Testament Theology in Outline*, 17–58; cf. Smith, *Old Testament Theology*, 94–233. Smith opens with God's self-revelation and name but then discusses election and covenant before considering God's deeds and character.

68. Routledge, *Old Testament Theology*, 81–123; Walton, *Old Testament Theology for Christians*, 29–70.

69. B. Donald Keyser and H. Wayne Ballard, *From Jerusalem to Gaza: An Old Testament Theology* (Macon, GA: Smith and Helwys, 2002), 23–45; Provan, *Seriously Dangerous Religion*, 21–46; Hafemann, *God of Promise and the Life of Faith*, 23–39; Babcock, Spencer, and Meek, *Trajectories*, 1–16.

TABLE 3.1: Initial Themes

Initial Theme	Emphasis	Author
God	Monotheism	Youngblood
	Personal knowledge and experience of God	Kinlaw
	God's nature and character	Goldingay (*Israel's Faith* and *Biblical Theology*), Feldmeier/Spieckermann
	God's self-revelation in his name and deeds	Bauks, Köhler, Zimmerli (cf. Smith)
	God in relation to other so-called gods and supernatural beings	Routledge, Walton
Humanity	Israelites and gentiles	Keyser/Ballard
Creation	God as creator and the nature of creation	Provan, Hafemann, Allen, Babcock/Spencer/Meek

Most of the theologies that do not begin with creation cover it either as part of God's self-revelation as creator or as a separate theme immediately following their treatment of God.[70] But after creation, their paths diverge. Other themes that appear frequently include wisdom, election, the nations, worship and/or sacrifice, kingship (of God or of Israel's human kings), sin, threat or suffering, and hope, but we will highlight just two: law and covenant. The theologies in this category differ over the primary term used for the theme of law, sometimes opting instead for *commandment, instruction,* or the Hebrew word *Torah* (which can mean "law" but often refers more broadly to "instruction"). They also demonstrate considerable variety in the significance they give to the topic and how they relate it to other themes. Zimmerli emphasizes it by devoting one of his five major sections to "Yahweh's commandment" and discussing the Decalogue in great depth.[71] By contrast, Walton subordinates the Torah to the temple, arguing that "the Torah gave direction concerning how to maintain access to God's presence."[72]

Bauks pairs instruction *(die Weisung)* with covenant in her treatment

---

70. As part of God's self-revelation: Bauks, *Theologie des Alten Testaments,* 94–126; Kinlaw and Oswalt, *Lectures in Old Testament Theology,* 39–55; Zimmerli, *Old Testament Theology in Outline,* 32–43; Routledge, *Old Testament Theology,* 124–58; Köhler, *Old Testament Theology,* 85–88; Feldmeier and Spieckermann, *God of the Living,* 251–70. As a separate theme: Walton, *Old Testament Theology for Christians,* 71–104; Keyser and Ballard, *From Jerusalem to Gaza,* 71–86. Goldingay considers creation after both "God's Person" and "God's Insight" (*Biblical Theology,* 134–214).

71. Zimmerli, *Old Testament Theology in Outline,* 109–40.

72. Walton, *Old Testament Theology for Christians,* 157.

of God's self-revelation at Sinai,[73] whereas Keyser and Ballard discuss the instruction of Moses along with prophecy and wisdom as various means of knowing God.[74] Feldmeier and Spieckermann consider commandment along with prayer, which together "stand for the whole relationship between God and human beings."[75] Köhler opens his section titled "Judgment and Salvation" with a discussion of "commandment and law."[76] Intriguingly, he begins with the creation mandate to "be fruitful and increase in number" in Genesis 1:28, which he sees as "God's first act of grace towards man."[77] Finally, Goldingay discusses how the Torah provides direction by casting an ethical vision, not by supplying a law code to be enacted by the courts.[78] In his whole-Bible theology, he gives considerable attention to Jesus as the fulfillment of the Torah.[79]

Covenant is sometimes connected with the themes of election and law, but Walton also relates it to God's kingdom.[80] Whereas Allen and Youngblood emphasize covenant by devoting significant attention to tracing the theme through the Old Testament, Keyser and Ballard summarize the covenants in a single paragraph.[81] Köhler describes the covenant as "*the* form of the relationship between Jahweh and Israel," while Feldmeier and Spieckermann argue that scholars have "significantly overvalued the concept of the covenant . . . as an interpretive category in biblical theology for the relationship among God, nation, and human being," particularly in the Old Testament.[82] Nevertheless, they give some attention to outlining their view of how the covenant concept developed, culminating in an emphasis on promise that is rooted in YHWH's faithfulness rather than the faithfulness of his covenant partners.[83]

---

73. Bauks, *Theologie des Alten Testaments*, 126–65. Bauks also uses the term *law* (*das Gesetz*, e.g., pp. 151–56) but gives primacy to *instruction*. See also Allen, *Theological Approach to the Old Testament*, 67–70, 75, 79–88; Routledge, *Old Testament Theology*, 173–74, 188–95, 242–45. Routledge treats the law under the themes of covenant and ethics.

74. Keyser and Ballard, *From Jerusalem to Gaza*, 55–60.

75. Feldmeier and Spieckermann, *God of the Living*, 425–40, esp. 426.

76. Köhler, *Old Testament Theology*, 201.

77. Ibid.

78. Goldingay, *Israel's Life*, 31–35, 37–45, esp. 39–42; see also Smith, *Old Testament Theology*, 337–72. Smith sees law as one source of OT ethics.

79. Goldingay, *Biblical Theology*, 439–49; see also Russell L. Meek, "Torah," in *Trajectories*, 78–92, esp. 79–80.

80. Routledge, *Old Testament Theology*, 159–74, though he treats the Davidic covenant in his later discussion of kingship (pp. 233–36); Smith, *Old Testament Theology*, 122–63; Zimmerli, *Old Testament Theology in Outline*, 48–58; Walton, *Old Testament Theology for Christians*, 105–42; see also the brief discussion in Goldingay, *Biblical Theology*, 220–22.

81. Allen, *Theological Approach to the Old Testament*, 54–88, 102–12. For Allen, covenant also serves as a governing theme for his discussion of certain other topics, and he devotes a chapter to the relationship between creation and covenant (pp. 141–51). Also Youngblood, *Heart of the Old Testament*, 39–58; Keyser and Ballard, *From Jerusalem to Gaza*, 31.

82. Köhler, *Old Testament Theology*, 60, italics ours; Feldmeier and Spieckermann, *God of the Living*, 447.

83. Feldmeier and Spieckermann, *God of the Living*, 448–58.

Interpretive Methods Used

Finally, scholars who take a multiplex thematic approach use a variety of interpretive methods to discern the theology of the Old Testament. Several employ word studies, especially to analyze the various Hebrew terms used to describe aspects of the human person, such as soul *(nephesh)*, spirit *(ruakh)*, flesh *(basar)*, and heart *(lev)*.[84] From there, however, their paths diverge widely, and we will highlight just a few to offer a glimpse of their diversity. Routledge identifies his approach as primarily canonical and narrative.[85] Like the authors who will be discussed in chapter 5 ("Canonical Old Testament Theology"), he takes the final form of the biblical text as the subject of his study, rather than trying to discern earlier sources or assuming "that what is later and so not 'original' is, in some way, of lesser value."[86]

Routledge's focus on narrative derives from his view that God's character must be understood within the context of the Old Testament story, a perspective he shares with those who structure their theology around Israel's history.[87] He contends that when propositions about God's nature and character are abstracted from the text, they are often understood through the theological grid of the interpreter. For example, "'God is love' means he will do nothing *we consider* to be unloving."[88] He also argues that a "narrative substructure" underlies the whole of the Old Testament, which revolves around "God's purpose to reveal his glory" to the nations, using Israel as his "agent."[89] However, the people of Israel fail to fulfill their mission, so they need to be renewed. The prophets variously identify "the agent of that renewal" as the Servant (Isaiah), the Messiah (Jeremiah), and the Spirit (Ezekiel). Together these figures will enable the people of Israel to live out their calling so that God's purpose will be fulfilled.[90]

Like Routledge, Walton also identifies the canon as fundamental to his approach, but he interprets the Old Testament using what he calls "cognitive environment criticism."[91] The term cognitive environment designates "how people think about the world including the place of the gods and the role of humanity."[92] Walton contends that if we do not understand Old Testament

---

84. See, e.g., Goldingay, *Biblical Theology*, 188–96; Keyser and Ballard, *From Jerusalem to Gaza*, 88–92; Routledge, *Old Testament Theology*, 143–47; Smith, *Old Testament Theology*, 264–72; Walton, *Old Testament Theology for Christians*, 88–91; Köhler, *Old Testament Theology*, 136–45.

85. Routledge, *Old Testament Theology*, 70–71.

86. Ibid., 70.

87. See chap. 1.

88. Routledge, *Old Testament Theology*, 71, italics original.

89. Ibid., 325; cf. Goldingay, *Biblical Theology*, 334.

90. Routledge, *Old Testament Theology*, 325.

91. Walton, *Old Testament Theology for Christians*, 16.

92. Ibid.

theology within its own cognitive environment, which is firmly situated in the ancient Near Eastern world, then we will unwittingly interpret it in light of the cognitive environment of the modern Western world. Therefore he gives considerable attention to explaining how people thought in the ancient Near East and then considers in what ways the Israelites simply reflect their cognitive environment and in what ways their theology is unique. He also describes what he sees as the "enduring theology" that emerges from the Old Testament.[93]

Walton's approach is evident in his treatment of creation, where he argues that in the minds of people in the ancient Near East, "something did not come into existence when it had materiality," as we tend to think today.[94] Instead "it came into existence when it had been given a role, function, and purpose in an ordered system. . . . Bringing order was the main job of the Creator, and it was something that was carried out continually, rather than as a one-time act."[95] He then uses an analogy to explain Genesis 1: to move into a new house involves both constructing the physical house and ordering the furniture and possessions to make it into a home, and that ordering is a continual process. Walton maintains that while the ancient Israelites would undoubtedly have seen God as the one who built the house (the physical universe), Genesis 1 focuses instead on God making the house into a home (an ordered cosmos) by giving everything its place and function.[96] Therefore he suggests that part of the enduring theology of the Old Testament is the emphasis on generating and preserving order as a significant aspect of creation. He also points out differences between Israel's creation narratives and those of the ancient Near East. Unlike their neighbors, the Israelites did not view creation as arising out of divine conflict.[97] Also, in the Old Testament God creates people to be servant-kings who live in relationship with him, rather than slaves to provide for his needs.[98]

For Zimmerli, historical criticism is more prominent.[99] He accepts the traditional source-critical division of the Pentateuch into four original sources—the Yahwist (J), Elohist (E), Deuteronomist (D), and priestly source (P)—and frequently discusses the theological perspectives of each of them. However, in his discussion of the patriarchs in Genesis, he notes that his

---

93. Ibid., 14–16.
94. Ibid., 72.
95. Ibid.
96. Ibid., 77.
97. Ibid., 77–82.
98. Ibid., 96–98.
99. Historical criticism is also employed by Bauks, *Theologie des Alten Testaments*; Köhler, *Old Testament Theology*; Feldmeier and Spieckermann, *God of the Living*.

aim is to determine what these "accounts in Genesis of how God acted with and toward the patriarchs contribute to 'what the Old Testament has to say about God.'"[100] His purpose is not to work out the details of what early Israelite religious belief and practice actually looked like, which he sees as a history of religion approach.[101] Highlighting the theme of promise (and "its delayed fulfillment") as central to the patriarchal narratives, he identifies the distinctive "emphases" of each source: "P, deriving from the worship of Israel, focuses on God's great decree; E stresses to a much greater degree how the fear of God . . . exhibited by the agent of the promise is put to the test; in J, failure and obedience reveal how truly human the patriarchs of Israel are."[102]

TEST CASE: EXODUS

Since theologies in this category are arranged thematically, the book of Exodus appears in various places, particularly in connection with the themes of covenant and Torah (Exodus 19–24). Routledge emphasizes the link between the covenant God made with Israel at Sinai and the promises of the Abrahamic covenant. First, at Sinai Israel becomes a nation, partially fulfilling God's promise to make Abraham "a great nation" (Gen. 12:2). Second, the exodus and Sinai accounts are intimately connected with God's promise to bring Abraham's offspring into the promised land. Third, when God declares to the enslaved Israelites, "I will take you as my own people, and I will be your God" (Ex. 6:7), it echoes his promise to Abraham's descendants, "I will be their God" (Gen. 17:8). Finally, the promise that Abraham would bring blessing to the nations is taken up by Israel's covenantal vocation to be "a kingdom of priests" (Ex. 19:6) so that they can mediate God's presence to the rest of the world.[103]

Examining Israel's Torah in relation to ancient Near Eastern legal collections, Walton concludes that both "fit into the category of 'list compilation'" and function "to circumscribe the nature of cosmic order."[104] However, whereas in the ancient Near East, legal texts could serve to legitimate kings by portraying them as just rulers, the aim of Israel's Torah is to enable the nation to fulfill its covenantal calling. By following the Torah, "Israel identifies as the people of Yahweh who are honoring the covenant relationship, properly reflecting its holy status, and maintaining the necessary sanctity of sacred

---

100. Zimmerli, *Old Testament Theology in Outline*, 28.
101. Ibid.
102. Ibid., 29.
103. Routledge, *Old Testament Theology*, 169.
104. Walton, *Old Testament Theology for Christians*, 158.

space."[105] Goldingay draws extensively on the legal material in Exodus in his discussion of Israel's life in community. He addresses both family concerns, such as the sanctity of marriage and respect for parents, and communal issues, such as care for resident aliens and poor Israelites, respect for others' property, conflict, retribution and restitution, capital punishment, and servanthood.[106]

Hafemann emphasizes the importance of the Sabbath command, seeing it as "the central pillar" of God's plan for his people, which "is carefully orchestrated to illustrate the depth of God's love, the trustworthiness of his commitments, the necessity of his commands, the disastrous consequences of idolatry, and the contours of the salvation to come in Christ."[107] Arguing that when Adam and Eve rebelled against God, they essentially "broke the Sabbath,"[108] he suggests that the Sabbath command given at Sinai is the final step in a process designed to reestablish the rest that God had always intended for his people. As Hafemann puts it, "The institution of the Sabbath after the Exodus is God's declaration that he has committed himself to meet Israel's needs, thereby restoring the same kind of Sabbath relationship with Israel that existed between God and Adam and Eve in the garden."[109]

The exodus event itself plays a considerably lesser role in some of these theologies than, for example, theologies rooted in Israel's history (chap. 1),[110] but it is not entirely absent. Youngblood considers the exodus event in a chapter on the broader theme of redemption, noting that the exodus serves as a type of (an event that prefigures) the greater redemption from sin accomplished through Christ's death. He also contends that Israel's redemption "was both external and internal" because they were enslaved not only to the Egyptians but also to the worship of other gods (Josh. 24:14).[111] Therefore the plagues display the power of Israel's God over the gods of Egypt in order to free the Israelites from their idolatrous tendencies.[112]

Allen discusses the exodus when he describes "God's side of the covenant"

---

105. Ibid., 159; cf. Goldingay's comment that the Torah "was designed to shape the life of people who have already been granted life. . . . It works out the implications of the exodus and the covenant making at Sinai" (*Biblical Theology*, 118); see also Routledge, *Old Testament Theology*, 175.

106. Goldingay, *Israel's Life*, 371, 399, 420, 430–31, 436, 442–43, 444–47, 449–51, 466–73.

107. Hafemann, *God of Promise and the Life of Faith*, 44.

108. Ibid., 61.

109. Ibid., 81; James Spencer also gives significant attention to the Sabbath in connection with the exodus event ("Liberation and Deliverance," in *Trajectories*, 70–73).

110. See, e.g., Walton, *Old Testament Theology for Christians*, 52, 225; Keyser and Ballard, *From Jerusalem to Gaza*, 56, 171, 173. References to the exodus are more plentiful in the theologies of Routledge and Feldmeier and Spieckermann, but mostly in connection with other topics (e.g., Routledge, *Old Testament Theology*, 88, 113, 162, 169, 226, 229, 245; Feldmeier and Spieckermann, *God of the Living*, 21, 25, 28, 34, 102, 428, 433)). Nowhere do they offer an extensive discussion of the exodus.

111. Youngblood, *Heart of the Old Testament*, 106–7.

112. Ibid., 107.

with Israel, observing that "the exodus establishes an archetypal role for Yahweh as Israel's God" and that "the covenant with Israel rests on the exodus from Egypt as its foundation."[113] He also considers YHWH's battle with Pharaoh under the topic of YHWH's dealings with the nations.[114] Analyzing the theme of the hardening of Pharaoh's heart, Allen declares that Pharaoh first hardens his own heart (Ex. 8:15, 32) until ultimately YHWH responds "with a 'So be it!' reaction of his own. Yahweh's reaction locks Pharaoh into his negative state of mind in a punitive way and inaugurates judgment" (9:12; 10:1).[115]

Bauks gives the most attention to the exodus, emphasizing its importance as Israel's chief foundation story.[116] She observes that the Old Testament portrays Israel's God as unlike the gods of the other nations, who were linked to nature (like Shamash, the Babylonian sun god) or a particular social institution (like Horus, the Egyptian god of kingship). Instead he is intimately bound up with Israel's historical narrative and particularly his deliverance of Israel from slavery in Egypt (Ex. 20:2; Hos.13:4).[117] Although Bauks does not view the exodus narratives as strictly historical, she sees them as performative texts that act upon each later generation as they reenact the exodus through the Passover.[118]

---

113. Allen, *Theological Approach to the Old Testament*, 56–61, esp. 58, 60.

114. Ibid., 116–18.

115. Ibid., 118. He contends that YHWH's statement about hardening Pharaoh's heart in Exodus 4:21 reflects his foreknowledge of what will happen.

116. Bauks, *Theologie des Alten Testaments*, 48–71; cf. Spencer, "Liberation and Deliverance," 65–77, esp. 70.

117. Bauks, *Theologie des Alten Testaments*, 49.

118. Ibid., 60–61; on the legendary character of Moses, see pp. 64–70.

Chapter 4

OLD TESTAMENT THEOLOGY FOCUSED AROUND A CENTRAL THEME

In contrast to the multiplex thematic theologies we surveyed in the last chapter, the theologies in this category seek to find unity in the Old Testament by looking for a single coherent organizing theme within the Old Testament. However, while this approach has been popular, the search for a center (often designated by the German word *Mitte*) has led to a wide proliferation of suggestions.

> **DEFINITION:** Old Testament theologies focused around a central theme assume that the Old Testament has a center, emphasize the unity of the Old and New Testaments, and are prescriptive. Points of tension for theologies in this category include the identity of that center, the incorporation of nonnarrative literature, and the role of historical-critical methods.

Central Texts Covered in This Chapter

Bernhard W. Anderson, *Contours of Old Testament Theology* (1999)

Stephen G. Dempster, *Dominion and Dynasty* (2003)

William J. Dumbrell, *Covenant and Creation* (1984; 2nd ed.: 2013)

J. Scott Duvall and J. Daniel Hays, *God's Relational Presence* (2019)

Walther Eichrodt, *Theology of the Old Testament* (German: 1933–39; English: 1961–67)[1]

James M. Hamilton Jr., *God's Glory in Salvation through Judgment* (2010)

Otto Kaiser, *Der Gott des Alten Testaments* (1993–2003)

Walter C. Kaiser Jr., *Toward an Old Testament Theology* (1978)

▶

---

1. The English vol. 1 was translated from the sixth German edition, published in 1959, and vol. 2 from the fifth German edition, of 1964.

John Kessler, *Old Testament Theology* (2013)

Rolf P. Knierim, *The Task of Old Testament Theology* (1995)

Elmer A. Martens, *God's Design* (1981; 4th ed.: 2015)

Eugene H. Merrill, *Everlasting Dominion* (2006)

Horst Dietrich Preuss, *Old Testament Theology* (German: 1991–92; English: 1995–96)

Thomas R. Schreiner, *The King in His Beauty* (2013)

Samuel Terrien, *The Elusive Presence* (1978)

Th. C. Vriezen, *An Outline of Old Testament Theology* (Dutch: 1949; 2nd English ed.: 1970)[2]

Christopher J. H. Wright, *The Mission of God* (2006)

COMMON FEATURES

Assumption of a Center

As seen in the previous chapter, many scholars working in the area of Old Testament theology dismiss the very idea that the Old Testament has a center. John Collins claims that in light of ideological and historical challenges to the Old Testament, finding a center "can only be compared to rearranging the chairs on the Titanic."[3] In contrast, the scholars surveyed in this chapter see the Old Testament as unified around a central theme or idea that can be found in the text itself. This belief that such a center may be identified appears sometimes to be simply assumed. The Old Testament is a single, cohesive book; therefore it must have a center. For example, Elmer Martens' arguments for seeing a center in the Old Testament revolve around its usefulness. He contends first that "the large amount of material and its disparate nature—genealogy, poetry, narrative, prophetic oracle—is vastly simplified if a theological center can be discerned. By means of a central concept one gets a handle on material that otherwise seems quite unmanageable."[4] Second, he suggests that using a center as an organizing principle "is intellectually satisfying."[5]

---

2. The second English edition was translated from the third Dutch edition, of 1966.

3. John J. Collins, "Biblical Theology between Apologetics and Criticism," in *Beyond Biblical Theologies*, ed. Heinrich Assel, Stefan Beyerle, and Christfried Böttrich, Wissenschaftliche Untersuchungen zum Neuen Testament 295 (Tübingen: Mohr Siebeck, 2012), 232.

4. Elmer A. Martens, *God's Design: A Focus on Old Testament Theology*, 4th ed. (Eugene, OR: Wipf and Stock, 2015), 323.

5. Ibid. Walther Eichrodt likewise assumes the unity of the Old Testament, articulating his aim as addressing *"the problem of how to understand the realm of OT belief in its structural unity and how, by examining on the one hand its religious environment and on the other hand its essential coherence with the NT, to illuminate its profoundest meaning"* (Walther Eichrodt, *Theology of the Old Testament*, trans. J. A. Baker, 2 vols., Old Testament Library [Philadelphia: Westminster, 1961–67], 1:31, italics original).

Those scholars who articulate more of an argument for a center tend to focus on the unified narrative of the Old Testament or Bible as a whole. For example, James Hamilton bases his concept of a center on the story of the Bible, which he says has four parts: *"creation, fall, redemption, restoration."*[6] He then contends that "the center of biblical theology is the theme that organizes this metanarrative, the theme out of which all others flow."[7] Rolf Knierim carefully frames his proposal in this way: "Old Testament theology is not concerned with finding a unifying topic that replaces all others. Instead, it is concerned with criteria by which the various theologies can be correlated in terms of theological priorities, including the ultimate priority governing all others."[8]

Scott Duvall and Daniel Hays argue that "the center of biblical theology is that prevalent theme that is continually advancing the plot forward and interconnecting the other themes."[9] They also propose a novel metaphor to depict how a center functions.

> Instead of using the analogy of a wheel, which has a hub (the center) and equally balanced spokes (the central themes) connected to the hub, to describe the center of biblical theology, we prefer the analogy of a spiderweb. The major themes of biblical theology would be like the main threads in the web, connected in one way or another to the center, but not always directly. . . . In the wheel analogy, everything must connect directly to the hub of the wheel, which can result, theologically speaking, in forcing an artificial orderliness on the diversity of the Bible. The center of a web, on the other hand, conveys a sense of interconnectedness that still allows for canonical flexibility.[10]

Unity of the Old and New Testaments

Scholars in this category tend to emphasize the unity between the Old and New Testaments, with the majority seeing their proposed center as the center of the whole Bible. While this is most obvious in the work of those who write biblical theologies of the entire Christian canon,[11] even those scholars

---

6. James M. Hamilton Jr., *God's Glory in Salvation through Judgment: A Biblical Theology* (Wheaton, IL: Crossway, 2010), 49, italics original.

7. Ibid., 51.

8. Rolf P. Knierim, *The Task of Old Testament Theology: Method and Cases* (Grand Rapids: Eerdmans, 1995), 17.

9. J. Scott Duvall and J. Daniel Hays, *God's Relational Presence: The Cohesive Center of Biblical Theology* (Grand Rapids: Baker Academic, 2019), 5.

10. Ibid., 4–5.

11. Hamilton, *God's Glory in Salvation through Judgment*; Thomas R. Schreiner, *The King in His*

who write theologies specifically of the Old Testament usually still see their proposed theme as relevant for both testaments. The clearest example of this is Walter Kaiser, who first wrote an Old Testament theology proposing promise as the center of the OT, and then later wrote a theology showing how it was also the unifying theme of the entire Christian Bible.[12]

Many authors provide justification for treating the two testaments as a unit. James Hamilton compares those who would read the Old Testament by itself to "a botanist examining an acorn in order to predict what will sprout from the seed. How seriously would we take such a botanist professing openness to the idea that the acorn might make potatoes?"[13] The Old Testament (an acorn) by its very nature leads to the New Testament (an oak tree). One of the main goals of Walther Eichrodt's Old Testament theology is *that this comprehensive picture does justice to the essential relationship [of the OT] with the NT.*"[14] He argues that Judaism never appeared complete without the New Testament, because the diversity within Judaism never presented a unified picture until Jesus combined the streams together in his offer of salvation.[15] While most of the authors in this category give precedence to the New Testament in some measure, Knierim desires that the testaments be treated as equals: "The Old and the New Testaments complement each other in that each helps rectify the deficiency of the other and in that each is partly in need of reconceptualization in light of the legitimate emphasis of the other."[16]

In contrast, Bernhard Anderson argues for the "relative independence of the Old Testament," in which it is allowed to speak for itself. Therefore any center of the Old Testament is not necessarily the center of the New Testament.[17] However, in his final chapter he still shows how the New Testament employs his central theme of covenant. He concludes, "In the New Testament these covenant perspectives are employed to confess our faith in Jesus, the Christ, whose life, death, and resurrection signify that 'God is with us.'"[18]

Beauty: A Biblical Theology of the Old and New Testaments (Grand Rapids: Baker, 2013); Samuel Terrien, *The Elusive Presence: Toward a New Biblical Theology* (New York: Harper and Row, 1978); Christopher J. H. Wright, *The Mission of God: Unlocking the Bible's Grand Narrative* (Downers Grove, IL: InterVarsity, 2006); Duvall and Hays, *God's Relational Presence.*

12. Walter C. Kaiser Jr., *Toward an Old Testament Theology* (Grand Rapids: Zondervan, 1978); idem, *The Promise-Plan of God: A Biblical Theology of the Old and New Testaments* (Grand Rapids: Zondervan, 2008).

13. Hamilton, *God's Glory in Salvation through Judgment,* 46–47.

14. Eichrodt, *Theology of the Old Testament,* 1:27, italics original.

15. Ibid., 1:510. Eichrodt even refers to "the torso-like appearance of Judaism in separation from Christianity" (1:26), a description that has brought charges of anti-Semitism against him in recent years.

16. Knierim, *Task of Old Testament Theology,* 137.

17. Bernhard W. Anderson, *Contours of Old Testament Theology* (Minneapolis: Augsburg Fortress, 1999), 9–15.

18. Ibid., 342. One exception to this general consensus is Horst Preuss. At a basic level, his *Old*

Prescriptive

In general, scholars who see a center in the Old Testament also read it prescriptively, viewing the Old Testament as authoritative for our lives as Christians today. John Kessler says that his Old Testament theology "formulates the message of the OT in ways that are closest to the concerns of my heart, the vision I hold for human life, and my own understanding of authentic spirituality."[19] Anderson argues that the Old Testament "is—or should be—used in worship, preaching and education," as well as "when formulating Christian doctrine (e.g., creation) or when seeking guidance on ethical issues."[20] Hamilton rejects the recovery of historical facts as the primary goal of biblical theology, saying that its goal is instead to "help people know God."[21] Given his proposal of mission as the center of Old Testament theology, Christopher Wright not surprisingly emphasizes its connection to Christian life today. He argues that "all mission or missions which we initiate, or into which we invest our own vocation, gifts and energies, flow from the prior and larger reality of the mission of God. *God* is on mission, and we, in that wonderful phrase of Paul, are 'co-workers with God' (1 Cor 3:9)."[22]

The German scholars tend not to emphasize the prescriptive nature of the Old Testament, but even they do not generally view their work as solely descriptive. Otto Kaiser identifies three roles of Old Testament theology for every new generation: instructing about how the Old Testament contributes to the Christian faith, providing historical context for how prior generations of Christians read the Old Testament, and teaching Christians about the nature of God.[23] Horst Preuss explicitly denies the prescriptive nature of Old Testament theology,[24] yet he also declares, "The discovery and the development of these fundamental structures of Old Testament faith, however, cannot remain only historically oriented and purely descriptive.

Testament Theology contains very few references to the New Testament. The index lists almost as many references to the Apocrypha as to the New Testament. In Preuss's view, seeing election as the center of the Old Testament would be valid for all scholars—Jewish and Christian—but attempting to integrate the New Testament into the question is legitimate only for Christian scholars. Therefore he argues that "the 'openness of the Old Testament' does not directly imply or even mean only an openness to the New Testament. Only a Christian theologian is able to speak of the Old Testament's openness to the New Testament" (Horst Dietrich Preuss, *Old Testament Theology*, trans. Leo G. Perdue, 2 vols., Old Testament Library [Louisville: Westminster John Knox, 1995–96], 2:306).

19. John Kessler, *Old Testament Theology: Divine Call and Human Response* (Waco, TX: Baylor Univ. Press, 2013), xvii.

20. Anderson, *Contours of Old Testament Theology*, 8.

21. Hamilton, *God's Glory in Salvation through Judgment*, 38.

22. Wright, *Mission of God*, 531–32, italics original.

23. Otto Kaiser, *Grundlegung*, vol. 1 of *Der Gott des Alten Testaments: Theologie des Alten Testaments* (Göttingen: Vandenhoeck and Ruprecht, 1993), 75.

24. Preuss, *Old Testament Theology*, 1:20.

Old Testament theology shall have to join in the endeavor within Christian theology to produce 'biblical theology,' . . . in order for the Christian faith to receive and keep its significance."[25]

POINTS OF TENSION

The Identity of the Center

The major point of tension for Old Testament theologies that adopt a center is the identity of that center. For the sake of clarity, their proposals will be grouped into four categories: covenant, kingdom of God, divine-human relationship, and other centers.

Covenant

Associated particularly with Eichrodt, covenant is the most well-known center proposed for the Old Testament. Eichrodt argues that "the concept of the covenant was given this central position in the religious thinking of the Old Testament so that, by working outward from it, the structural unity of the OT message might be made more readily visible."[26] He organizes the first volume of his Old Testament theology around the theme of covenant, discussing the covenant statutes, the covenant God, the leaders of the covenant (prophets, priests, and kings), and means of breaking and fulfilling the covenant.[27]

William Dumbrell structures his theology around the covenant with Noah (which, he argues, began at creation), the Abrahamic covenant, the Sinai covenant, the covenant with David, and the new covenant, seeing them as subsets of one primary covenant.[28] In his discussion of the new covenant, he contends that the catastrophe of the exile forced a shift from a concentration on the structures of Israel, such as the monarchy and the temple, to a sole focus on God's grace as the foundation of the covenant.[29] While Otto Kaiser refers to the law as the center of the Old Testament, his argument is based largely on covenant ideas. He observes that the covenant formula, "I shall be your God, and you shall be my people," is found throughout the Old Testament, from the patriarchs through the exilic period (Gen. 17:7–8; Lev.

---

25. Ibid., 2:306–7.
26. Eichrodt, *Theology of the Old Testament*, 1:17.
27. However, his second volume (second and third volumes in German) focuses less on the covenant as he addresses "God and the World" (including topics like creation and the spirit realm) and "God and Man" (focusing on God's relationship with the individual).
28. William J. Dumbrell, *Covenant and Creation: An Old Testament Covenant Theology*, rev. ed. (Milton Keynes, UK: Paternoster, 2013).
29. Ibid., 164–200.

26:12; Jer. 7:21–23), and argues that it "is in fact the chief thread through the labyrinth of the Bible."[30] Since the covenant is at the core of the Torah, the Torah functions as a canon within the canon. The rest of the Old Testament is marked by its dependence upon the Torah.[31]

Taking his cue from Paul's list of YHWH's gifts to Israel in Romans 9:4–5 (election, promises, covenants, adoption, the glory, and the law), Anderson identifies these items as the heart of Old Testament theology. However, he suggests that focusing on the covenants will encapsulate all of these themes.[32] He divides his book into three sections. First, he studies YHWH as the character who initiates the covenants. Second, he covers the three major covenants (Abrahamic, Mosaic, and Davidic), connecting a variety of topics to each covenant. While the biblical account portrays these three covenants as chronological, Anderson argues that they are most likely simultaneous, "like the trajectories of three jet planes whose jet streams parallel each other in the course of flight."[33] Finally, Anderson discusses the covenantal crisis brought about by the exile, as well as various responses to that crisis.

Kingdom of God

Another general category of proposed centers revolves around the idea of the kingdom of God. Grounding this theme primarily in Genesis 1:26–28, Eugene Merrill describes the kingdom of God as "the arena in which the God and man cooperative program is enacted."[34] He devotes his largest major section to outlining the kingdom of God and examining how it functions in the Mosaic covenant, the Deuteronomistic History (Deuteronomy–Kings), and the postexilic history books (Chronicles and Ezra–Nehemiah).[35] However, the theme also influences his other major sections, particularly his discussion of the Prophets.[36]

Although Thomas Schreiner recognizes that other selections of a central theme are just as valid, he proposes viewing the kingdom of God as the primary theme of the whole Bible. In particular, he contends that the Bible describes how the kingdom of God is being regained for the glory of God and includes both God's love for his people and his judgment of those opposed to

---

30. Otto Kaiser, "The Law as Center of the Hebrew Bible," in *"Sha'arei Talmon": Studies in the Bible, Qumran, and the Ancient Near East Presented to Shemaryahu Talmon*, ed. Michael Fishbane, Emanuel Tov, and Weston W. Fields (Winona Lake, IN: Eisenbrauns, 1992), 96.

31. Ibid., 96–100; idem, *Grundlegung*, 329–53.

32. Anderson, *Contours of Old Testament Theology*, 33.

33. Ibid., 239.

34. Eugene H. Merrill, *Everlasting Dominion: A Theology of the Old Testament* (Nashville: Broadman and Holman, 2006), 27, 31.

35. Ibid., 275–488.

36. Ibid., 489–566.

his divine rule.[37] According to Stephen Dempster, land (dominion) and kingship (dynasty) are the main themes of the Old Testament, and he summarizes the Old Testament narrative as a story "about the reclamation of a lost human dominion over the world through a Davidic dynasty."[38]

Knierim prefers to speak of a criterion to evaluate the plurality of the Old Testament rather than using the terminology of a center, but his choice of that criterion is *the universal dominion of Yahweh in justice and righteousness.*"[39] Finally, Martens centers his study of the Old Testament on the theme of building the kingdom of God as described in Exodus 5:22–6:8.[40] Working his way chronologically through the Old Testament, he examines four aspects of God's design for his kingdom in each time period: "deliverance, community, knowledge of God, and the abundant life."[41]

Divine-Human Relationship

The third category includes a variety of proposals that in some broad way highlight the divine-human relationship. For example, David Carr suggests passion for God as a center, focusing on the marriage metaphor used to describe the relationship between God and his people.[42] Rudolf Smend advocates for "YHWH the God of Israel and Israel the people of God" as the center of the Old Testament, showing how it connects to the New Testament, in which "the name of Jesus has replaced the two names YHWH and Israel."[43] Th. C. Vriezen concludes that "Old Testament theology must centre upon Israel's God as the God of the Old Testament in His relations to the people, man, and the world, and that it must be dependent upon this central element for its structure."[44] Roberto Ouro proposes that the sanctuary, in its role as the meeting place with God, is the center of Old Testament theology: "God and humanity are present in the sanctuary, together carrying out the plan of salvation. . . . Taken together, the physical and conceptual components of

---

37. Schreiner, *King in His Beauty*, xii–xiii.

38. Stephen G. Dempster, *Dominion and Dynasty: A Theology of the Hebrew Bible*, New Studies in Biblical Theology 15 (Downers Grove, IL: InterVarsity, 2003), 231.

39. Knierim, *Task of Old Testament Theology*, 15, italics original.

40. Martens, *God's Design*, 3–18.

41. Ibid., xi. Although we have included him in the canonical chapter (chap. 5), Bruce Waltke could easily be placed in this chapter as well. He argues that "a universal that embraces all the biblical text is the irruption of the holy God's merciful kingship" (Bruce K. Waltke and Charles Yu, *An Old Testament Theology: An Exegetical, Canonical, and Thematic Approach* [Grand Rapids: Zondervan, 2007], 147).

42. David M. Carr, "Passion for God: A Center in Biblical Theology," *Horizons in Biblical Theology* 23 (2001): 1–24.

43. Rudolf Smend, "Die Mitte des Alten Testaments," in *Die Mitte des Alten Testaments: Exegetische Aufsätze* (Tübingen: Mohr Siebeck, 2002), 73, translation ours.

44. Th. C. Vriezen, *An Outline of Old Testament Theology*, trans. S. Neuijen, 2nd ed. (Newton, MA: Branford, 1970), 150.

the sanctuary form a macroconcept that governs the meaning of all the major theological themes of the OT."[45]

Kessler identifies six streams within an overarching center of divine-human relationship.

- "Creation Theology: The Relationship of Knowing God as Creator and God's Purposes for Creation"
- "Sinai Covenant Theology: The Relationship of Grateful Obligation"
- "Promise Theology: The Relationship of Confident Expectation"
- "Priestly Theology: The Gift of Yahweh's Holy Presence"
- "The Theology of Divine Accessibility: Speaking to God amidst the Manifold Experiences of Life"
- "Wisdom Theology: The Relationship of Faith Seeking Understanding"[46]

These streams allow Kessler to demonstrate diversity in the Old Testament but still find coherence in the midst of that diversity, which he finds helpful for students. He explains, "I can personally attest to the fact that when students begin with an analysis of the OT in terms of the 'theological traditions' or 'theological streams' that constitute the core chapters of this book, they express a far greater ability to understand and appropriate the OT than when they begin with the text in its canonical presentation."[47] However, even with his broad theme of divine-human relationship, he is still concerned that he left out some important Old Testament material, such as "messianic ideology or apocalyptic thought."[48]

A similar proposal comes from Preuss, who has selected election as the center of his Old Testament theology, defining it as "'*YHWH's historical activity of electing Israel for communion with his world' and the obedient activity required of this people (and the nations).*"[49] This center allows him to engage with the history of the people of Israel in the Old Testament, but it also provides him with an avenue for discussing topics that are somewhat broader. Each of his chapters begins with a short statement about how it connects to the theme of election. For example, a chapter on YHWH describes him as "the God Who Elects," while a chapter on priests and Levites observes that they "were chosen by YHWH."[50]

---

45. Roberto Ouro, "The Sanctuary: The Canonical Key of Old Testament Theology," *Andrews University Seminary Studies* 50 (2012): 174.

46. Kessler, *Old Testament Theology*.

47. Ibid., xiv.

48. Ibid., 531.

49. Preuss, *Old Testament Theology*, 1:25, italics original.

50. Ibid., 1:139, 2:52. However, even a lack of connection to the theme of election does not prevent him from discussing a particular topic. For example, his section on the Prophets begins with the notice that "there is a dearth of statements about election in the Old Testament prophets" (2:67).

Divine presence as the center of the Old Testament is a proposal that has gained ground in recent years.[51] Bernd Janowski offers an example of this approach, with his suggestion of a theology focusing on God's presence in the temple and Jerusalem in the Old Testament and in Jesus in the New Testament.[52] Duvall and Hays have also recently published a book proposing the relational divine presence as the center of the Bible: "In arguing that the relational presence of God is the 'cohesive center' of biblical theology, we are neither ignoring nor downplaying the importance of other prevalent and highly significant biblical themes (e.g., covenant, kingdom of God), but rather suggesting that the cohesive central megatheme of God's relational presence connects all of these other themes into the big overarching plot of the biblical story."[53] Duvall and Hays trace this theme from the garden of Eden at the beginning of the Bible to new creation at the end, concluding, "At the center of it all is God—the Triune God, who has created and redeemed and invited his people to enjoy his relational presence for eternity."[54]

In an interesting twist on this theme, Samuel Terrien argues that "the reality of the presence of God stands at the center of biblical faith. This presence, however, is always elusive."[55] In his view, while God often reveals himself to his people in the biblical text, that presence is usually temporary. The cult (religious system) and Sabbath (sacred time) provide a way to experience that presence but do not guarantee access to it. The divine presence "is neither absolute nor eternal but elusive and fragile, even and especially when human beings seek to prolong it in the form of cultus. . . . It is when presence escapes man's grasp that it surges, survives, or returns."[56]

Other Centers

Other proposed centers do not fit neatly into these categories. Walter Kaiser proposes promise as the center of Old Testament theology. Although he structures his book according to historical time period, his aim is to trace the trajectory of promise throughout biblical history. He sees the promise theme as appearing throughout the Old Testament in such places as the major

---

51. John Walton sees divine presence as a theme that pervades the whole Bible, though he does not describe it as a center and follows a multiplex structure for his Old Testament theology (John H. Walton, *Old Testament Theology for Christians: From Ancient Context to Enduring Belief* [Downers Grove, IL: IVP Academic, 2017], 7). Therefore he is discussed in chap. 3.

52. Bernd Janowski, "The One God of the Two Testaments: Basic Questions of a Biblical Theology," *Theology Today* 57 (2000): 297–324.

53. Duvall and Hays, *God's Relational Presence*, 5.

54. Ibid., 336.

55. Terrien, *Elusive Presence*, xxvii.

56. Ibid., 476.

covenants, the fear of YHWH in the wisdom literature, the day of YHWH in the Prophets, and YHWH's continued dedication to his promise in the exilic and postexilic literature.[57]

James Hamilton suggests that the Bible's center is God's glory in salvation through judgment. Recognizing that God's glory is too broad to be an effective center, he focuses on these two particular ways that God brings glory to himself. Since these categories encapsulate much of the plan of God in history, Hamilton is able to draw on most of the biblical narrative. For example, in Exodus, God brings glory to himself by saving the Israelites from oppression and judging the Egyptians who have enslaved them.[58]

Finally, Wright argues that the mission of God is the center of the Bible.[59] The heart of his theology consists of three main sections. First, he describes how "the God of mission" is known through Israel and Jesus, challenging idolatry. Second, in regard to "the people of mission," Wright focuses on Israel's role as a people chosen to bless the world, with particular reference to the Old Testament. Third, "the arena of mission" includes discussion of the role of creation, the image of God, and the nations.[60] Wright moves beyond the texts usually associated with missions by examining such themes as the exodus, the jubilee, and ethics.[61] Bungishabaku Katho of the Democratic Republic of Congo suggests a similar view concerning mission and Old Testament theology.[62]

Incorporation of Nonnarrative Literature

One of the problems of attempting to find a unified center in a diverse work is that invariably some pieces remain outside the center. Since the proposed central themes often revolve around the Old Testament narratives, the nonnarrative literature, especially the wisdom literature, is often neglected.[63] For example, Eichrodt has less than fifteen pages on wisdom in a two-volume

---

57. Kaiser, *Toward an Old Testament Theology*, 43–51.

58. Hamilton, *God's Glory in Salvation through Judgment*, 90–96.

59. Christopher J. H. Wright, "Mission as a Matrix for Hermeneutics and Biblical Theology," in *Out of Egypt: Biblical Theology and Biblical Interpretation*, ed. Craig Bartholomew et al., Scripture and Hermeneutics Series 5 (Grand Rapids: Zondervan, 2004), 102–43; idem, *Mission of God*, 29.

60. Wright, *Mission of God*, 71–530.

61. Ibid., 265–323, 357–392. Wright extends his treatment of this theme in idem, *The Mission of God's People: A Biblical Theology of the Church's Mission*, Biblical Theology for Life (Grand Rapids: Zondervan, 2010).

62. Bungishabaku Katho, "Faire la théologie de l'Ancien Testament en Afrique aujourd'hui: Défis et perspective," *Old Testament Essays* 23 (2010): 88–89.

63. This is not always the case. For example, Carr's proposal of passion for God as the center of the Old Testament is based on the Song of Songs and neglects much of the history in the Old Testament ("Passion for God," 23–24).

work that totals around a thousand pages.[64] Walter Kaiser recognizes the difficulties of incorporating wisdom into his outline, declaring that "no period of time is more difficult to relate to the whole of a continuing OT theology than that of the wisdom literature."[65] His solution to the problem is to include a topical chapter on wisdom titled "Life in the Promise: Sapiential [Wisdom] Era" in the midst of a series of chapters otherwise based on historical periods.

However, others have found creative ways to include wisdom and other parts of the Old Testament that often do not fit into neat categories. One strategy to incorporate wisdom literature is to view it as a human response. Merrill's solution is to include a final section on the poetic and wisdom literature, titled "Human Reflection on the Ways of God."[66] Dempster resolves the problem by reading the nonnarrative books as commentary on the narrative storyline.[67] Otto Kaiser's approach is to look at how the Torah functions as a foundation for other parts of the canon. For example, the Prophets proclaim the blessings and curses of the covenant, the Psalms call forth blessing on the one who meditates on the Torah, and the Song of Songs can be read as an allegory of the relationship between YHWH and his people.[68] Vriezen includes wisdom in his discussion of the revelation of God but then mitigates its place in this category: "Wisdom cannot be considered a direct source of the revelation of God in the Old Testament; it speaks only indirectly of Him in so far as it speaks of the Creation and unfolds the Creation ordinances."[69]

In general, those who focus on themes broader than covenant or kingdom are more successful at incorporating all parts of the Old Testament. Since Kessler emphasizes diversity within his wide-ranging theme of divine-human relationship, he is able to include an entire chapter on wisdom theology as one stream of the divine-human relationship.[70] The theme of divine presence provides Terrien with an easy way to include diverse material as well. He declares, "It is the Hebraic theology of presence, not the covenant ceremonial, that constitutes the field of forces which links—across the biblical centuries—the fathers of Israel, the reforming prophets, the priests of Jerusalem, the psalmists of Zion, the Jobian poet, and the bearers of the gospel."[71] Likewise, Hamilton's theme of God's glory in salvation through judgment is broad enough to allow

---

64. Eichrodt, *Theology of the Old Testament*, 2:80–92. The wisdom books are also discussed under a few other headings, such as Job in the category of immortality (2:517–23).

65. Kaiser, *Toward an Old Testament Theology*, 46.

66. Merrill, *Everlasting Dominion*, 567–640.

67. Dempster, *Dominion and Dynasty*, 159–210.

68. Kaiser, "Law as Center of the Hebrew Bible," 96–100; idem, *Grundlegung*, 329–53.

69. Vriezen, *Outline of Old Testament Theology*, 244–45.

70. Kessler, *Old Testament Theology*, 447–505.

71. Terrien, *Elusive Presence*, 31.

him to find it in the wisdom literature by connecting the wise and foolish paths with salvation and judgment. He states that "through the judgments announced against the company of evil men, against the folly of sexual immorality, and against wicked and deceitful practices that undermine one's integrity, the book of Proverbs seeks to deliver the simple son of Solomon to a life of wisdom."[72]

Role of Historical-Critical Methods

The final point of tension in this category is the extent to which these theologies use historical criticism. Rather than accepting the biblical account of Israel's history, some scholars use historical-critical reconstructions of the text extensively.[73] For example, Terrien employs Wellhausen's views on the origin of the Pentateuch, and he sees the patriarchal accounts as reflecting "tribal migrations" of legendary heroes.[74] These critical viewpoints play a significant role in the construction of his Old Testament theology. Terrien sees the Sabbath as originating not early in Israelite history—as would be suggested by texts like Exodus 20:8—but only after the destruction of Jerusalem in 587/586 BCE. He argues, based on this dating, that the divine space that was lost in the exile with the destruction of the temple was replaced by the concept of divine time, primarily through the Sabbath.[75]

Eichrodt works within the historical criticism of his day but generally has an optimistic perspective on the historicity of the text, including some kind of historical Moses. He contends that "only a Mosaic law-giving can explain the remarkable force and persistence of the true personality of Israel, in spite of all the cases of adaptation and receptive borrowing in their new home."[76] Likewise, he argues that the ark of the covenant goes back to Mosaic times.[77] This optimism often allows him to work with the historical claims of the text.[78] In particular, the historicity of YHWH's saving events is very important to him: "For on one point all the various expressions of the hope of salvation are agreed, that they make *a real entry of God into history* the centre of their belief."[79]

---

72. Hamilton, *God's Glory in Salvation through Judgment*, 300.

73. For more details on these historical reconstructions, see chap. 2.

74. Terrien, *Elusive Presence*, 10, 66.

75. Ibid., 391–94.

76. Eichrodt, *Theology of the Old Testament*, 1:84.

77. Ibid., 1:108–9.

78. Naturally, he is not always optimistic. Just as one example, he is skeptical about the biblical account of the origin of the Levites (ibid., 1:393–94).

79. Ibid., 1:490, italics original. One of Eichrodt's main arguments against Gerhard von Rad is that von Rad dispenses with true history by creating a rift between historical events and Israel's confession about the acts of God: "Since such an approach must also throw doubt on all the later historical evidence in the OT, one is forced to ask whether a religious testimony which possesses no assured connection with historical reality can be regarded as valid evidence of a historical revelation?" (1:514).

Similarly, Preuss assumes the critical theory current at the time of writing his Old Testament theology.[80] However, he suggests that he would rather err on the side of trusting the authenticity of texts too much rather than too little and rejects the late dating of Old Testament texts.[81] Therefore he denies the exact historicity of the exodus, contending that "no apparent consideration was given to the historical accuracy or even probability of what happened. Theology was more important than history."[82] However, he still argues for some kind of historical kernel of truth about a Moses group who "experienced their deliverance from an Egyptian military unit (a border guard?) as an act of YHWH."[83] These critical theories also affect how he constructs his theology, as evident in his discussion of how the various sources present the Sinai traditions.[84]

Other scholars in this category eschew historical criticism entirely. Hamilton's comment is representative: "Rather than interpreting a disputed scholarly reconstruction, I will interpret the claims the texts make."[85] Likewise, Walter Kaiser argues that "biblical theology will always remain an endangered species until the heavy-handed methodology of imaginary source criticism, history of tradition, and certain types of form criticism are arrested."[86] He contends that the history recorded must be true history; otherwise "it was both unworthy of personal belief and liable to internal collapse from the sheer weight of its own contrivances."[87] Finally, Duvall and Hays say that "we see very limited benefit to the development of Christian biblical theology from the numerous evolving compositional theories and accompanying historical settings that frequently are being discussed and debated within the broader academy, especially in the field of OT studies."[88]

TEST CASE: EXODUS

The events of the exodus play a major role in some of the Old Testament theologies in this category. For example, Preuss reads the exodus as the central electing event in the OT, declaring that "in this decisive act, the Old

---

80. For example, Preuss assumes a Yahwist from the tenth century BCE (*Old Testament Theology*, 1:112). Otto Kaiser also employs historical criticism extensively in his work.
81. Preuss, *Old Testament Theology*, 1:25–26.
82. Ibid., 1:48.
83. Ibid., 1:42.
84. Ibid., 1:64–69.
85. Hamilton, *God's Glory in Salvation through Judgment*, 44.
86. Kaiser, *Toward an Old Testament Theology*, 7.
87. Ibid., 8.
88. Duvall and Hays, *God's Relational Presence*, 4.

Testament witness to God finds both its origins and its center."[89] Further, the exodus serves as the foundation for such aspects of Israelite life as the rejection of foreign gods and the gift of the land.[90] As already noted, Martens centers his study of the Old Testament on God's promise to Moses to deliver Israel from Egypt in Exodus 5:22–6:8 and the theme of building the kingdom of God.[91]

On the other hand, those theologies that focus on covenant or presence tend to emphasize the latter half of Exodus (Sinai) rather than the exodus event. For example, Terrien highlights theophany in Exodus, without giving much attention to the exodus from Egypt.[92] Eichrodt also spends little time discussing the exodus event, because his focus on covenant leads him to pay more attention to the revelation of the divine name (Exodus 3, 6) and to the book of the covenant (Exodus 20–23).[93] Likewise, Dumbrell, who also sees covenant as a center, primarily examines Exodus 19–40. He highlights the connection with the promises to the patriarchs, the missional focus of the covenant for the good of all the world, and the understanding of the law as guidance for life within the covenant.[94] In his section on Exodus, Walter Kaiser focuses on the status of Israel as YHWH's people, mainly based on Exodus 19.[95]

However, many scholars give significant attention to both parts of the book. Wright devotes an entire chapter to the exodus, arguing that it "provided the primary model of God's idea of redemption, not just in the Old Testament but even in the New, where it is used as one of the keys to understanding the meaning of the cross of Christ."[96] He rejects spiritualizing and politicizing interpretations in favor of an understanding that combines aspects of both, concluding that "mission without social compassion and justice is biblically deficient."[97] The description of Israel as "a kingdom of priests and a holy nation" in Exodus 19:6 highlights for Wright the relationship between the calling and actions of God's people. He contends that "Israel's *identity* (to be a priestly kingdom) declares a *mission*, and Israel's *mission* demands an *ethic* (to be a holy nation)."[98]

Hamilton sees the events of the exodus as paradigmatic for his theme of God's glory in salvation through judgment, saying that God "wants Egypt,

---

89. Preuss, *Old Testament Theology*, 1:40.
90. Ibid., 1:47.
91. Martens, *God's Design*, 3–18.
92. Terrien, *Elusive Presence*, 106–60.
93. Eichrodt, *Theology of the Old Testament*, 1:70–97, 187–92.
94. Dumbrell, *Covenant and Creation*, 80–126.
95. Kaiser, *Toward an Old Testament Theology*, 103–21.
96. Wright, *Mission of God*, 265.
97. Ibid., 288.
98. Ibid., 375, italics original.

Israel, and all the earth to know that he is Yahweh. And they will know that he is simultaneously just and merciful, so much so that the finite mind can scarcely perceive the glory of the justice and the mercy as they intermingle and radiate with the blinding splendor of the one they reveal. Yahweh glorifies himself at the exodus by saving Israel through the judgment of Egypt."[99] Tying in the second half of the book to his central theme by looking at the story of the golden calf (Exodus 32–34), Hamilton declares that "when the people did not honor Yahweh as God and give thanks to him, Yahweh judged their sin, and through the judgment, he saved them from themselves even as thousands died."[100]

Duvall and Hays likewise include material from both portions of the book in their study of divine presence. In the context of the revelation of the divine name in Exodus 3, they argue that "there is a strong case that one of the most core characteristics reflected in the revelation and in the basic meaning of the name Yahweh is his relational presence."[101] They also see the presence of God as emphasized in the exodus, for example, in YHWH's presence with Moses in Egypt. They point out that "there is no mention of Moses trying to communicate with God up in the heavens or God appearing to him in dreams."[102] However, they contend that the theme of divine presence reaches a climax in the final portion of Exodus: "God has brought the Israelites out of Egypt to Mount Sinai, where he will encounter them with his very real and intense presence, establish a covenant relationship with them, and then actually move into their midst to dwell with them in the tabernacle and to travel with them."[103]

Finally, Dempster sees his theme of "dominion and dynasty" as found throughout Exodus. The first half of the book reveals that against the opposition of the Egyptians, "the goal of Exodus is thus the building of the Edenic sanctuary so that the Lord can dwell with his people" as at creation.[104] Interestingly, Dempster argues that the second half of the book suggests that "Sinai, not Egypt, is Israel's largest roadblock to Canaan."[105] In this case, Sinai stands for Israel's rebellion against the covenant in their worship of the golden calf (Exodus 32), which leads to YHWH's revelation of his character (Ex. 34:6–7) and to what Dempster understands as the creation of a new covenant (Ex. 34:10–35).[106]

---

99. Hamilton, *God's Glory in Salvation through Judgment*, 106.

100. Ibid., 107.

101. Duvall and Hays, *God's Relational Presence*, 26.

102. Ibid., 27–28.

103. Ibid., 29.

104. Dempster, *Dominion and Dynasty*, 100.

105. Ibid., 101.

106. Ibid., 106.

Part 3

CONTEXT

Although the approaches we describe in part 3 differ from one another in substantial ways, they all share a focus on the importance of context. Chapter 5, "Canonical Old Testament Theology," examines theologies that see the Christian canon as the proper context for Old Testament theology and therefore highlight connections with the New Testament. By contrast, chapter 6, "Jewish Biblical Theology," covers theologies that read the Hebrew Bible from the context of a Jewish background. Finally, chapter 7, "Postmodern Old Testament Theology," considers theologies that emphasize the particular contexts of individual interpreters and interpretive communities, while also pointing out the significant diversity found within the Old Testament.

Chapter 5

CANONICAL OLD TESTAMENT THEOLOGY

In this chapter, we will discuss an approach to Old Testament theology that identifies the primary context for understanding Old Testament texts as the biblical canon—the collection of books accepted by the community of faith as authoritative. The dominant figure behind this approach is Brevard Childs. Rejecting the domination of biblical theology by historical-critical concerns, which he saw as making the biblical text "theologically mute,"[1] Childs called for a new approach in his landmark *Biblical Theology in Crisis*, published in 1970.[2] Since the Bible has been recognized as the canon of sacred Scripture for the church, he contended that the biblical texts "must be interpreted in relation to their function within the community of faith that treasured them."[3] Childs' influence has been massive, prompting many scholars to follow in his wake and produce a wide range of self-described canonical Old Testament theologies.[4] Recent years have also seen the growth of a movement known as the theological interpretation of Scripture.[5] Since it shares considerable overlap

---

1. Brevard S. Childs, *Old Testament Theology in a Canonical Context* (Philadelphia: Fortress, 1985), 17.
2. Idem, *Biblical Theology in Crisis* (Philadelphia: Westminster, 1970).
3. Ibid., 99.
4. James Sanders has also been a dominant figure in the development of a canonical approach. However, in using the term "canonical criticism" (which Childs rejects), Sanders categorizes it as one among other critical interpretive methods, and he has not made any thoroughgoing attempt to relate it to the construction of an Old Testament theology. He also focuses much more than did Childs on the canonical process, which he sees as continuing up to the present day as biblical traditions are continually reappropriated in new contexts (see James A. Sanders, *Canon and Community: A Guide to Canonical Criticism* [Philadelphia: Fortress, 1984]; idem, *Torah and Canon*, 2nd ed. [Eugene, OR: Cascade, 2005]).
5. The theological interpretation of Scripture unfortunately suffers from the same definitional confusion as does biblical theology. For an introduction to the field, see Stephen E. Fowl, ed., *The Theological Interpretation of Scripture: Classic and Contemporary Readings*, Blackwell Readings in Modern Theology (Malden, MA: Blackwell, 1997); Stephen E. Fowl, *Theological Interpretation of Scripture*, Cascade Companions (Eugene, OR: Cascade, 2009); Daniel J. Treier, *Introducing Theological Interpretation of Scripture: Recovering a Christian Practice* (Grand Rapids: Baker, 2008); Kevin J. Vanhoozer, "Introduction: What Is Theological Interpretation of the Bible?" in *Theological Interpretation of the Old Testament: A Book-by-Book Survey*, ed. Kevin J. Vanhoozer, Craig G. Bartholomew, and Daniel J. Treier (Grand Rapids: Baker, 2008), 15–28.

with the canonical approach, particularly when applied to biblical theology, we will include it in this chapter as well.[6]

DEFINITION: Canonical Old Testament theologies focus on the final canonical form of the biblical text, interpret texts in light of their broader Old Testament context, read the Old Testament as Christian Scripture, and see Old Testament theology as prescriptive. Points of tension among proponents of this approach include which canon is followed, the significance of the history of interpretation, and the role of historical-critical methods.

Central Texts Covered in This Chapter

Gary A. Anderson, *Christian Doctrine and the Old Testament* (2017)

Mark J. Boda, *The Heartbeat of Old Testament Theology* (2017)

Brevard S. Childs, *Biblical Theology of the Old and New Testaments* (1992)

Brevard S. Childs, *Old Testament Theology in a Canonical Context* (1985)

Sigurd Grindheim, *Introducing Biblical Theology* (2013)

Paul R. House, *Old Testament Theology* (1998)

R. W. L. Moberly, *Old Testament Theology* (2013)

Rolf Rendtorff, *The Canonical Hebrew Bible* (German: 2001; English: 2005)

John H. Sailhamer, *Introduction to Old Testament Theology* (1995)

Charles H. H. Scobie, *The Ways of Our God* (2003)

Christopher R. Seitz, *The Elder Testament* (2018)

Bruce K. Waltke with Charles Yu, *An Old Testament Theology* (2007)

Francis Watson, *Text and Truth* (1997)

Ben Witherington III, *Biblical Theology* (2019)

---

6. Only a couple of scholars who have written biblical theologies identify themselves with this movement—Francis Watson and R. W. L. Moberly—and they have somewhat different conceptions of what the theological interpretation of Scripture involves (see Francis Watson, *Text and Truth: Redefining Biblical Theology* [London: T&T Clark, 1997], 1–29; R. W. L. Moberly, "What Is Theological Interpretation of Scripture?" *Journal of Theological Interpretation* 3 [2009]: 161–78). Although Christopher Seitz discusses the "Theological Interpretation of the Elder Testament," he does not seem to associate himself with the theological interpretation movement (Christopher R. Seitz, *The Elder Testament: Canon, Theology, Trinity* [Waco, TX: Baylor Univ. Press, 2018], 35–50).

The category in this chapter corresponds to "BT4: Biblical Theology as Canonical Approach" and "BT5: Biblical Theology as Theological Construction" in Edward W. Klink III and Darian R. Lockett, *Understanding Biblical Theology: A Comparison of Theory and Practice* (Grand Rapids: Zondervan, 2012), 125–82.

COMMON FEATURES

Focus on the Final Canonical Form

The key characteristics of a canonical approach all flow out of the conviction that the biblical canon is the primary context for doing Old Testament theology. The first common feature is that theologies in this category focus their efforts on examining the theology of the final canonical form of the biblical text.[7] Whereas historical-critical approaches often give greater weight to earlier stages of composition, it is the final form that the church accepted as canonical Scripture. Mark Boda states the point forcefully: "For it to be a truly *biblical*-theological reading it must focus on the witness of the canonical text, that final literary form of books that now constitute an authoritative collection."[8]

Since the church never recognized the Yahwist source by itself as authoritative Scripture,[9] in Childs' view it has meaning and significance for the church only when read in light of its present location within the Pentateuch. In his discussion of the priesthood, Childs avoids the historical-critical tendency to reconstruct the theologies of various traditions concerning the priests and Levites. Instead he focuses on how the final form highlights the priest's role "as the guardian of the will of God to separate the clean and the unclean, the pure and the sacred."[10]

Christopher Seitz contends that in some historical-critical interpretation, "the [biblical] text as a complex and coherent statement of its own disappears like the dirt around so many shards of pottery."[11] Whereas historical-critical scholarship on the Pentateuch has focused on four continuous sources (JEDP) interwoven together, Seitz argues that scholars should "acknowledge the peculiar shape and form each one of the five books presents and see this factor as significant in itself."[12] For example, when Leviticus is used simply to reconstruct the history of Israel's religion and text traditions, scholars fail

---

7. Childs, *Biblical Theology in Crisis*, 102–3; idem, *Old Testament Theology in a Canonical Context*, 11–12.

8. Mark J. Boda, *The Heartbeat of Old Testament Theology: Three Creedal Expressions*, Acadia Studies in Bible and Theology (Grand Rapids: Baker Academic, 2017), 161, italics original; see also Ben Witherington III, *Biblical Theology: The Convergence of the Canon* (Cambridge: Cambridge Univ. Press, 2019), 117.

9. On the Yahwist, see p. 44.

10. Childs, *Old Testament Theology in a Canonical Context*, 153.

11. Seitz, *Elder Testament*, 77.

12. Ibid., 137. See also Paul R. House, *Old Testament Theology* (Downers Grove, IL: InterVarsity, 1998), 57. House takes a book-by-book approach to demonstrate the "unique theological contribution" of each book within the Old Testament.

to recognize that it offers "canonical speech from the tabernacle of the text."[13] Divine encounter happens in and through the book of Leviticus in its final form.

Charles Scobie counters the tendency of many historical-critical scholars to subordinate creation to a theology of redemption because they see creation theology as emerging only late in Israel's history and so view redemption as primary to Israel's understanding of God. For a canonical biblical theology, Scobie argues that "what is most significant is that canonical Scripture begins and ends with God's concern for all creation and all humankind and places everything else within that overall framework."[14] In the structure of the canon, creation is given the more dominant position, and redemption serves the aim of restoring creation.

Interpreting Texts in Light of Their Broader Old Testament Context

A second common feature of canonical Old Testament theologies is that they interpret texts in light of their broader Old Testament context. Engaging in intertextual reflection, they examine how Old Testament texts illuminate and sometimes intentionally use each other. According to Childs, the impulse to draw connections between disparate traditions is evident already in the canonical process. For example, he observes the use of the Decalogue in the Prophets (Hos. 4:2; Jer. 7:9) and also contends that "the narrative material offers a major commentary within scripture as to how these commands now function within the canon."[15] The commandment against adultery is treated in the story of Joseph and Potiphar's wife (Genesis 39), while other narratives interact with the purity laws (Num. 12:1–15; 2 Sam. 11:4).[16] This encourages biblical theologians to do likewise, bringing biblical texts from different genres and historical periods into conversation with one another.[17]

Paul House highlights intertextual connections in his frequent "Canonical Synthesis" sections. Concerning Isaiah 40–55, he contends that "this section of Isaiah is a minicanon unto itself. It mentions Eden, Abraham and Sarah, Jacob, the exodus, the law, Zion, David, the return from exile and the uniting of Israelites and Gentiles as a holy remnant to the holy God. All the Old

---

13. Seitz, *Elder Testament*, 137.

14. Charles H. H. Scobie, *The Ways of Our God: An Approach to Biblical Theology* (Grand Rapids: Eerdmans, 2003), 183.

15. Childs, *Old Testament Theology in a Canonical Context*, 13, 64.

16. Ibid., 64, 88–89.

17. See also John H. Sailhamer, *Introduction to Old Testament Theology: A Canonical Approach* (Grand Rapids: Zondervan, 1995), 212–13.

Testament's major redemption themes converge here."[18] House also examines the role of God's servant, through whom "God will bless all nations (cf. Gen 12:1–9), make Israel a holy nation (cf. Ex 19:5–6), legitimate the law (cf. Deut 8:3), give David an everlasting kingdom (cf. 2 Sam 7:7–17) and provide a future for the remnant."[19]

Bruce Waltke gives significant attention to what he calls "transformative" intertextuality—when "later writers interpret earlier writings to meet new historical situations and so advance our understanding."[20] For example, he observes the clear parallel between the near-rape of Lot's daughters by the Sodomites in Genesis 19 and the brutal rape leading to the death of a Levite's concubine by the Benjamite city of Gibeah in Judges 19. He concludes that this intentional intertextual link "subtly indicts the tribe of Benjamin for having become like the Sodomites, whom I AM utterly destroyed. But unlike his treatment of Sodom, I AM spares a remnant of Benjamin (Judg. 20–21)."[21]

R. W. L. Moberly demonstrates his use of intertextuality when he discusses the thorny problem of Deuteronomy 6:4 (often called the *Shema* after its first word in Hebrew). The verse is typically translated, "Hear, O Israel: The LORD our God, the LORD is one [*'ekhad*]," but it is not entirely clear what it means for YHWH to be "one."[22] Moberly observes that the verse has often been connected to the idea of monotheism (the belief in only one God) and that it was frequently used in Trinitarian debates.[23] However, noting that the verse is connected to the command to love YHWH wholeheartedly (v. 5), he offers a different approach. He interprets it in light of an intertextual connection with Song of Songs 6:8–9, the only other place in the Old Testament where he sees "one" (*'ekhad*) linked to the idea of love. In those verses, the lover acknowledges the many other women around but says of his beloved, "My dove, my perfect one, is the only one [*'ekhad*]" (NRSV).[24] As Moberly puts it, "It is the reality of one singling out another in such a way as, 'forsaking all others,' to focus solely on her."[25] Therefore he contends that in Deuteronomy

---

18. House, *Old Testament Theology*, 292.

19. Ibid.

20. Bruce K. Waltke and Charles Yu, *An Old Testament Theology: An Exegetical, Canonical, and Thematic Approach* (Grand Rapids: Zondervan, 2007), 126.

21. Ibid., 133.

22. Moberly notes that some commentators translate the Hebrew word *'ekhad* in this verse as "alone" (see the NLT: "The LORD is our God, the LORD alone"). However, he points out that the early Greek translation of the Old Testament and most interpreters throughout the history of the church have understood it as meaning "one" (R. W. L. Moberly, *Old Testament Theology: Reading the Hebrew Bible as Christian Scripture* [Grand Rapids: Baker Academic, 2013], 9–10).

23. Ibid., 10–13.

24. Ibid., 19.

25. Ibid., 20.

6:4, "the point is that, whatever 'other gods' there may be, such 'other gods' should be of no existential interest to Israel, but rather are to be displaced, rejected, and disregarded, since Israel's focus is to be on YHWH alone."[26]

For Boda, intertextual connections are central to what he calls his "selective intertextual-canonical approach," in which he identifies "certain topics in the biblical witness [that] seem to constitute its 'inner structure'" and "focuses on repeated use of particular phrases, expressions, and structures throughout the breadth of the OT and the NT."[27] For example, one of the "three basic rhythms" that he detects in "the heartbeat of the OT" is the "character creed."[28] This creed is summarized in Exodus 34:6–7, and its significance is demonstrated by the number of passages that quote or allude to it.[29] It testifies to YHWH's core characteristics as "compassionate and gracious, slow to anger, abundant in steadfast love and truth" and highlights his typical acts of showing steadfast love and forgiving sin but also disciplining when necessary.[30]

Reading the Old Testament as Christian Scripture

Scholars in this category also tend to argue that Old Testament theology is necessarily a Christian enterprise, since the term Old Testament implies a New Testament. For Childs, this means reading the Old Testament "as Christian Scripture."[31] He sees the two testaments as a unity, whose central subject is Christ.[32] Therefore he denies the possibility of Christians reading the Old Testament from a pre-Christian vantage point or understanding it in the same way as Jews.[33] However, he acknowledges "the legitimacy, even necessity,

---

26. Ibid.

27. Boda, *Heartbeat of Old Testament Theology*, 7.

28. Ibid., 7, 27. The others are the "historical creed," concerning YHWH's acts on behalf of his people, and the "relational creed," which highlights his covenantal relationship with his people.

29. For example, Numbers 14:18; Psalms 86:15; 103:8; 111:4; 145:8; Joel 2:13; Jonah 4:2; Nehemiah 9:17; 2 Chronicles 30:9 (see ibid., 28).

30. Ibid., 35–41, translation his. Boda also observes that elsewhere these characteristics are connected to YHWH's jealousy, which arises from his "exclusive relationship with his people," as well as to his incomparability and power (see Ex. 20:5–6; 1 Kings 8:23; Neh. 9:32; pp. 44–47).

31. Childs, *Old Testament Theology in a Canonical Context*, 9; see also Sailhamer, *Introduction to Old Testament Theology*, 22–23.

32. Brevard S. Childs, *Biblical Theology of the Old and New Testaments* (Minneapolis: Fortress, 1992), 78–79; see also Sigurd Grindheim, *Introducing Biblical Theology* (New York: Bloomsbury T&T Clark, 2013), 1.

33. Childs, *Old Testament Theology in a Canonical Context*, 9. By contrast, Rendtorff, who was shaped by his context in post–World War II Germany and highly attuned to the devastating effects of the Holocaust and Christian anti-Semitism, is concerned that Christians not steal the Hebrew Bible away from Jews. Therefore he argues that Christians should interpret the Hebrew Bible first without reference to the New Testament or Christian theology, and he contends that they should work together with Jews to form a shared Jewish-Christian theological understanding (see esp. Rolf Rendtorff, "Toward a Common Jewish-Christian Reading of the Hebrew Bible," in *Canon and Theology: Overtures to an Old Testament Theology*, trans. and ed. Margaret Kohl, Overtures to Biblical Theology [Minneapolis: Fortress, 1993], 31–45).

of serious theological reflection on the old covenant [Old Testament] in its own right as scripture of the church."[34]

Childs' *Old Testament Theology in a Canonical Context* is an attempt to do just that, but his ultimate goal of a whole-Bible theology, which reads the two testaments together as one book, is realized in his *Biblical Theology of the Old and New Testaments*. There he traces trajectories of key themes through both testaments, noting points of continuity and discontinuity, before concluding with biblical-theological and systematic reflections. Charles Scobie takes a similar approach, though he uses a fourfold scheme, drawing an arc from Old Testament "proclamation" and "promise" to New Testament "fulfillment" and "consummation."[35] He is also concerned to point out that a truly biblical theology is more than the sum of its parts (Old Testament theology plus New Testament theology), since it entails describing the dynamic relationship between the testaments.[36]

Reading the Old Testament as Christian Scripture can also involve reinterpreting Old Testament texts in light of the New Testament. Some, such as Ben Witherington, are more cautious about this endeavor. On the one hand, he declares, "I am not merely interested in doing what came to be called 'canonical' theology, if by that is meant doing Christian readings of the OT which either ignore or do not allow the OT text to have its own say in its own original context. . . . I take it as a basic matter of fairness that we should allow the OT to have its own say, since, after all, it is just as much God's Word as any portion of the NT."[37] Yet on the other hand, in his treatment of creation, he states that "the first Adam began the process which climaxed in the second Adam. This is to see Genesis in a canonical context and in light of the NT, but that is what the NT authors, especially Paul, do."[38] For Witherington, it is important to note the progressive development between the testaments so as not to flatten the Old Testament witness, but he suggests that we should also follow how the New Testament authors understand the Old Testament in light of the Christ event.[39]

Others go farther in offering Christian rereadings of the Old Testament. For example, in discussing the identity of the serpent in Genesis 3, Scobie acknowledges that the snake was not originally understood as a Satan-like

---

34. Childs, *Old Testament Theology in a Canonical Context*, 30.

35. Scobie, *Ways of Our God*, 93–99.

36. Ibid., 59.

37. Witherington, *Biblical Theology*, 2, also 442.

38. Ibid., 116. See also Witherington's reading of the new covenant, which is, to some degree, influenced by the understanding of the New Testament writers (pp. 306–38).

39. See ibid., 438–40, including Witherington's comments on Paul's use of the Abrahamic narrative.

figure. However, noting that an understanding of a personal force of evil emerged gradually within the biblical canon, he concludes, "Canonically, it is legitimate and indeed necessary to read Gen 3 in the light of that later development and to recognize that here at the outset of human history battle is joined between the forces of good and the forces of evil."[40] Sigurd Grindheim takes a similar approach to Isaiah's prophecy that "the virgin will conceive and give birth to a son, and will call him Immanuel" (Isa. 7:14). Although he observes that most scholars see this promised son as a child born during Isaiah's day (perhaps King Hezekiah or Isaiah's son),[41] he contends that "in the canonical context, Isaiah's prophecy refers to the future Messiah," Jesus Christ (see Matt. 1:23; Luke 1:34).[42]

As a proponent of the theological interpretation of Scripture, Francis Watson reinterprets the Old Testament in light of the New more thoroughly than most canonical interpreters. He maintains that "from the standpoint of Christian faith, it must be said that *the Old Testament comes to us with Jesus and from Jesus, and can never be understood in abstraction from him.*"[43] After Jesus' death and resurrection, Old Testament Scripture is reoriented "as its true scope and telos [aim] now for the first time come to light."[44] Responding to potential objections to his approach, he declares, "It might be said that Old Testament theology can and should reflect theologically on themes such as creation or suffering without reference to any christological center. Yet such a theology could only operate by interpreting certain texts in isolation from their context within the Christian Bible, the centre of which is marked by the figure of Jesus."[45] Watson concludes that "the Old Testament itself would be dissolved by a theological reflection basing itself exclusively on Old Testament texts."[46]

Watson sees this christological rereading of the Old Testament as exemplified by the use of Psalm 8 in Hebrews 2:5–9. In his view, the way Hebrews applies the psalm's reflection on the role and significance of humanity to Christ is not a spurious misinterpretation, as some Old Testament scholars

---

40. Scobie, *Ways of Our God*, 244.

41. Grindheim notes that the Hebrew word *'almah* found in this verse is often translated simply as "young woman," but he argues that it usually denotes "an unmarried girl." He also points out that the early Greek translation of the Old Testament uses *parthenos*, which does mean "virgin" (*Introducing Biblical Theology*, 78).

42. Ibid; see also Moberly, *Old Testament Theology*, 39. Moberly suggests that "one should be open to the potential value of later understandings for re-reading earlier texts."

43. Watson, *Text and Truth*, 182, italics original. Although Childs also sees Christ as the center of the Bible, Watson critiques Childs for merely placing the two testaments next to each other so that the Old Testament's "dialectical relationship to the New virtually disappears" (p. 14).

44. Ibid., 182.

45. Ibid., 209.

46. Ibid.

may think, but a careful reflection on the psalm in light of the Christ event. The complete dominion of humanity over creation envisaged by Psalm 8 does not seem to reflect reality on the ground, so Hebrews reads the psalm as prophetically pointing toward the dominion accomplished by Christ, in which those who follow him will one day share. As Watson points out, "There is no subjection of all things to humankind apart from the one that is taking place in Jesus."[47] For Paul, the psalm's declaration, "You put everything under their feet" (v. 6) also anticipates Jesus' defeat of death (1 Cor. 15:25–27). Watson concludes that "to be human is therefore to share with Jesus a way which has its final goal in the overcoming of death. The promise of human transcendence of the creaturely sphere finally amounts to nothing less than that."[48]

Prescriptive

A final common feature of canonical Old Testament theologies is that they view the Old Testament as prescriptive.[49] According to Childs, "The appeal to the canon understands Scripture as a vehicle of a divine reality, which indeed encountered an ancient people in the historical past, but which continues to confront the church through the pages of Scripture."[50] Therefore biblical theologians must place themselves within the sphere of Israel's witness to God and wrestle with the biblical text so that they may perceive God's word to the modern church by the illumination of the Spirit.[51] Childs offers prescriptive comments in his discussion of humanity, where he observes that the Old Testament condemns individual autonomy, portraying humans as completely dependent on God and created to live in community. He also sees the Old Testament as confronting the still-prevalent Gnostic tendency to view people as "having a spiritual core which is tragically locked into a mortal body,"

---

47. Ibid., 297.
48. Ibid., 298.
49. See, e.g., Childs, *Old Testament Theology in a Canonical Context*, 12; Sailhamer, *Introduction to Old Testament Theology*, 224; Scobie, *Ways of Our God*, 47–49; Richard Schultz, "What Is 'Canonical' about a Canonical Biblical Theology? Genesis as a Case Study of Recent Old Testament Proposals," in *Biblical Theology: Retrospect and Prospect*, ed. Scott J. Hafemann (Downers Grove, IL: InterVarsity, 2002), 96; Boda, *Heartbeat of Old Testament Theology*, 121–41, though he intentionally seeks "to avoid the language of description versus prescription" (p. 121). While Rendtorff also recognizes the importance of the Old Testament in developing a Christian theology for the church (see Rolf Rendtorff, *The Canonical Hebrew Bible: A Theology of the Old Testament*, trans. D. E. Orton, Tools for Biblical Study 7 [Leiden: Deo, 2005], 720), his concern to promote a shared theological understanding between Christians and Jews leads him to take a purely descriptive approach to Old Testament theology, seeing prescriptive reflection as a later step. However, he is clearly an outlier in this regard and has been critiqued for inconsistency in advocating for a canonical but nonprescriptive Old Testament theology (see R. Kendall Soulen, "Panel Review of *The Canonical Hebrew Bible: A Theology of the Old Testament*, by Rolf Rendtorff," *Horizons in Biblical Theology* 28 [2006]: 31–38).
50. Childs, *Biblical Theology in Crisis*, 100.
51. Idem, *Old Testament Theology in a Canonical Context*, 15.

by instead depicting the human person as a united whole.[52] Finally, in light of God's creation of humanity as male and female, Childs contends that "all attempts to assess sexuality merely as a style of life, or orientation of choice, seriously misconstrue the biblical witness which links sexual differentiation to particular functions within God's good creation."[53]

Boda insists that the inclusion of various texts and genres in a single canon "demands a certain reading strategy . . . because of the ultimate generic context of authoritative Scripture, which captures the imagination, demands obedience, and shapes the values of the receiving community."[54] In a chapter titled "Taking the Old Testament Pulse in the Christian Life," he discusses the significance of the "character creed" for the church. He contends that "the present generation more than any other needs to experience God as a divine parent in whom they will find security through his tender mercy as well as his measured discipline. . . . Crying 'Abba, Father' means that we are open to all aspects of God's parenting and trust him implicitly with our development as his children."[55]

In a discussion of the relationship between "theology, ethics, and praxis [practice]," Witherington points out that God "is not just interested in what we believe. . . . He is interested in replicating his moral character in us."[56] House emphasizes the importance of biblical theology for the faith and life of the church by declaring, "If biblical theology becomes integral to the thinking of students and pastors, if it becomes the heart of pastoral theology, if it becomes the basis for discussions on worship, if it becomes the basis for doctrinal debates, then the church will be a better place for the next generation."[57] Scobie offers a number of specific ways in which biblical theology can serve the church. For example, he suggests that it can help identify the root problem that has led to the current ecological crisis: "Humankind has a wrong relationship to creation because it has a wrong relationship to the Creator."[58] Later, in a chapter on the biblical command to love your neighbor, Scobie considers how the Bible provides teaching that can address a whole host of modern ethical issues, such as abortion, euthanasia, the status of women in the home and in society, racial tension, and war.[59]

---

52. Idem, *Biblical Theology of the Old and New Testaments*, 590.

53. Ibid.

54. Boda, *Heartbeat of Old Testament Theology*, 122.

55. Ibid., 132.

56. Witherington, *Biblical Theology*, 420.

57. Paul R. House, "Biblical Theology and the Wholeness of Scripture: Steps toward a Program for the Future," in *Biblical Theology: Retrospect and Prospect*, 278; see also idem, *Old Testament Theology*, 53.

58. Scobie, *Ways of Our God*, 187.

59. Ibid., 861–79.

Finally, using the analogy of a drama or a musical piece, which is best interpreted through reenactment, Moberly contends that "the crowning achievement of a theological interpretation of Scripture should be performance, that is ways of living, on the part of believers and those sympathetically interested, who are enabled to realize more fully that wholeness of life to which God calls."[60] At the heart of this performance should be "a love supreme"—a deep love for God—which "will purify all other loves and order them aright, so that they can be what they should be, and be less likely to become unhealthy or idolatrous."[61]

POINTS OF TENSION

Which Canon?

The most obvious point of tension for canonical Old Testament theologies is, which canon? This question involves two choices. First, should a canonical approach use the broader Roman Catholic canon and include the Apocrypha (called deuterocanonical books by the Catholic Church; see table 5.1 for a list), or should it restrict itself to the narrower canon accepted by Jews and Protestants?

TABLE 5.1: Apocrypha (Deuterocanonical Books)

Tobit	Wisdom of Solomon	Additions to Daniel
Judith	Sirach (Ecclesiasticus)	1 Maccabees
Additions to Esther	Baruch (and Letter of Jeremiah)	2 Maccabees

Since the vast majority of scholars working in biblical theology are Protestant, the Apocrypha plays only a minor role in most of the works covered in this chapter. House explicitly rejects its relevance, since the New Testament does not quote the apocryphal books as authoritative revelation.[62] Likewise, Waltke adopts the Protestant canon, which includes the books "shared by all branches of historic Christianity."[63]

However, Childs seeks to maintain the tension between the broader and narrower canons as part of what he calls "the church's ongoing *search* for the

---

60. Moberly, *Old Testament Theology*, 288.

61. Ibid., 32, 40.

62. House, *Old Testament Theology*, 55; see also Witherington, *Biblical Theology*, 8, though he gives some attention to the Apocrypha as offering glimpses into early Jewish theological understandings and providing background for New Testament thought (see, e.g., pp. 60, 77, 208, 344).

63. Waltke and Yu, *Old Testament Theology*, 36.

Christian Bible."[64] Thus references to apocryphal books may be found scattered throughout his work. He cites 1 Maccabees concerning Israel's postexilic hope for the return of prophecy and refers to Sirach, Baruch, and the Wisdom of Solomon when discussing the connection between wisdom and Israel's redemptive history.[65] As a Roman Catholic scholar, Gary Anderson takes the incorporation of the deuterocanonical books into the canon even more seriously. For example, Tobit plays a minor role in his defense of creation *ex nihilo* and a major role in his Christology, since he views Tobit as a righteous sufferer who foreshadows the suffering of Jesus.[66]

The second choice concerns whether canonical theology should follow the Jewish or Protestant canonical orders. The Jewish (Hebrew) canon is divided into a three-part structure—Torah, Prophets *(Nevi'im)*, and Writings *(Ketuvim)*—and is often called the Tanak, which is an acronym for the Hebrew names of its three major sections.[67] The Protestant (Greek) canon, on the other hand, divides its books into four parts: Pentateuch, History, Poetry, and Prophecy.

TABLE 5.2: Jewish (Hebrew) Canon

Torah	Prophets *(Nevi'im)**	Writings *(Ketuvim)***
Genesis	Joshua	Psalms
Exodus	Judges	Job
Leviticus	1 & 2 Samuel	Proverbs
Numbers	1 & 2 Kings	Ruth
Deuteronomy	Isaiah	Song of Songs
	Jeremiah	Ecclesiastes
	Ezekiel	Lamentations
	Book of the Twelve	Esther
	(Hosea–Malachi)	Daniel
		Ezra
		Nehemiah
		1 & 2 Chronicles

* Joshua–Kings is designated as the Former Prophets, and Isaiah–Malachi as the Latter Prophets.

** Hebrew manuscripts vary in the order of the books in the Writings, but the sequence presented here follows the order of the standard scholarly version of the Hebrew Bible, the *Biblia Hebraica Stuttgartensia*. For more details about the various orders, see Roger Beckwith, *The Old Testament Canon of the New Testament Church and Its Background in Early Judaism* (Grand Rapids: Eerdmans, 1985), 449–68.

---

64. Childs, *Biblical Theology of the Old and New Testaments*, 67, italics original.

65. Ibid., 171, 189–90.

66. Gary A. Anderson, *Christian Doctrine and the Old Testament: Theology in the Service of Biblical Exegesis* (Grand Rapids: Baker Academic, 2017), 55–56, 135–49.

67. TaNaK comes from the first letters of *Torah*, *Nevi'im*, and *Ketuvim*.

TABLE 5.3: Protestant (Greek) Canon*

Pentateuch	History	Poetry	Prophecy
Genesis	Joshua	Job	Isaiah
Exodus	Judges	Psalms	Jeremiah
Leviticus	Ruth	Proverbs	Lamentations
Numbers	1 & 2 Samuel	Ecclesiastes	Ezekiel
Deuteronomy	1 & 2 Kings	Song of Songs	Daniel
	1 & 2 Chronicles		Minor Prophets
	Ezra		(Hosea–Malachi)
	Nehemiah		
	Esther		

* The Roman Catholic canon follows the order of the Protestant canon but intersperses the deuterocanonical books throughout the three final sections.

Since the canonical approach emphasizes the importance of the church tradition accepting the Bible as canonical Scripture, we might expect that proponents of this approach would use the canonical order of their own church tradition. Yet that has not typically been the case.[68] As already noted, most of the scholars covered in this chapter hail from a Protestant background, but only Scobie clearly advocates for grounding biblical theology in the Protestant canonical order.[69] Rolf Rendtorff, John Sailhamer, and Paul House, on the other hand, explicitly take the Jewish Tanak as their starting point. As Rendtorff observes, its three-part order may be traced back to the beginnings of canon consciousness (see the prologue to the second-century BCE book of Sirach).[70] They also give attention to the shape of the canon, finding theological significance in the placement of books within the three-part structure of the Tanak. Rendtorff, for example, draws a connection between Ruth and Song of Songs, which are placed together among the *Megillot*,[71] noting that women act in surprisingly independent ways in these two books, considering the generally male-dominant culture of ancient Israel.[72]

---

68. Jewish scholar Marvin Sweeney also discusses the significance of the differences between the Jewish and Christian canonical orders. (See pp. 112–13.)

69. Scobie, *Ways of Our God*, 65–71.

70. Rendtorff, *Canonical Hebrew Bible*, 5; see also Sailhamer, *Introduction to Old Testament Theology*, 238–39; House, *Old Testament Theology*, 55. Childs' Old Testament theology seems to be based on the Jewish canonical order, though he does not make his choice entirely clear (*Old Testament Theology in a Canonical Context*, 10, 13). Boda's work seems to exhibit some tension between his identification with the Protestant canon (*Heartbeat of Old Testament Theology*, 7) and his reference to the three-part Jewish canon (p. 82).

71. That is, the "Five Scrolls," which also include Ecclesiastes, Lamentations, and Esther.

72. Rendtorff, *Canonical Hebrew Bible*, 374; on the significance of the canonical order, see also Sailhamer, *Introduction to Old Testament Theology*, 239–52; House, *Old Testament Theology*, 197–98, 408, 525.

Seitz points out that the order of books in the Christian canon was not standardized for several centuries, so the early church did not seem to see any theological significance in a particular sequence of books. Therefore he suggests that we should not limit ourselves to a single canonical order but instead observe how various orders highlight different connections.[73] For example, he asks whether Ruth should be considered between Judges and 1 Samuel (as in the Protestant canon) or between Proverbs and Song of Songs (as in the Jewish canon) and then declares, "The answer is simple: 'Both.' . . . Proverbs ends by extolling the virtuous woman, and Ruth follows to give a stellar example [see Prov. 31:10; Ruth 3:11]. . . . Judges ends on a hopeless note, with no king in the land as well, and Ruth comes to establish the line of David, and bring a ray of hope in the darkness, anticipating the Song of Hannah in 1 Samuel to follow."[74]

The Significance of the History of Interpretation

Canonical biblical theologies also differ over the degree of significance given to the history of biblical interpretation. Recovering the history of interpretation is a primary concern for Childs, who rebukes modern biblical scholars for unfairly judging earlier interpreters by historical-critical standards and therefore rejecting their work wholesale. While he acknowledges that premodern Christian interpretation should not be accepted uncritically, he argues that we can gain much from the careful and insightful reflection of renowned thinkers like Augustine and the Reformers, who read the Bible as the Word of God to the church and interpreted Scripture in light of Scripture.[75] Similarly, Moberly hopes that his own "attempt to reintegrate Old Testament study with classic Christian understandings and priorities may in its own way have an impact on people's ability to read the biblical texts freshly and to acquire a deeper understanding of some of their dimensions."[76]

Rendtorff focuses more attention on Jewish rabbinic and medieval interpretation than on early Christian exegesis. He observes that for many centuries Christian interpretation was almost wholly based on the Septuagint (the Greek translation of the Old Testament), so rabbinic texts provide the only early interpretation of the Hebrew text.[77] Concerning the difficult statement about God "punishing the children for the sin of the parents to the third and

---

73. Seitz, *Elder Testament*, 123; see also Gregory Goswell, "Should the Church Be Committed to a Particular Order of the Old Testament Canon?" *Horizons in Biblical Theology* 40 (2018): 17–40.

74. Seitz, *Elder Testament*, 125.

75. Childs, *Biblical Theology in Crisis*, 143–47.

76. Moberly, *Old Testament Theology*, 4; see also the frequent reference to premodern interpreters by Scobie, *Ways of Our God*; Sailhamer, *Introduction to Old Testament Theology*, 272–89.

77. Rolf Rendtorff, "Rabbinic Exegesis and the Modern Christian Bible Scholar," in *Canon and Theology*, 17–24.

fourth generation of those who hate [him]" (Ex. 20:5), he cites the medieval Jewish exegete Rashi's qualification, "if they hold firmly on to the work of their fathers," which is based on Deuteronomy 7:9–10 and Jewish texts like the Targumim and Talmud.[78] According to this Jewish tradition, the verse does not indicate that God will punish children for their father's sins regardless of their own behavior. Instead each generation will be judged on its own merits.

With a driving concern to break down the dividing wall between the disciplines of biblical studies and theology, Watson suggests that critical attention to the history of interpretation "can assist in the renewal of theologically-oriented biblical interpretation in our own time."[79] He illustrates this by analyzing the second-century dialogue between the Christian Justin Martyr and the Jewish Trypho, who have fundamentally different readings of the Scriptures because of their differing theological starting points. Ultimately, Watson contends that "the 'orthodox' Christology of Justin and others . . . is able to demonstrate the greatest coherence with Old Testament scripture, since it can appeal not only to traditional messianic proof-texts but also to the entire theology of the covenant and of the covenantal God who is both distant and near, holy and merciful."[80]

Anderson goes farther than most canonical interpreters by taking traditional Catholic doctrines as a starting point.[81] However, he does not see this as in conflict with hearing the witness of the Old Testament: "I make the rather audacious claim that theological doctrines need not be a hindrance to exegesis but, when properly deployed, play a key role in uncovering a text's meaning."[82] He aims to show how each of his selected doctrines "illumines what the biblical writers wish to accomplish."[83] Anderson interacts extensively with a wide range of interpreters, both ancient and modern, Jewish and Christian. For example, in his discussion of the enigmatic death of Aaron's sons Nadab and Abihu (Lev. 10:1–3), he cites the medieval Jewish exegetes Rashi and Rashbam and argues for an interpretation that follows the postmodern

---

78. Idem, *Canonical Hebrew Bible*, 486.

79. Watson, *Text and Truth*, 306; see also pp. 2–5.

80. Ibid., 324.

81. Similarly, many practitioners of the theological interpretation of Scripture employ the rule of faith and theological doctrines as a hermeneutical guide for interpretation. Daniel Treier argues that interpreters should not jettison their theological baggage before interpreting a biblical text, because that baggage provides what they need for good interpretation (*Introducing Theological Interpretation of Scripture*, 202).

82. Anderson, *Christian Doctrine and the Old Testament*, xi.

83. Ibid. See also Kevin J. Vanhoozer, "Toward a Theological Old Testament Theology? A Systematic Theologian's Take on Reading the Old Testament Theologically," in *Interpreting the Old Testament Theologically: Essays in Honor of Willem A. VanGemeren*, ed. Andrew T. Abernethy [Grand Rapids: Zondervan, 2018], 302–5).

reading of Jewish scholar Edward Greenstein, mediated through the Christian mystical theology of Pseudo-Dionysius (from around 500 CE).[84]

By contrast, other scholars who claim the canonical label do not see the history of interpretation as an important source. Waltke is concerned that church doctrine might function as a distorting lens for viewing the Old Testament. He declares that the interpretations of church tradition, "though intended to maintain orthodoxy, many times nullify the Word of God, as Jesus complained (Mark 7:13)."[85] House observes the practical difficulties involved in interacting with the history of interpretation. Since premodern interpreters were not writing books solely focused on Old Testament theology, "their ideas must be gleaned from literally dozens of sermons, commentaries and other works."[86] Others, like Grindheim and Boda, simply do not make it a priority to interact with the history of interpretation, though without addressing the issue.

The Role of Historical-Critical Methods

Finally, canonical Old Testament theologies vary widely in their attitude toward and use of historical-critical methods. For Childs, despite some commonalities with Christian exegesis prior to the Enlightenment, the canonical approach does not signify a return to the interpretive methods of earlier centuries before the rise of historical criticism but is instead a *post*-critical enterprise. While his approach goes beyond historical criticism to examine the significance of the final canonical form, it is still deeply wedded to modern critical methods as a necessary stage in the exegesis of biblical texts.[87] Historical critics may have become like surgeons cutting away at their patient to reveal the inner workings of his body, only to leave the parts strewn about. However, Childs' view is not that scholars should stop doing surgery but that they should sew the parts back together and then examine the whole living patient in light of what they have discovered.

Therefore Childs accepts the "assured results" of historical criticism and sees critical methods as highlighting a "depth dimension" within the Scriptures.[88] In his treatment of Exodus, he discusses at considerable length historical-critical views concerning the composition of the exodus traditions and legal material. He agrees with the basic historical-critical positions that

---

84. Anderson, *Christian Doctrine and the Old Testament*, 7–22.

85. Waltke and Yu, *Old Testament Theology*, 76; similarly, Witherington, *Biblical Theology*, 386–401, 448.

86. House, *Old Testament Theology*, 13. House makes this comment when deciding where to begin his review of the history of Old Testament theology, but presumably it also applies to his quite limited interaction with the history of interpretation throughout his work.

87. Childs, *Old Testament Theology in a Canonical Context*, 11–14.

88. Ibid., 11, 53.

- the exodus from Egypt represents an early tradition that was only later combined with the Passover festival and the account of the crossing of the Red Sea;
- the legal texts derive from various times and social contexts in Israel's history but were later subsumed under the authority of Moses and God's appearance at Mount Sinai.[89]

However, in his effort to draw out the canonical significance of these traditions, he highlights "the centrality of the exodus . . . throughout the entire Old Testament" as the key event that "established Israel's identity."[90] He also points out the legal moorings of the prophetic literature, the authority of the law of Moses in the historical books, and the "joyous celebration of the law" in the Psalms.[91]

While Rendtorff also accepts traditional historical-critical conclusions,[92] these issues occupy considerably less space in his work, as he primarily engages in a theological retelling of the Hebrew Bible, adhering closely to the biblical text.[93] Therefore for him the historical-critical views about the exodus and legal materials noted by Childs receive only passing comment.[94] He is more interested in explaining what the exodus reveals about God—for example, how it demonstrates God's sovereignty over the gods of Egypt and over Pharaoh, who "represents the anti-divine power."[95] Similarly, Seitz accepts historical criticism as offering valid insights, but he gives more emphasis to how traditions work in harmony in the final form of the canon, pointing readers to a transcendent reality.[96] He also challenges certain historical-critical conclusions, such as the traditional source-critical view of the Pentateuch.[97]

Other scholars have adopted a canonical approach that gives little or no attention to historical criticism.[98] Although Watson does not advocate a

---

89. However, Childs also challenges the classic historical-critical views of Wellhausen on a number of points (*Biblical Theology of the Old and New Testaments*, 130–37).

90. Ibid., 131.

91. Ibid., 137–38.

92. See Rendtorff, *Canonical Hebrew Bible*, 719–21.

93. This demonstrates the influence of Rendtorff's PhD mentor, Gerhard von Rad, on his work, though Rendtorff's retelling is grounded in the final form of the text rather than in tradition-historical reconstructions (see ibid., 1–2).

94. Ibid., 45–46, 53.

95. Ibid., 45.

96. See, e.g., Seitz, *Elder Testament*, 77–84; see further idem, "Biblical Authority in the Late Twentieth Century: The Baltimore Declaration, Scripture-Reason-Tradition, and the Canonical Approach," in *Word without End: The Old Testament as Abiding Theological Witness*, Old Testament Studies (Grand Rapids: Eerdmans, 1998), 97–101.

97. Seitz, *Elder Testament*, 85–117.

98. In an early response to Childs' approach, James Barr expressed the concern that Childs' position would be taken by conservative scholars to suggest the end of historical criticism (James Barr, "Childs'

complete rejection of historical-critical methods, he critiques them for their demand that Christians check their faith commitments at the door in order to participate and gives them no discernible role in his discussion of the Old Testament.[99] Similarly, Scobie warns, "It should always be remembered that the results of historical criticism are far from assured, and often are highly speculative."[100] His brief treatments of the exodus narrative and the laws given at Sinai do not even address historical-critical concerns,[101] and he argues elsewhere (with reference to the exodus) that biblical theology "can hardly proceed without assuming at least the basic historicity of the biblical narratives."[102] In response to James Barr's historical-critical approach to biblical theology, Waltke argues that Barr's "faith in human reason is not one to which I could and/or would commit and entrust my life and my eternal destiny."[103] He also comments that the "assumptions of the historico-critical approach directly contradict the assumptions of the biblical writers to whom God was a passionate, powerful, awesome, and not necessarily predictable reality."[104]

Likewise, Sailhamer draws a clear dichotomy between critical and canonical approaches.[105] With a concern to uphold the authority and reliability of the Bible, he takes both the historical and authorship claims found within the biblical text at face value, thereby rejecting most uses of historical criticism.[106] Nevertheless, he does employ a form of redaction criticism by seeking to analyze the theological significance of seams created by later editors to join diverse texts together.[107] An example of his approach may be found in his discussion of Deuteronomy 34:9–12 and Joshua 1:1–9 along with Malachi 4:4–6 and Psalm 1, which he sees as seams placed in those strategic locations

---

Introduction to the Old Testament as Scripture," Journal for the Study of the Old Testament 16 [1980]: 14–15). Childs' response indicates his view that a canonical approach is inextricably bound to historical-critical methods (Brevard S. Childs, "Response to Reviewers of *Introduction to the OT as Scripture*," *Journal for the Study of the Old Testament* 16 [1980]: 58–59), but some scholars who have followed Childs have thought it possible to separate the canonical kernel from its historical-critical shell. See Richard Schultz, "Brevard S. Childs' Contribution to Old Testament Interpretation: An Evangelical Appreciation and Assessment," *The Princeton Theological Review* 14 (2008): 69–93, though not focused specifically on Old Testament theology.

99. Watson, *Text and Truth*, 6, 209.

100. Scobie, *Ways of Our God*, 30. Scobie still suggests that "the recognition that all biblical texts are to some degree historically conditioned means that historical study of the texts and of their background must continue to be part of the hermeneutical process," but he contends that historical criticism "must recognize its limitations and moderate its claims" and that historical analysis is *"preliminary"* to biblical theology (p. 34, italics original). See also House, *Old Testament Theology*, 55–56.

101. Scobie, *Ways of Our God*, 194–95, 749–50.

102. Ibid., 229.

103. Waltke and Yu, *Old Testament Theology*, 73.

104. Ibid., 74. The historical-critical assumptions that Waltke rejects include skepticism, antisupernaturalism, and analogy (the idea that past events must conform to present events).

105. Sailhamer, *Introduction to Old Testament Theology*, 86–114.

106. Ibid., 198.

107. Ibid., 100–101.

by editors to connect the three sections of the Tanak. Sailhamer observes that at the time the canon was completed, prophecy had ceased in Israel. Therefore he argues that while these texts anticipate a future for prophecy, they primarily direct readers to focus on wisdom—linked to meditating on the Torah—as the locus of authority and means of seeking divine direction in the present.[108]

TEST CASE: EXODUS

Canonical treatments of Exodus often note points of connection between that book and other biblical texts. For example, Rendtorff observes that the exodus is viewed within the canon as the primary event that reveals YHWH's character to Israel: "As a result of this fundamental event in its history Israel is to acknowledge and constantly remind itself of the fact that Yhwh alone is God and that he leads his people everywhere and saves them from all calamities" (see, e.g., Exodus 15; Psalms 105; 135; 136).[109] However, some texts trace the nation's persistent disobedience against God back to the time of the exodus, so "Israel's behavior stands in sharp contrast to God's saving act in leading them out of Egypt" (see Psalms 78; 106; Hosea 11; Mic. 6:2–8).[110] Ultimately, Israel's rebellion leads God to declare that judgment is coming in the form of exile, which Hosea describes as a return to Egypt (8:13; 9:3). However, exile is not the end of the story. Isaiah envisions a second exodus, in which "God will make a way in the sea" as he did before, allowing the people to return to their land (43:14–21).[111] The narrative account of this return in Ezra 1 echoes the exodus in the gifts the Jews receive from their neighbors when they leave their place of exile.[112]

Waltke traces the theme of exodus back into the life of the patriarchs. When Pharaoh takes Abraham's wife, Sarah, into his harem, God delivers them from Egypt, bringing them out with great possessions (Gen. 12:10–20). Likewise, when Jacob is mistreated by his uncle Laban, God rescues him and leads him out of Laban's land with considerable wealth (Genesis 31–32).[113] Waltke also looks forward to the New Testament's use of the exodus theme to describe how "in the present age, Christ is delivering his people out of the satanic world system . . . in order to worship God in the heavenly Mount Zion."[114] He observes further how Jesus is identified as a Passover lamb (1 Cor. 5:7) and how

---

108. Ibid., 248–49.
109. Rendtorff, *Canonical Hebrew Bible*, 472.
110. Ibid., 474–75.
111. Ibid., 476.
112. Ibid.
113. Waltke and Yu, *Old Testament Theology*, 390.
114. Ibid., 392.

he describes his coming death as an *exodus* ("departure") at the transfiguration (Luke 9:30–31).[115] In a similar fashion, Scobie notes that the coming of John the Baptist is connected to new exodus language in Isaiah (Isa. 40:3; Mark 1:3). He also points out that Christ is portrayed as "the new Moses, the deliverer not just of Israel but of all humankind" and that Paul identifies him with the rock that the Israelites drank from in the wilderness (1 Cor. 10:4; Ex. 17:1–7).[116]

In his intentionally selective theology, Moberly gives the greatest attention to the narrative of the Israelites receiving manna in Exodus 16. Citing Deuteronomy 8:2–5, he describes the enforced routine of collecting manna six days a week (not on the Sabbath) as a program of discipline, which sought to teach Israel that "not by bread alone is human life sustained, but by responsiveness to the divine will" (cf. Matt. 4:4).[117] Moberly also observes that the reference to manna as "bread from heaven" (Ex. 16:4) has led interpreters to adopt metaphorical readings. Jews have often understood manna as symbolizing wisdom, and Christians have connected it to Jesus, following John 6:30–59. In that narrative, Jesus responds to a request for a sign like the manna Moses gave the Israelites in the wilderness by identifying himself as the "bread of life" (vv. 35, 48). He then invites his listeners to eat his flesh, using language reminiscent of the Eucharist (vv. 53–58).[118] Finally, Moberly suggests that "the need to start each day with collecting fresh manna readily becomes metaphorical for wider patterns of starting each day through deliberate engagement with God so as to receive grace afresh," and he draws a connection with the request for God to "give us today our daily bread" in the Lord's Prayer (Matt. 6:11).[119]

Anderson's theology is also selective, but he discusses the tabernacle in connection with the incarnation, suggesting that in the perspective of the Old Testament, the furniture of the tabernacle and the tabernacle itself become attached to the presence of God. This explains texts that describe seeing the articles of the tabernacle in a manner reminiscent of seeing God (Num. 4:20; 2 Sam. 15:25).[120] Anderson observes that when John 1:14 describes Jesus as a tabernacle, it connects that idea with seeing God's glory.[121] Therefore the divine presence in the tabernacle furniture becomes, among the church fathers, an illustration of the incarnation: "As God became one with his furniture, so God became one with flesh."[122]

---

115. Ibid.
116. Scobie, *Ways of Our God*, 216–17.
117. Moberly, *Old Testament Theology*, 97.
118. Ibid., 98–101.
119. Ibid., 101–2.
120. Anderson, *Christian Doctrine and the Old Testament*, 102–9.
121. Ibid., 101, 114.
122. Ibid., 119.

Chapter 6

JEWISH BIBLICAL THEOLOGY

Although the field of biblical theology has been dominated by Christian scholars, work in Jewish biblical theology has recently seen an explosion of growth.[1] In general, this category does not describe a specific method of doing biblical theology, and many of the examples included here fit in other categories, particularly historical-critical biblical theology. However, the links that bind this group of biblical theologians together are sufficiently strong to merit a separate category. While the New Testament authors were Jewish biblical theologians in the broadest sense of the phrase, this chapter surveys contemporary Jewish scholars who work in the field of biblical theology, often from the faith perspective of one of the branches of modern Judaism.

DEFINITION: Jewish biblical theology follows the extent and order of the Jewish canon, emphasizes diversity, and focuses on topics of importance for Jews. The points of tension for Jewish biblical theology include the question of its existence, the role of postbiblical Jewish material, and the influence of the Holocaust on biblical theology.

Central Texts Covered in This Chapter

Shimon Gesundheit, "Gibt es eine jüdische Theologie der Hebräischen Bibel?" (2005)

Shimon Gesundheit, "Das Land Israels als Mitte einer jüdischen Theologie der Tora" (2011)

M. H. Goshen-Gottstein, "Tanakh Theology" (Hebrew: 1981; English: 1987)

▶

---

1. For recent surveys of Jewish biblical theology, see Leo G. Perdue, *Reconstructing Old Testament Theology: After the Collapse of History*, Overtures to Biblical Theology (Minneapolis: Fortress, 2005), 183–238; Ziony Zevit, "Jewish Biblical Theology: Whence? Why? And Whither?" *Hebrew Union College Annual* 76 (2005): 289–340; Ehud Ben Zvi, "Constructing the Past: The Recent History of Jewish Biblical Theology," in *Jewish Bible Theology: Perspectives and Case Studies*, ed. Isaac Kalimi (Winona Lake, IN: Eisenbrauns, 2012), 31–50.

Isaac Kalimi, "History of Israelite Religion or Hebrew Bible / Old Testament Theology?" (2002)

Isaac Kalimi, "Models for Jewish Bible Theologies" (2017)

Isaac Kalimi, ed., *Jewish Bible Theology* (2012)

Jon D. Levenson, *Sinai and Zion* (1985)

Jon D. Levenson, "Why Jews Are Not Interested in Biblical Theology" (1993)

Gershom M. H. Ratheiser, Mitzvoth *Ethics and the Jewish Bible* (2007)

Dalit Rom-Shiloni, "Hebrew Bible Theology" (2016)

Benjamin D. Sommer, "Dialogical Biblical Theology" (2009)

Marvin A. Sweeney, *Reading the Hebrew Bible after the Shoah* (2008)

Marvin A. Sweeney, *Tanak* (2012)

Marvin A. Sweeney, "Tanak versus Old Testament" (1997)

Matitiahu Tsevat, "Theology of the Old Testament" (1986)

Ziony Zevit, "Jewish Biblical Theology" (2005)

COMMON FEATURES

Extent and Order of the Jewish Canon

Since Jews do not accept the New Testament as authoritative, the most distinguishing characteristic of Jewish biblical theology is that it interprets the Old Testament—or, as it is known among Jews, the Hebrew Bible or Tanak—on its own as a complete canon. While Christian biblical theology has often been preoccupied with examining the nature of the connection between the Old and New Testaments, Jewish biblical theology addresses different questions.

Beyond rejecting the New Testament, Jewish biblical theologians also follow the three-part Hebrew canon rather than the four-part Greek (Protestant Christian) canon.[2] Marvin Sweeney has even argued that Christians and Jews read different texts because the Old Testament and the Hebrew Bible are structured differently.[3] In his view the Christian order focuses on finding Christ in the Old Testament, with the prophets serving as the link between the testaments. The Jewish order, on the other hand, concludes with Chronicles, which recites Israel's history from creation to the end of the exile to provide

---

2. On the differences between the canonical orders, see tables 5.2 and 5.3 on pp. 102–3.

3. Marvin A. Sweeney, "Tanak versus Old Testament: Concerning the Foundation for a Jewish Theology of the Bible," in *Problems in Biblical Theology: Essays in Honor of Rolf Knierim*, ed. Henry T. C. Sun and Keith L. Eades (Grand Rapids: Eerdmans, 1997), 353–72; idem, "Jewish Biblical Theology," in *The Hebrew Bible: New Insights and Scholarship*, ed. Frederick E. Greenspahn (New York: New York Univ. Press, 2008), 195–98; idem, "Foundations for a Jewish Theology of the Hebrew Bible: Prophets in Dialogue," in *Jewish Bible Theology: Perspectives and Case Studies*, 163–65.

a model for how the returned exiles should live. Therefore it focuses more on a cyclical view of history, living by the Torah, and life in the land, with an emphasis on the Davidic monarchy and the temple. However, an important argument against Sweeney's view is that many Christian biblical theologians also follow the Hebrew canonical order.[4]

Emphasis on Diversity

Another common feature of Jewish biblical theology is its emphasis on diversity. While Jewish tradition has focused on systematizing law, the same has not been the case for its theology.[5] Jewish scholars, such as Michael Fishbane, have been at the forefront of research on intertextuality in the Hebrew Bible, showing how the biblical authors themselves engage in conversation with each other.[6] Later rabbinic tradition also emphasizes diverse opinions on biblical texts; rabbinic Bibles even include competing interpretations on the same page. This trend has continued with Jewish biblical theologians, who are far less concerned with finding central themes in the Hebrew Bible than are their Christian counterparts. For example, Sweeney says that "given the fundamental disagreement so frequently apparent among biblical books, interpreters must recognize that the Bible does not posit a consistent understanding of truth, at least not in the way that rational theology or philosophy might envision."[7]

In a study on the Psalms, Marc Brettler states that Jewish biblical theology needs to recognize the plurality of voices "not only because this principle stands at the core of the structure of the rabbinic (and transitional, prerabbinic) world view, but also because it stands at the core of the structure of the book of Psalms."[8] Brettler considers this emphasis on diversity as such an important aspect of Jewish biblical theology that he is even tempted to consider it a sufficient condition to mark a biblical theology as Jewish, but quickly recognizes that some Christian scholars have also stressed diversity.[9]

Likewise, Benjamin Sommer argues for what he calls "dialogical biblical

---

4. See, e.g., the work of John Sailhamer, Rolf Rendtorff, and Stephen Dempster.

5. M. H. Goshen-Gottstein, "Tanakh Theology: The Religion of the Old Testament and the Place of Jewish Biblical Theology," in *Ancient Israelite Religion: Essays in Honor of Frank Moore Cross*, ed. Patrick D. Miller Jr., Paul D. Hanson, and S. Dean McBride (Philadelphia: Fortress, 1987), 627.

6. Michael Fishbane, *Biblical Interpretation in Ancient Israel* (Oxford: Clarendon, 1985).

7. Marvin A. Sweeney, "What Is Biblical Theology? With an Example on Divine Absence and the Song of Songs," in *Methodological Studies*, vol. 1 of *Theology of the Hebrew Bible*, ed. Marvin A. Sweeney, Resources for Biblical Study 92 (Atlanta: Society of Biblical Literature, 2019), 37. See also idem, *Tanak: A Theological and Critical Introduction to the Jewish Bible* (Minneapolis: Fortress, 2012), 32–35.

8. Marc Zvi Brettler, "Psalms and Jewish Biblical Theology," in *Jewish Bible Theology: Perspectives and Case Studies*, 189.

9. Ibid., 197. For a survey of some of these scholars, see chap. 7.

theology," which he defines as "an attempt to construct a discussion between biblical texts and a particular postbiblical theological tradition."[10] One major reason for this is that he sees the Hebrew Bible itself as exhibiting this kind of dialogue between different positions. Since he does not understand the task of biblical theology as systematizing the contents of the Hebrew Bible, he calls for a biblical theology that focuses on particular texts or themes rather than seeking to be comprehensive and limiting "itself to large, hard-cover two-volume works."[11]

An example of this focus on diversity may be found in Jon Levenson's work *Sinai and Zion*, in which Sinai stands for the Mosaic covenant, including the law, and Zion symbolizes the Davidic covenant.[12] Seeing a contrast between the obligations in the Mosaic covenant and the promises to David, many critical scholars have suggested that the Northern Kingdom (Israel) was responsible for creating the Sinai tradition, and the Southern Kingdom (Judah) the Zion tradition. They assume that the diversity between the two traditions must have derived from originally separate sources. In contrast, Levenson sees both traditions as originating from the Southern Kingdom, and he also seeks to demonstrate how hints of strong dynastic tendencies associated with the Zion tradition existed even in the Northern Kingdom. Rather than attempting to flatten out one theme or assign each theme to a particular historical-geographical location, he asserts that "the two complexes were quite capable of coexistence without tension."[13]

However, it should be noted that Jewish biblical theologians do not completely deny the presence of unifying themes in the Hebrew Bible. For example, in a study of the figure of Moses, Asa Kasher argues that fighting idolatry is a key theme in both the Hebrew Bible and Jewish tradition.[14] Likewise, after citing various attempts to find a center in biblical theology, Sommer concludes, "All these works attempt—in my opinion, successfully—to find unity amid the diversity of material, genre, and period in the Hebrew Scriptures."[15] Jewish biblical theologians like Sommer simply contend that none of these key themes holds together the entire Hebrew Bible in all of its various parts.

---

10. Benjamin D. Sommer, "Dialogical Biblical Theology: A Jewish Approach to Reading Scripture Theologically," in *Biblical Theology: Introducing the Conversation*, ed. Leo G. Perdue, Robert Morgan, and Benjamin D. Sommer, Library of Biblical Theology (Nashville: Abingdon, 2009), 21.

11. Ibid., 50.

12. Jon D. Levenson, *Sinai and Zion: An Entry into the Jewish Bible*, New Voices in Biblical Studies (Minneapolis: Winston, 1985).

13. Ibid., 206.

14. Asa Kasher, "Fighting Forms of Idolatry: The Meaning of an Image of Moses in Jewish Theology," in *Jewish Bible Theology: Perspectives and Case Studies*, 53–62.

15. Sommer, "Dialogical Biblical Theology," 4.

Topics of Importance for Jews

A third common characteristic of Jewish biblical theology relates to the topics it covers. While it focuses on many of the same themes as does Christian biblical theology—such as covenant and creation—Jewish biblical theology gives greater attention to certain topics that are more highly valued in Jewish tradition. For example, Jewish interpreters tend to place less emphasis on divine action and more on human responsibility. Zvi Shimon rejects God as the center of the Hebrew Bible and proposes humans as the center instead: "An anthropocentric-focused theology will tend to see history as determined by human action, and view humanity as capable of bringing spiritual-moral progress and salvation."[16] Other important topics for Jewish biblical theology include the Sabbath, the chosenness of Israel, the temple, and ritual, but we will examine just two in more detail—the law and the land.[17]

First, although some Christian scholars, such as Daniel Block, take a more positive view of the law,[18] many in the Christian tradition tend to downplay the law because of the influence of some of the New Testament's apparently negative statements about it (Romans 3; 7; Galatians 3). From his Jewish perspective, Sweeney summarizes the Christian view of the Torah as developed by Paul in this way: "In subsequent Christian thought, 'Law' is frequently characterized as legalistic priestly ritual lacking in efficacy, spirituality, and rationale."[19] Julius Wellhausen provides a classic example of this kind of thinking from the late 1800s: "The law thrusts itself everywhere; it commands and blocks up the access to heaven; it regulates and sets limits to the understanding of the divine working on earth. As far as it can, it takes the soul out of religion and spoils morality."[20] Sommer surveys various Christian interpreters, mostly following Gerhard von Rad, who see a dichotomy between law and grace in the book of Deuteronomy and argue that grace is more important than law.[21]

In contrast to these negative perspectives by Christian scholars, Jewish

---

16. Zvi Shimon, "The Place of God in the Bible: Between Jewish and Christian Theology," in *Biblical Theology: Past, Present, and Future*, ed. Carey Walsh and Mark W. Elliott (Eugene, OR: Cascade, 2016), 200.

17. For a suggested list of such topics, see Isaac Kalimi, "Models for Jewish Bible Theologies: Tasks and Challenges," *Horizons in Biblical Theology* 39 (2017): 128.

18. Daniel I. Block, *How I Love Your Torah, O Lord! Studies in the Book of Deuteronomy* (Eugene, OR: Cascade, 2011); idem, *The Gospel according to Moses: Theological and Ethical Reflections on the Book of Deuteronomy* (Eugene, OR: Cascade, 2012); idem, *Deuteronomy*, NIV Application Commentary (Grand Rapids: Zondervan, 2012).

19. Sweeney, "Jewish Biblical Theology," 199.

20. Julius Wellhausen, *Prolegomena to the History of Ancient Israel: With a Reprint of the Article Israel from the "Encyclopaedia Britannica"* (Edinburgh: Adam and Charles Black, 1885; repr. New York: Meridian, 1957), 509.

21. Sommer, "Dialogical Biblical Theology," 8–12. Von Rad's emphasis on grace in the Old Testament was important in his Nazi German context to show why the Old Testament was still important for the

scholars view the law much more highly and give it greater significance in their work. For example, Sommer points out that in certain prominent forms of modern Jewish thought that highly esteem Torah study, "Psalms is less important than the Pentateuch, and prayer is less important than study."[22] However, he also observes the role of meditating on the law in Psalm 1, explaining that "The Psalter that begins with Ps 1 is a textbook, to which one turns for guidance and instruction. One recites or sings a psalm; one reads or studies the book of Psalms. In short, Ps 1 attempts to convert the book of Psalms into another form of Torah."[23] Gershom Ratheiser employs the cultic system found within the law as the basis for his work on the Jewish Bible: "It will be demonstrated that the Jewish cultic system, with its prime *locus* in the tabernacle/temple cult, served as the place of orientation for the search for behavioural/ethical patterns in ancient Jewish society."[24]

Second, while it has received some recent attention by non-Jewish scholars,[25] the theme of the land has also typically been deemphasized in Christian traditions. In the eschatological view common throughout church history, the land of Israel is understood as a type of heaven, and the land promise is seen as being universalized in the New Testament. For example, according to Bruce Waltke, "Interpreting the Old Testament promises and prophecies about the Land with reference to life in Christ is not allegorizing a reluctant Old Testament text but showing how the New Testament reveals doctrines regarding the Land that the Old Testament conceals. Accordingly, the promise that Israel will inherit a land flowing with milk and honey becomes a metaphor for the milk and honey of life in Christ, a participation in heaven itself and in a world that is beyond what saints could imagine or think."[26]

In contrast, the physical reality of the land is given greater emphasis by Jewish scholars.[27] M. H. Goshen-Gottstein argues that Jewish biblical theol-

---

German church (Bernard M. Levinson, "Reading the Bible in Nazi Germany: Gerhard von Rad's Attempt to Reclaim the Old Testament for the Church," *Interpretation* 62 [2008]: 247).

22. Sommer, "Dialogical Biblical Theology," 36.

23. Ibid., 34–35. In line with his dialogical biblical theology, in which two emphases interact, Sommer goes on to highlight the view of Psalms that focuses on prayer, an interpretation that is generated when Psalm 150 is placed as its conclusion.

24. Gershom M. H. Ratheiser, Mitzvoth *Ethics and the Jewish Bible: The End of Old Testament Theology*, Library of Hebrew Bible / Old Testament Studies 460 (New York: T&T Clark, 2007), 5–6, italics original.

25. Christopher J. H. Wright, *God's People in God's Land: Family, Land, and Property in the Old Testament* (Grand Rapids: Eerdmans, 1990); Walter Brueggemann, *The Land: Place as Gift, Promise, and Challenge in Biblical Faith*, 2nd ed., Overtures to Biblical Theology (Minneapolis: Augsburg Fortress, 2002).

26. Bruce K. Waltke and Charles Yu, *An Old Testament Theology: An Exegetical, Canonical, and Thematic Approach* (Grand Rapids: Zondervan, 2007), 586.

27. For example, a recent edited volume on the conquest of the Canaanites from a Jewish perspective highlights the theological question of the land: Katell Berthelot, Joseph E. David, and Marc Hirshman,

ogy could help Christian theology to recognize the significance of this theme: "It would be the task of Tanakh theology to point out that this [the importance of the land] is not just a matter of opinion, since ignoring the centrality runs counter to the facts . . . that is, the number and density of occurrences as well as the issues connected with promises and threats concerning the land."[28]

Shimon Gesundheit suggests that the land should be the center of a Jewish theology of the Torah, offering support for his view from two directions. First, he employs historical criticism to argue for a Hexateuch (Genesis–Joshua) that ends with the conquest of Canaan in Joshua, thus increasing the emphasis on the land.[29] Second, he contends that the final version of the Torah implies a difference between the roles of Moses and Joshua. In Deuteronomy 34:9–12 Moses is the great prophet who will never have an equal. By contrast, the prophetic role of Joshua is downplayed, as he receives only the spirit of wisdom rather than the spirit of prophecy (v. 9) and is portrayed as a scholar rather than a prophet (Josh. 1:8). The prophet (Moses) is greater than the scholar (Joshua) because the prophet provides the words of God, which the scholar then studies and obeys. This comparison then enables Gesundheit to connect each of them with a view of the land: "Moses' book and deeds are of eternal value; Joshua's work is fleeting. The land *promise* in the Law of Moses is *eternal*, the land *seizure* is *fleeting*. The existential situation of Israel in exile is again doubtlessly reflected here: Israel lived during its long exile without a land, but in the certainty and faith in the eternal value of the land promise."[30]

The theology of the land has important practical implications because of the current Israeli-Palestinian conflict. For example, one group of Christians, sometimes called Christian Zionists, actively supports the government of Israel in its claim to the land, based on their reading of the land promises in the Old Testament.[31] Also, in recent decades some religious Jews have employed the land promise in a politically aggressive manner as part of their attempt to remove the Palestinians from the West Bank.[32] Naim Stifan

eds., *The Gift of the Land and the Fate of the Canaanites in Jewish Thought* (Oxford: Oxford Univ. Press, 2014).

28. Goshen-Gottstein, "Tanakh Theology," 630.

29. Gesundheit argues that Deuteronomy 34:8 requires a main clause to follow it, but since vv. 9–12 happened before Moses' death, the only logical clause that could follow Deuteronomy 34:8 is Joshua 1:1. Hence these books were originally designed to be a unit as part of the Hexateuch (Shimon Gesundheit, "Das Land Israels als Mitte einer jüdischen Theologie der Tora: Synchrone und diachrone Perspektiven," *Zeitschrift für die alttestamentliche Wissenschaft* 123 [2011]: 327–30).

30. Ibid., 334, translation ours, italics original.

31. H. Wayne House, ed., *Israel: The Land and the People: An Evangelical Affirmation of God's Promises* (Grand Rapids: Kregel, 1998); Gerald R. McDermott, ed., *The New Christian Zionism: Fresh Perspectives on Israel and the Land* (Downers Grove, IL: InterVarsity, 2016).

32. For a summary and critique of this position, see Moshe Greenberg, "On the Political Use of the Bible in Modern Israel: An Engaged Critique," in *Pomegranates and Golden Bells: Studies in Biblical,*

Ateek, a Palestinian Anglican priest who lives in Jerusalem as an Arab citizen of Israel, summarizes the existential problem that this has presented for Palestinian Christians in this way: "Before the creation of the State [of Israel], the Old Testament was considered to be an essential part of Christian Scripture, pointing and witnessing to Jesus. Since the creation of the State, some Jewish and Christian interpreters have read the Old Testament largely as a Zionist text to such an extent that it has become almost repugnant to Palestinian Christians."[33]

Although this is surely not what Goshen-Gottstein intended when he called for greater attention to the land in Christian theology, Palestinian Christians have ironically begun to fulfill his desire as they have responded to this crisis by investigating the issue of land much more closely.[34] Mitri Raheb, a Palestinian Lutheran living in Bethlehem, focuses on how the land of Israel has always had other nations living in it, even during biblical times.[35] Therefore he contends that the land should continue to be shared because the Bible does not present a paradigm of *sole* ownership of the land by Israel. In his view, "the land happens to be the homeland of two peoples. Each of them should understand this land to be a gift of God to be shared with the other. Peace and the blessing on the land and on the two peoples will depend on this sharing. Only then will the biblical promises be fulfilled."[36]

More radically, Ateek has developed a Palestinian liberation theology by examining difficult Old Testament passages to see if they match the character of God as revealed in Jesus: "If it does, then that passage is valid and authoritative. If not, then I cannot accept its validity or authority."[37] He further develops two principles related to the land. First, "the land that God has chosen at one particular time in history for one particular people is now perceived as a paradigm, a model, for God's concern for every people and land."[38] Second, readers of the Old Testament must understand how the people of Israel grew in their understanding from an earlier exclusivist view of YHWH

Jewish, and Near Eastern Ritual, Law, and Literature in Honor of Jacob Milgrom, ed. David P. Wright, David Noel Freedman, and Avi Hurvitz (Winona Lake, IN: Eisenbrauns, 1995), 461–71.

33. Naim Stifan Ateek, *Justice and Only Justice: A Palestinian Theology of Liberation* (Maryknoll, NY: Orbis, 1989), 77.

34. For a summary of various views, see Will Stalder, *Palestinian Christians and the Old Testament: History, Hermeneutics, and Ideology*, Emerging Scholars (Minneapolis: Fortress, 2015). See also the various essays from both sides of the debate in Salim J. Munayer and Lisa Loden, eds., *The Land Cries Out: Theology of the Land in the Israeli-Palestinian Context* (Eugene, OR: Cascade, 2012).

35. Mitri Raheb, *Faith in the Face of Empire: The Bible through Palestinian Eyes* (Maryknoll, NY: Orbis, 2014), 70–73.

36. Idem, *I Am a Palestinian Christian*, trans. Ruth C. L. Gritsch (Minneapolis: Augsburg Fortress, 1995), 80.

37. Ateek, *Justice and Only Justice*, 82.

38. Ibid., 108.

as tied to Israel and its land to a later inclusivist view of YHWH as the God
of all nations. He concludes that "the blessing will only come when Israel
transcends the narrow concept of a nationalist God and embraces the more
universal image of God."[39]

Many Jewish scholars have also opposed modern political readings of the
land promise. David Frankel, a religious Jew living in Israel, emphasizes the
diversity of the biblical texts about the land. He concludes with a call to
Israel to fulfill God's purpose for them and their land, contending that "if
the vocation of Israel is to live in the land, not in isolation from the nations,
but with an eye toward them and in accordance with laws that will evoke
their admiration for Israel's wisdom and sense of justice, then both political
and halakic [rabbinic] calculations must be strongly informed by universal
ethical concerns."[40] In a later essay, he fleshes out what this looks like in
practical terms for religious Jews living in the land of Israel today, concluding,
"Unfortunately, there are some who point to 'texts of terror' in the Bible in
order to justify the unethical in Israel today. I believe that it is particularly
incumbent upon Jewish scholars of the Bible, both in Israel and abroad, to
counter this trend by finding and foregrounding what we might refer to as
'texts of tolerance.'"[41]

POINTS OF TENSION

The Question of Its Existence

Somewhat strangely, one of the main questions for Jewish biblical theology
has been whether it even exists.[42] One reason for this is sociological: the situation of Jewish scholars living in Israel directs them to focus more on history
than on theology, because the search for historical roots is so important for
them geographically, psychologically, and politically.[43] However, the primary

---

39. Ibid., 112. In a later book, he cites a contemporary baptismal liturgy as the kind of exclusivism
to avoid: "'We thank you, Almighty God, for the gift of water. Over it the Holy Spirit moved in the
beginning of creation. Through it you led the children of Israel out of their bondage in Egypt into the
land of promise.' What value does the last sentence have? Some scholars doubt that it ever happened,
theologically it is absurd, spiritually it is not edifying. Why is it included?" (idem, *A Palestinian Theology
of Liberation: The Bible, Justice, and the Palestine-Israel Conflict* [Maryknoll, NY: Orbis, 2017], 101).

40. David Frankel, *The Land of Canaan and the Destiny of Israel: Theologies of Territory in the Hebrew
Bible*, Siphrut 4 (Winona Lake, IN: Eisenbrauns, 2011), 399.

41. David Frankel, "Toward a Constructive Jewish Biblical Theology of the Land," in *Methodological
Studies*, 176.

42. The question under discussion here is specifically about Jewish *biblical* theology, as the broader
field of Jewish theology is clearly alive and flourishing (see, e.g., Michael Fishbane, *Sacred Attunement:
A Jewish Theology* [Chicago: Univ. of Chicago Press, 2008]).

43. Isaac Kalimi, "History of Israelite Religion or Hebrew Bible / Old Testament Theology? Jewish
Interest in Biblical Theology," in *Early Jewish Exegesis and Theological Controversy: Studies in Scriptures in*

reason for Jewish avoidance of biblical theology is that it has historically been viewed as a strictly Christian practice. For example, Brevard Childs claims that biblical theology "has as its fundamental goal to understand the various voices within the whole Christian Bible, New and Old Testament alike, as a witness to the one Lord Jesus Christ, the selfsame divine reality."[44] If this is the core of biblical theology, then clearly Jews are unable to participate in the discipline.

Therefore some Jews have denied the possibility of Jewish biblical theology. Levenson addresses this issue in an article titled "Why Jews Are Not Interested in Biblical Theology," in which he provides several reasons why Jews should not practice it.[45] First, the focus of Old Testament theology has generally been intrinsically connected to the New Testament and the role of Jesus. Second, Levenson cites the negative comments about Judaism by Walther Eichrodt, and the lack of reference to later Judaism by Gerhard von Rad, to show that biblical theology has a strong anti-Semitic strain that would prevent Jews from honestly partaking in the exercise. Third, he argues that other Christian presuppositions, such as the content of Christian theology and the desire to harmonize tensions in the biblical text, have colored the way that scholars do biblical theology and made Jews uninterested in the endeavor.

However, other Jewish scholars have argued for a Jewish biblical theology, calling for a broader definition of the discipline than that cited by Childs. For example, Ehud Ben Zvi contends that biblical theology should include all research related to theology that is based on the Bible.[46] Likewise, Sweeney has been a vocal advocate for more Jewish biblical theology, arguing that while it focuses on different issues than does its Christian counterpart, it still fundamentally counts as biblical theology and can contribute to Christian studies precisely by highlighting those areas neglected by Christians.[47]

Several Jewish scholars have also responded directly to Levenson's arguments. Sommer notes that the field of biblical theology has changed sufficiently in the years since Levenson's essay to allow Jews to gain an interest in it. The main difference is that Christian scholars like Walter Brueggemann and Erhard Gerstenberger are now more interested in highlighting diversity, which fits

---

the Shadow of Internal and External Controversies, Jewish and Christian Heritage 2 (Assen: Van Gorcum, 2002), 129–30.

44. Brevard S. Childs, Biblical Theology of the Old and New Testaments: Theological Reflection on the Christian Bible (Minneapolis: Fortress, 1992), 85.

45. Jon D. Levenson, "Why Jews Are Not Interested in Biblical Theology," in The Hebrew Bible, the Old Testament, and Historical Criticism: Jews and Christians in Biblical Studies (Louisville: Westminster John Knox, 1993), 33–61. Another example is Ratheiser, Mitzvoth Ethics and the Jewish Bible. Ratheiser argues that a Jewish approach should focus on nonconfessional ethics rather than theology because the intention of the biblical authors is to offer instruction on how to live.

46. Ben Zvi, "Constructing the Past," 41–50.

47. Sweeney, "Foundations for a Jewish Theology of the Hebrew Bible," 162–63.

better with a Jewish hermeneutic.[48] Also, even though Levenson is correct that Jewish scholars have not written comprehensive theologies of the Hebrew Bible, Isaac Kalimi shows the unhelpfulness of this argument by comparing it to the production of technical commentaries. The scarcity of commentary series from a Jewish viewpoint surely does not mean that Jews are not interested in exegesis! He sees the minimal Jewish contribution to biblical theology as more a result of the recent entry of Jewish scholarship into that field than a sign of Jewish disinterest. He also notes that the presence of anti-Semitism in the history of Israelite religion has not caused Jewish scholars to avoid that field of study.[49]

Ironically, many scholars have noted that Levenson himself is a good example of a Jewish biblical theologian! James Barr's comment is typical: "No one looks more like a successful Jewish biblical theologian than he himself does."[50] In an unpublished letter summarized in an article by Ziony Zevit, Levenson says that he would agree with that ascription given a definition of biblical theology broad enough to include scholarship that "engaged in enriching the encounter of bible readers with sacred texts."[51]

Role of Postbiblical Jewish Material

As with Christian scholars, an important point of debate for Jewish scholars is the role of postbiblical material—especially the Mishna, the Talmud, and the midrashim—in the practice of biblical theology. The Mishna and the Talmud are early collections of Jewish oral traditions that largely deal with issues related to the law, while the midrashim are commentaries on texts from the Hebrew Bible. Jewish biblical theologians, like their Christian counterparts, lie on a spectrum, ranging from those on one side, who focus almost solely on the scriptural text, to those on the other side, who employ rabbinic materials as authoritative guides for the biblical text.[52]

In an early article on Jewish biblical theology, Matitiahu Tsevat says that the road from the Hebrew Bible to the rabbinic material consists of "sparse and uncertain paths," while the road from the rabbinic material to the Hebrew Bible is "broad and well passable."[53] In his view, the rabbinic material is not

---

48. Sommer, "Dialogical Biblical Theology," 8–15. This response to Levenson's argument is widespread; see also Perdue, *Reconstructing Old Testament Theology*, 192–93.

49. Kalimi, "History of Israelite Religion or Hebrew Bible / Old Testament Theology?" 123–26.

50. James Barr, *The Concept of Biblical Theology: An Old Testament Perspective* (Minneapolis: Fortress, 1999), 294; see also Ben Zvi, "Constructing the Past," 36.

51. Zevit, "Jewish Biblical Theology," 325.

52. For a threefold categorization of Jewish biblical theology similar to that presented here, see Kalimi, "Models for Jewish Bible Theologies."

53. Matitiahu Tsevat, "Theology of the Old Testament: A Jewish View," *Horizons in Biblical Theology* 8 (1986): 46.

the authoritative interpretation of the Hebrew Bible but merely one possible way forward. He continues by declaring, "He who reads in Talmud and Midrash is rewarded with an image of the Old Testament which is entirely wrong, to be sure, but which is, in recompense, extraordinarily wondrous."[54]

Likewise, Goshen-Gottstein argues for a greater focus on the biblical text. He recognizes that the Old Testament theologies of Christian scholars like von Rad and Eichrodt provide real benefit to the larger academy, even if they employ explicitly Christian beliefs. Therefore he proposes that Jews similarly contribute to the academy by engaging in Tanak theology, which would focus primarily on the biblical text in an effort to explain "what the Tanakh is all about."[55] However, it would not completely ignore later rabbinic interpretations. As Goshen-Gottstein puts it, while Tanak theologians are not responsible to examine the structures of later biblical interpretation (e.g., in sources like the Talmud), "it is not necessary to close one's eyes to later structures even as the earlier ones are analyzed so long as one does not confuse the facts."[56]

Other Jewish scholars express similar views. Tikva Frymer-Kensky is appreciative of a renewed study of the Hebrew Bible because it reveals the many ambiguities in Scripture and highlights a way out of the control of rabbinic interpretation.[57] Gesundheit cites several texts from the Middle Ages to show that interpreting Scripture apart from the midrashim and Talmud was already a part of Jewish practice even then.[58] Dalit Rom-Shiloni argues for a Hebrew Bible theology (HBT) that focuses strictly on the biblical text: "My critical interest in HBT is with the ancient thought, restricted to the Tanakh as my corpus, self-contained as it is and studied from a critical-descriptive point of view that utilizes philological tools to read the HB and comparative methodologies to tap its ANE [ancient Near Eastern] counterparts, maintaining clear distinctions from later Jewish or Christian traditions."[59]

At the other end of the spectrum, Rabbinic Judaism views Jewish post-biblical material as authoritative. According to Frymer-Kensky, "The Bible is the source of halakic [rabbinic] authority, but it does not function on its

---

54. Ibid., 48.

55. Goshen-Gottstein, "Tanakh Theology," 626–33.

56. Ibid., 633.

57. Tikva Frymer-Kensky, "The Emergence of Jewish Biblical Theologies," in *Jews, Christians, and the Theology of the Hebrew Scriptures*, ed. Alice Ogden Bellis and Joel S. Kaminsky, Society of Biblical Literature Symposium Series 8 (Atlanta: Society of Biblical Literature, 2000), 116–21.

58. Shimon Gesundheit, "Gibt es eine jüdische Theologie der Hebräischen Bibel?" in *Theologie und Exegese des Alten Testaments / der Hebräischen Bibel: Zwischenbilanz und Zukunftsperspektiven*, ed. Bernd Janowski, Stuttgarter Bibelstudien 200 (Stuttgart: Katholisches Bibelwerk, 2005), 81–83.

59. Dalit Rom-Shiloni, "Hebrew Bible Theology: A Jewish Descriptive Approach," *Journal of Religion* 96 (2016): 181–82.

own and is not an independent source of authority in traditional Judaism. A new reading of the Bible has never had the power to upset rabbinic laws or attitudes."[60] Among recent scholars, Sommer argues strongly for the necessity of employing postbiblical material in biblical theology, declaring that "all forms of Jewish theology must base themselves on tradition at least as much as Scripture, and hence they cannot be primarily biblical; conversely, any theology that limits itself to Scripture is by definition Protestant and not Jewish."[61] Building on the work of Christian scholars who employ the New Testament and church tradition to understand the Old Testament, Sommer suggests that Jewish scholars can do something comparable with rabbinic material in a "dialogical biblical theology."[62] This dialogue between biblical and rabbinic texts should be bidirectional. Just as the later rabbinic texts can help us understand the biblical material, so also the biblical text can illuminate the rabbinic sources. Even non-Jews can learn from observing this dialogue, as it may raise important questions that do not emerge within their own traditions.

Another example of this kind of interaction with rabbinic literature can be found in Kasher's study of the image of Moses.[63] Following hints in the midrashim, Kasher argues that the negative portrayals of Moses are important because they prevent Jews from viewing him as a divine figure, especially in a Christian context where the human Jesus is understood as divine. Sweeney occupies a more moderate position in this debate. He recognizes that the Bible must be interpreted as a product of its ancient world. However, he also argues that "in the Jewish tradition, the Bible serves as the foundation. As such, it enters into dialog with the other elements of Jewish tradition, viz., the subsequent sacred literature, practices, and socio-political and cultural expressions of the Jewish people throughout history, including Jewish life in the land of Israel and in the Diaspora."[64]

The Influence of the Holocaust on Biblical Theology

A final topic of debate among Jewish biblical theologians is whether and how the Holocaust should affect biblical theology. While some Jewish scholars have not referred to it in their work, the death of six million Jews in the

---

60. Frymer-Kensky, "Emergence of Jewish Biblical Theologies," 111.
61. Benjamin D. Sommer, "Psalm 1 and the Canonical Shaping of Jewish Scripture," in *Jewish Bible Theology: Perspectives and Case Studies*, 199. For a similarly strong statement, see idem, "Dialogical Biblical Theology," 1–2.
62. Idem, "Dialogical Biblical Theology," 21.
63. Kasher, "Fighting Forms of Idolatry."
64. Sweeney, *Tanak*, 28; see also idem, "Jewish Biblical Theology," 203.

Holocaust (often called the Shoah in Jewish writings) is a tremendously significant event in modern Jewish history, which has led some scholars to reconsider various aspects of biblical theology. At a basic level, the Holocaust has led to strong calls to reject anti-Semitism of any kind in scholarly research on the Hebrew Bible. Kalimi speaks for many Jewish scholars when he declares, "It should be understood that the Christian theologian may not introduce anti-Semitic and anti-Jewish theology; the defining of Christianity through the negation of Judaism; [or] portraying the Jewish people in an unfavorable light to show the superiority of the Christian faith, as has been done many times."[65] However, other Jewish scholars have denied that anti-Semitism exists in academic circles after World War II.[66]

Another way that the Shoah has influenced Jewish biblical theology has been in prompting a reaction against Christian tendencies to universalize the Old Testament. For example, Christian liberation theologians commonly apply the exodus and the book of Amos to any situation of oppression worldwide, declaring that God is on the side of the oppressed. However, Levenson and Sweeney call theologians to pay closer attention to the text: YHWH acts on behalf of the oppressed people of *Israel*.[67]

On a grander scale, some Jewish scholars have developed a full-blown Holocaust theology that significantly affects how they read the Hebrew Bible and raises important questions. For example, after the Holocaust, how can we still believe that God is dedicated to his people? Many of these proposals are quite radical compared with traditional theology. Most provocatively, Richard Rubenstein associates himself with the death-of-God theology and argues that God died at Auschwitz.[68] David Blumenthal portrays YHWH as an abusive parent in the Shoah, calling on YHWH's followers to engage in a theology of protest. His book ends with a series of suggested prayers, one of which includes the following lines: "Our Father, our King, we have sinned before You. Our Father, our King, You have sinned before us."[69]

For Sweeney, the heart of the question is whether after the Holocaust, we can continue to view God as truly good: "The Shoah raises fundamental questions

---

65. Kalimi, "History of Israelite Religion or Hebrew Bible / Old Testament Theology?" 115.

66. For example, Zevit claims that he knows of no anti-Semitic statements after the Shoah ("Jewish Biblical Theology," 316). For similar arguments that anti-Semitic statements are rare, see Perdue, *Reconstructing Old Testament Theology*, 191.

67. Marvin A. Sweeney, "Reconceiving the Paradigms of Old Testament Theology in the Post-Shoah Period," in *Jews, Christians, and the Theology of the Hebrew Scriptures*, 155–72; Jon D. Levenson, "Liberation Theology and the Exodus," in *Jews, Christians, and the Theology of the Hebrew Scriptures*, 215–30.

68. Richard L. Rubenstein, *After Auschwitz: Radical Theology and Contemporary Judaism* (Indianapolis: Bobbs-Merrill, 1966).

69. David R. Blumenthal, *Facing the Abusing God: A Theology of Protest* (Louisville: Westminster John Knox, 1993), 291.

concerning the presence, power, and righteousness of G-d and the presumed guilt and sin of those portrayed as subject to divine judgment in the Hebrew Bible."[70] These questions would in particular affect the understanding of how the Hebrew Bible uses Shoah-like events, such as the destruction of Israel and Judah, as important elements in constructing its picture of God. If we are uncomfortable saying that the Holocaust was divine judgment on the Jews, then why are we comfortable agreeing with Scripture that the exile was divine judgment?

Building on the common Jewish perspective that the Hebrew Bible is in conversation with itself, Sweeney highlights various responses to Shoah-like events and other kinds of evil within the Hebrew Bible. For example, Kings ascribes the exile to the actions of Manasseh, who was long dead by the time of the conquest of Jerusalem (2 Kings 24:3). In contrast, Chronicles presents the current generation as the one at fault, while Manasseh has his own mini exile, followed by repentance and restoration (2 Chronicles 33). However, both texts agree that the responsibility for the exile lay with humans in some way.[71] The lament psalms, Lamentations, and Job, on the other hand, lay the blame for at least some calamities at the feet of God, encouraging us to act in similar ways.[72] Sweeney suggests that "such a dialogue points to a robust relationship between YHWH and the people in which both parties express themselves, forcefully and deliberately, when either perceives wrongdoing on the part of the other."[73] For example, he suggests that Isaiah should have confronted YHWH when YHWH informed him about his plan to make Israel unresponsive, leading to certain judgment (Isa. 6:9–10). As Sweeney puts it, "Isaiah ends with a portrayal of the bodies of the wicked strewn about; perhaps if Isaiah had stood up to YHWH and said 'No!' like Moses in the wilderness, . . . the book of Isaiah might have arrived at a different conclusion in which the goals of the book had been achieved."[74]

While overall the combined witness of the Hebrew Bible, New Testament, and rabbinic literature testifies to YHWH's righteousness, for Sweeney, "the modern experience of the Shoah and our examination of biblical literature demonstrates that the realization of such an ideal is questionable."[75] Since God

---

70. Marvin A. Sweeney, *Reading the Hebrew Bible after the Shoah: Engaging Holocaust Theology* (Minneapolis: Fortress, 2008), 1. Sweeney uses "G-d" to reflect the ancient Jewish practice of not pronouncing the name of God. For other works on Holocaust theology, see Emil L. Fackenheim, *The Jewish Bible after the Holocaust: A Re-reading* (Bloomington, IN: Indiana Univ. Press, 1990); Tod Linafelt, ed., *Strange Fire: Reading the Bible after the Holocaust* (New York: New York Univ. Press, 2000).

71. Sweeney, *Reading the Hebrew Bible after the Shoah*, 72–83.

72. Ibid., 167–87, 195–200.

73. Ibid., 187.

74. Idem, "What Is Biblical Theology?" 39.

75. Idem, *Reading the Hebrew Bible after the Shoah*, 239.

does not always help his people in times of trouble, Sweeney argues that we should emphasize another common theme in the Hebrew Bible: human responsibility for establishing righteousness in the world. Examples of such activity in the Hebrew Bible include Abraham bargaining on behalf of Sodom and Gomorrah, Moses confronting YHWH for the sake of Israel, and Esther acting for her people in a time of YHWH's absence. Therefore the call for Jewish believers today is to press on with assisting God in the task of sanctifying the world, even if we have no promise that his divine absence will end. Sweeney concludes that "like the child of an abusive parent, we must act in the aftermath of the Shoah because such action is necessary for us to rebuild and continue our lives and our roles as partners with G-d in the world of creation."[76]

TEST CASE: EXODUS

While Jewish scholars clearly value the exodus event (Exodus 1–15), Sinai and the Mosaic covenant (Exodus 19–40) play a much more dominant role in their biblical theologies, as seen in our earlier discussion of the role of the law in Jewish biblical theology.[77] As another example, Sommer focuses on Sinai in his monograph on the nature of revelation. Contradicting the traditional Jewish view that God revealed the Torah directly, he argues that the Torah is a response to God's revelation—or Moses' translation of the divine revelation to the people. In his perspective, the oral law in the rabbinic tradition, with its imperfections, is found already at the beginning of the Torah. Therefore the letter of the law, what he calls the *Gesetz*, can be changed as time passes. However, the nonspecific divine command behind the *Gesetz*—the *Gebot*—stays the same. Hence modern Jews are merely following the pattern of the biblical authors when they adapt specific laws to new situations.[78]

Sinai also plays a major role in Levenson's book *Sinai and Zion*. As discussed earlier, Levenson believes that both of these major streams are present simultaneously in the Hebrew Bible.[79] Sinai stands for the Mosaic covenant and the obligations it contains, while Zion symbolizes the promise of the Messiah in the Davidic covenant. Levenson contends that the early church, following the New Testament, subordinated the Mosaic covenant to the

---

76. Ibid., 240.
77. See pp. 115–16.
78. Benjamin D. Sommer, *Revelation and Authority: Sinai in Jewish Scripture and Tradition*, Anchor Yale Bible Reference Library (New Haven, CT: Yale Univ. Press, 2015), 241–51.
79. See p. 114.

Davidic covenant (symbolized by Jesus) by removing the necessity of following the law. In contrast, Judaism requires both covenants to be kept on equal footing: "The survival of these two ancient traditions endows the Jew with the obligation to become an active partner, in the redemption not only of his people, but of the world, to live in a simultaneous and indissoluble awareness of commandment and of promise."[80]

---

80. Levenson, *Sinai and Zion*, 217.

Chapter 7

POSTMODERN OLD TESTAMENT THEOLOGY

The final peak we will describe in the landscape of Old Testament theology is an approach that has emerged over the past few decades from the rise of postmodernism. Like those who take a canonical approach,[1] postmodern interpreters find historical-critical study insufficient to allow for meaningful engagement with the Old Testament in the contemporary era. However, rather than taking the biblical canon as their starting point, they begin with their own historical-cultural location. As noted earlier, postmodernism argues that each culture and religious community has its own narrative that offers a particular perspective on reality.[2] In its more radical forms, it leads to relativism—the idea that truth is always relative to a person's cultural location, so that there can be no absolute truth. However, more moderate forms of postmodernism simply recognize that all knowledge is perspectival. A person's perception of truth is always shaped by their viewpoint, which is rooted in their historical-cultural context. Since postmodern interpreters come from a wide array of contexts, the field of postmodern Old Testament theology offers a rich but sometimes bewildering variety of interpretive approaches and conclusions.

DEFINITION: Postmodern Old Testament theologies emphasize diverse perspectives within the Old Testament, reflect on the context of the interpreter, embrace subjective experience, and are attentive to interpretive interests and power dynamics. Points of tension for those who take this approach include the extent to which the biblical text is critiqued or deconstructed, the use of divergent interpretive methods leading to competing conclusions, and the criteria that are adopted for evaluating the legitimacy of theological conclusions.

---

1. See chap. 5.
2. See p. 20.

Central Texts Covered in This Chapter

Pablo R. Andiñach, *El Dios que está* (2014)

Dick Boer, *Deliverance from Slavery* (German: 2008; English: 2015)

Walter Brueggemann, *Old Testament Theology* (2008)

Walter Brueggemann, *Theology of the Old Testament* (1997)

Irmtraud Fischer, "Zwischen Kahlschlag, Durchforstung und neuer Pflanzung" (2005)

Kondasingu Jesurathnam, *Old Testament Theology* (2016)

Mark McEntire, *Portraits of a Mature God* (2013)

Leo G. Perdue, *Reconstructing Old Testament Theology* (2005)

John W. Rogerson, *A Theology of the Old Testament* (2009)

Phyllis Trible, "Five Loaves and Two Fishes" (1989)

Patricia K. Tull and Jacqueline E. Lapsley, eds., *After Exegesis* (2015)

Carey Walsh, *Chasing Mystery* (2012)

Jackson Wu, "Biblical Theology from a Chinese Perspective" (2013)

COMMON FEATURES

Emphasis on Diverse Perspectives within the Old Testament

A primary feature of postmodern Old Testament theologies is that they emphasize the diversity of perspectives within the Old Testament. It is a presupposition for most scholars who take this approach that the Old Testament contains a multitude of differing and sometimes competing voices. John Rogerson illustrates this by arguing that those who negatively evaluate the faith of the Teacher in Ecclesiastes (Qoheleth) "imply that there is only one genuine type of experience or knowledge of God and that Qoheleth lacks this."[3] In his view, "this brings with it the danger that the theological witness of the Old Testament becomes restricted and diminished, because those who approach it in this way know in advance what it says, or ought to say, about God."[4] Instead interpreters ought to acknowledge that the biblical texts present varying views on God and faith, and these perspectives should be held in tension.[5]

---

3. John W. Rogerson, *A Theology of the Old Testament: Cultural Memory, Communication, and Being Human* (Minneapolis: Fortress, 2009), 54.

4. Ibid.; see also Kondasingu Jesurathnam, *Old Testament Theology: History, Issues, and Perspectives*, Biblical Hermeneutics Rediscovered 3 (New Delhi: Christian World Imprints: 2016), 339–40.

5. See also Jacqueline E. Lapsley and Patricia K. Tull, "Introduction: Wisdom Rebuilds Her House," in *After Exegesis: Feminist Biblical Theology; Essays in Honor of Carol A. Newsom*, ed. Patricia K. Tull and

Carey Walsh speaks of the "shape-shifting" reflected in the biblical depictions of God revealing himself through a diverse array of forms, such as "angels, fire, thunder, storms, glory, name, [and] prophetic oracle," suggesting that it indicates "a resistance . . . to words themselves becoming idols."[6] Similarly, Walter Brueggemann contends that "it is the multiplicity of metaphors for YHWH that prevents the testimony of the Old Testament about YHWH from becoming idolatrous."[7] YHWH cannot be pinned down to a particular image that might allow people to manipulate him.

Brueggemann reflects the diversity of biblical faith in the structure of his *Theology of the Old Testament*, which is based on the metaphor of a trial. In a trial, witnesses offer testimony both for and against a particular supposition before a verdict is reached in which "reality is decided."[8] Therefore in part 1 Brueggemann presents Israel's core testimony about YHWH's actions in Israel's history, as well as his general character. Then in part 2 he examines Israel's countertestimony, which is found especially in the genre of complaint. This countertestimony arises from circumstances of injustice, when the experience of Israel (or particular individuals) does not seem to cohere with the core testimony's claims that "Yahweh's power and fidelity are operative."[9]

Mark McEntire sees even greater disparity in the biblical depictions of God. He contends that the beginning of the biblical narrative portrays God as "a playful, impetuous God who makes a person like a child playing with mud pies [Genesis 2], tosses the clay figure over the fence when it will not play as God wishes [Genesis 3], destroys the whole earth in a flash of angry regret [Genesis 6–7], and then almost immediately regrets the destructive act

---

Jacqueline E. Lapsley (Waco, TX: Baylor Univ. Press, 2015), 3; L. Juliana M. Claassens, "Biblical Theology as Dialogue: Continuing the Conversation on Mikhail Bakhtin and Biblical Theology," *Journal of Biblical Literature* 122 (2003): 127–44; Burke O. Long, "Letting Rival Gods Be Rivals: Biblical Theology in a Postmodern Age," in *Problems in Biblical Theology: Essays in Honor of Rolf Knierim*, ed. Henry T. C. Sun and Keith L. Eades (Grand Rapids: Eerdmans, 1997), 226–27; Dennis T. Olson, "Deuteronomy as De-Centering Center: Reflections on Postmodernism and the Quest for a Theological Center of the Hebrew Scriptures," *Semeia* 71 (1995): 119–32.

6. Carey Walsh, *Chasing Mystery: A Catholic Biblical Theology* (Collegeville, MN: Liturgical, 2012), 58.

7. Walter Brueggemann, *Old Testament Theology: An Introduction*, Library of Biblical Theology (Nashville: Abingdon, 2008), 140.

8. Idem, *Theology of the Old Testament: Testimony, Dispute, Advocacy* (Minneapolis: Augsburg Fortress, 1997), 135.

9. Ibid., 321. In part 3 Brueggemann covers what he terms "Israel's unsolicited testimony" about YHWH's relationships with Israel, the human person, the nations, and creation, and he abandons the courtroom metaphor in parts 4 and 5. Elsewhere he contends that we must continue to struggle with these different perspectives of YHWH rather than trying to "arrive at a settled, safe formulation," lest our theology dissolve into ideology (idem, "*Theology of the Old Testament: Testimony, Dispute, Advocacy* Revisited," *Catholic Biblical Quarterly* 74 [2012]: 30–31). He also insists that he has "no desire to be postmodern except as the polyvocal character of the text itself indicates such an interpretive perspective" (idem, *Old Testament Theology*, 1).

[Genesis 8–9]."[10] By contrast, the end of the Old Testament story (in Ezra, Nehemiah, Esther, and Daniel) depicts him as "a seasoned, detached, observer God who leaves the humans created so long ago to find their own way in the world, speaking to them only through the indirect majesty of literature."[11]

Reflection on the Interpreter's Context

In the modern era a primary goal of biblical interpretation was to read the Bible objectively, using scientific principles to ensure that interpretation consisted of sound *ex*egesis (drawing meaning out of the biblical text) rather than *eis*egesis (reading meaning into the biblical text). Postmodern scholars, however, recognize that purely objective interpretation is unattainable, since the theological and cultural contexts of interpreters shape their readings of the biblical text. Therefore a second common feature for those who take a postmodern approach is that they draw attention to what readers of the Old Testament contribute, from their specific contexts, to the process of interpretation.

Drawing on the work of Paul Ricoeur, Argentinian scholar Pablo Andiñach emphasizes the role of the reader by describing the biblical text as "an intimate relationship of signs that sleep . . . until a reader approaches who wakes them."[12] He contends that "without this participation of the reader, the text is not updated [or realized], and remains asleep. Without the reader, there is no text."[13] However, he also observes that the text itself "sets the limits of the reading" so that the reader is not an equal partner in the dialogue but is constrained by the text.[14] Like any literary text that seeks to reflect the complexity of human life, biblical texts are full of "ambiguity and polysemy"—they allow for a range of possible meanings that readers then produce from their personal or corporate engagement with the text.[15]

Scholars who take a postmodern approach to biblical theology acknowledge this dynamic of interpretation as dialogue between the text and the reader and typically identify their own theological and cultural contexts.[16]

---

10. Mark McEntire, *Portraits of a Mature God: Choices in Old Testament Theology* (Minneapolis: Fortress, 2013), 14.

11. Ibid.

12. Pablo R. Andiñach, *El Dios que está: Teología del Antiguo Testamento*, Estudios Bíblicos (Estella, Spain: Verbo Divino, 2014), 43, translation ours.

13. Ibid., 44, translation ours.

14. Ibid., 45, translation ours.

15. Ibid., 46, translation ours.

16. See Julia M. O'Brien, "Biblical Theology in Context(s): Jewish, Christian, and Critical Approaches to the Theology of the Hebrew Bible," in *Methodological Studies*, vol. 1 of *Theology of the Hebrew Bible*, ed. Marvin A. Sweeney, Resources for Biblical Study 92 (Atlanta: Society of Biblical Literature, 2019), 60; Lapsley and Tull, "Introduction," 2.

They also celebrate the diversity of viewpoints, contending that we see a more complete picture when we hear from a variety of perspectives. For example, Chinese scholar Jackson Wu observes, "Historically, most Christian theology is the product of reading the Bible with Western eyes. As a result, certain themes are especially prominent within western theology, such as law, judgment, and individual salvation. Particular books have been emphasized over others, particularly Romans and Galatians. . . . A Western lens is every bit as limiting as an Eastern one. Therefore, in order to gain a more comprehensive understanding of the grand biblical narrative, we need also to interpret Scripture from non-western vantage points."[17]

Wu proceeds to offer a framework for a Chinese biblical theology that emphasizes themes that are often neglected in the West, such as honor and shame, as well as family identity and responsibility. He contends that humans were created to be one family, with God as father and king, but they have rejected their divine father. In essence, Wu contends, "we have spit in our father's face. . . . We have no sense of shame. . . . People refuse to bring glory to the family name."[18] Evoking the Chinese concept of *lian* ("to lose face"), he declares that "as a result, our alienation causes us to lose face."[19] However, God makes a plan to "vindicate his honor, restore his kingdom, and bring reconciliation to his family" through the family of Abraham.[20] This plan is ultimately fulfilled through Jesus, who brings honor through his shameful death on the cross.[21]

The recognition that all theological accounts are perspectival and therefore partial also leads to a redefinition of what counts as Old Testament theology, by minimizing the importance of a comprehensive account. In the introduction to *After Exegesis*, a volume of essays offering a feminist biblical theology, Jacqueline Lapsley and Patricia Tull contend that "Feminist biblical theology resists the idea that a holistic or comprehensive treatment is necessary to qualify for the title 'biblical theology.' . . . Readings of individual texts, explicit engagement with present-day social and political realities, reflection on themes occurring in a minority of texts, and so on—these, without apology, are often the purview of feminist biblical interpretation."[22]

---

17. Jackson Wu, "Biblical Theology from a Chinese Perspective: Interpreting Scripture through the Lens of Honor and Shame," *Global Missiology* 4.10 (2013): 2.

18. Ibid., 12.

19. Ibid.

20. Ibid., 16.

21. Ibid., 24–25.

22. Lapsley and Tull, "Introduction," 6; see also Claassens, "Biblical Theology as Dialogue," 144. This emphasis also fits with the desire of Gunther Wittenberg and Jesurathnam to see theology done "from below"—by common people, not just scholars—which will necessarily be selective (see Gunther H.

Embrace of Subjective Experience

A third common feature for scholars who take a postmodern approach is that they view the way their subjective experience influences their interpretation as something to be embraced, for two reasons. First, rather than seeing subjective experience as a factor that skews their interpretation, they see it as offering perspective that can lead to a deeper understanding of the biblical texts. For example, Andiñach points out that those who have suffered from want of food are better able to grasp biblical references to hunger than those whose stomachs have always been full.[23]

For feminist scholars, the features of their subjective experience that serve as potential sources of knowledge and insight into the biblical text include their (female) embodiment, emotional capacity, and imagination. Katie Heffelfinger illustrates this by exploring "how attention to experience, embodiment, and emotion might help us better understand the vision of salvation" presented in Isaiah 51:9–52:12.[24] She observes how that text explicitly addresses YHWH's "arm" (51:9), which in Hebrew is a feminine noun. It then describes that feminine forearm as "she" who accomplished "the divine victories of the past."[25] The city of Zion is also personified as a female figure, and both her prior defeat and her coming salvation are depicted in bodily terms. In addition, Heffelfinger notes the references to the "beautiful" feet of the messenger who proclaims salvation (52:7) and the "embodied" response of the people, who are instructed to "depart, go out from there! Touch no unclean thing!" (v. 11).[26] She concludes that "body language clearly plays a key role in meaning-making in this text."[27] It "grounds this text's vision of salvation in concrete realities. . . . It happens to 'real bodies, lived lives,' even when they are portrayed in idealized, representative forms."[28]

Second, and more significantly, postmodern interpreters contend that their subjective readings produce interpretations that are relevant to their situation.[29]

Wittenberg, "Old Testament Theology, for Whom?" *Semeia* 73 [1996]: 230–32; K. Jesurathnam, "The Task of Old Testament Theology in the Indian Context: Some Methodological Explorations and Proposals," *Bangalore Theological Forum* 45 [2013], 23). McEntire, by contrast, argues that biblical theology should not be selective (*Portraits of a Mature God*, 207–8), though his concern is to give attention to passages that are typically neglected (particularly the postexilic narratives), a concern he shares with feminist interpreters like Lapsley and Tull.

23. Andiñach, *El Dios que está*, 44.

24. Katie M. Heffelfinger, "Embodiment in Isaiah 51–52 and Psalm 62: A Feminist Biblical Theology of Salvation," in *After Exegesis*, 64.

25. Ibid., 65.

26. Ibid., 66–67.

27. Ibid., 67.

28. Ibid.

29. Julia O'Brien sees the engagement between the context of the reader and the context of the biblical text as leading to a "search for a deeper understanding of human existence" ("Biblical Theology

Walsh's slim volume *Chasing Mystery* seeks to address the experience of "the modern situation where [divine] absences often seem more pressing than presences."[30] While most work in biblical theology has come from Protestant scholars, Walsh writes explicitly from a Catholic perspective, which she understands as influencing her in three primary ways. First, Catholicism emphasizes "the complementarity of faith and reason" and instills a deep appreciation for divine mystery.[31] Second, it views the world as "enchanted"—the world is full of objects "to see and smell and touch to help us worship the invisible God."[32] And third, Catholicism understands the biblical text as sacramental and thus as containing "spiritual meanings that are not immediately plain but instead reveal themselves in reflection."[33]

Central to Walsh's work is a desire to help readers experience the living God within the biblical text. She sees the narratives of the wilderness wanderings as generating multiple levels of meaning.

- Israel's complaints in the wilderness after the exodus
- "the restlessness of being in exile" after the fall of Jerusalem
- "the restlessness and grumbling condition of the current biblical reader in their cultural context" as they struggle to find meaning in the biblical text and particularly in the law[34]

Focusing in on the last of these, she contends that as we wade through the Old Testament law, "the unremitting sameness, the tedium, the effort, the ongoing disorientation, the cyclical fighting off of the urge to complain and giving in to the run of emotions is truly revealing of who *we* are," leading us to relate to the Israelites and ultimately to be transformed along with them.[35]

---

in Context[s]," 57). In contrast to most scholars in this chapter, despite her feminist leanings, Phyllis Bird calls for a descriptive biblical theology that is not "feminist, or liberationist, or Christian, or Jewish," though she also observes that "every version (and there can only be versions, never definitive statements) will be a distinctly individual creation, shaped by the peculiar sensitivities and biases of the author, including feminist sensitivities and biases" (Phyllis A. Bird, "The God of the Fathers Encounters Feminism: Overture for a Feminist Old Testament Theology," in *Methods*, vol. 3 of *Feminist Interpretation of the Hebrew Bible in Retrospect*, ed. Susanne Scholz, Recent Research in Biblical Studies 9 [Sheffield: Sheffield Phoenix, 2016], 151).

30. Walsh, *Chasing Mystery*, 4–5.

31. Ibid., 15; see also Kathleen M. O'Connor, "Stammering toward the Unsayable: Old Testament Theology, Trauma Theory, and Genesis," *Interpretation* 70 (2016), 301–2. O'Connor also comes from a Catholic background and speaks of the "divine ineffability, the 'unsayability' of God."

32. Walsh, *Chasing Mystery*, 16.

33. Ibid., 18.

34. Ibid., 45–46.

35. Ibid., 48, italics original. On the transformation of the reader, see also Andiñach, *El Dios que está*, 45.

Other scholars also recognize that intentionally reading the biblical text from their own subjective experience leads to interpretations that speak to their particular situation. Writing from an Indian context and concerned particularly with the situation of the Dalits (the untouchables in India's caste system), Kondasingu Jesurathnam gives considerable attention to drawing parallels between the Old Testament and the situation of modern India. For example, he notes connections between some Dalit literature and the Hebrew prophets: "With the same hope [as that of the Hebrew prophets] the Dalit prophets work towards the emancipation of millions of Dalits in India. It is with the same goal [that] the Dalit Prophetic voices emerged against their oppressors in order to show them that God is on their side."[36] He also links the situation of the Dalits to the innocent suffering of Job. Noting that the Dalits are often seen as getting what they deserve, according to the Hindu doctrine of Karma, he contends that "the wisdom writers of the Hebrew Bible squash such a traditional and mechanical understanding of retributive justice."[37]

This concern for a subjective theology that addresses the author's cultural context may also be seen in three essays written from different continents. Gunther Wittenberg calls for a South African Old Testament theology that reflects a concern for justice for the poor and marginalized. He suggests that such a theology should focus on "the establishment of royal-imperial power and the resistance to that power," which will provide "a model for struggles of resistance and theological reflection arising out of struggles" in South Africa.[38] From his location in Latin America, Valdir Steuernagel advocates for a biblical theology centered on the kingdom of God that would have a missiological focus and would speak to "the reality of a continent in deep political crisis, economic dependency, and absurd levels of poverty."[39] Finally, writing from Papua New Guinea, William Kenny Longgar urges the development of a distinctly Melanesian biblical theology, contending that foreign theologies do not "address key Melanesian religious and cultural realities facing Christians today: fear of evil spirits, fear of sorcery and witchcraft, fear of barrenness, fear of death, fear of failure, fear of the unknown, and the place of the ancestors in the lives of Christians."[40]

---

36. Jesurathnam, *Old Testament Theology*, 149.
37. Ibid., 167.
38. Wittenberg, "Old Testament Theology, for Whom?" 237.
39. Valdir Steuernagel, "Forty-Five Years of the FTL and Its Biblical Theology: A Bit of Theology along the Way . . . and Mary," *Journal of Latin American Theology* 11 (2016): 29–30.
40. William Kenny Longgar, "Authenticating Melanesian Biblical Theology: A Response to Foreign Theologies," *Point Series* 40 (2016): 47.

Attentiveness to Interpretive Interests and Power Dynamics

A final common feature of postmodern Old Testament theologies is that along with emphasizing the context of the interpreter, they also give attention to the interests (or ideologies) that are driving biblical interpretation and to the power dynamics that are at play in various uses of the biblical texts. They argue that everyone comes to the biblical text with particular aims and with the hope that certain preconceived notions will be confirmed, even when those desires are unacknowledged.[41] Therefore postmodern interpreters ask who benefits from a particular interpretation and whether a biblical text may have been misinterpreted (even if unconsciously) in order to support oppressive power structures. For example, Brueggemann questions the tendency of some scholars to challenge the character of God in the Old Testament but say nothing about "socio-economic, political matters," which he sees as prominent in the biblical text. Therefore they leave unchallenged a system that "has well-served the rise of entitled individuals at the expense of everyone else."[42]

Feminist biblical theology recognizes that in the history of interpretation, which has primarily been the purview of men, the biblical text has often been used to reinforce male domination. As Phyllis Bird points out, "Feminists who love these texts also know them as toxic, as dangerous to women's physical and mental health. They know that women's lives have been constricted, warped, and violated by these texts and their interpreters. Some have experienced denial of their vocation on the basis of these texts, others roadblocks to personal and professional fulfillment."[43] Therefore feminist biblical theology seeks to dismantle interpretations that it deems unjust to women, in many cases arguing that those interpretations reflect a misreading of the text. At the same time, it aims to illuminate neglected texts that offer a more positive perspective on women.[44]

For example, in an essay aptly titled "Between Deforestation, Thinning and New Planting," Irmtraud Fischer seeks to cut down the trees of gender-biased interpretation and plant new saplings that reflect a fairer treatment of women.[45] For example, she draws attention to how interpreters have often

---

41. See Brueggemann, *Theology of the Old Testament*, 62–63. Of course, engagement with the biblical text can also reshape an interpreter's presuppositions and interests.

42. Idem, "Futures in Old Testament Theology: Dialogic Engagement," *Horizons in Biblical Theology* 37 (2015): 41–42.

43. Bird, "God of the Fathers Encounters Feminism," 143.

44. See Phyllis Trible, "Five Loaves and Two Fishes: Feminist Hermeneutics and Biblical Theology," *Theological Studies* 50 (1989): 285–95.

45. Irmtraud Fischer, "Zwischen Kahlschlag, Durchforstung und neuer Pflanzung: Zu einigen Aspekten Feministischer Exegese und ihrer Relevanz für eine Theologie des Alten Testaments," in *Theologie und Exegese des Alten Testaments / der Hebräischen Bibel: Zwischenbilanz und Zukunftsperspektiven,*

downplayed the role of "the women who served at the entrance to the tent of meeting" (Ex. 38:8; 1 Sam. 2:22) because of their gendered assumptions.[46] Fischer also highlights female metaphors for YHWH, noting how Isaiah 42:14 portrays YHWH as "the potent deity . . . who with cries, snorting, and gasping like a woman in labor can bring to life."[47] She even contends that some divine metaphors that have traditionally been viewed as male images could be understood as female. After all, Rachel and Zipporah shepherd their fathers' sheep (Gen. 29:6; Ex. 2:16), and Deborah serves as a judge (Judg. 4:4–5).[48]

Anne Stewart's specific interest in promoting *gender* justice is central to her broader examination of a biblical theology of justice. She contends that the Old Testament's "cosmic vision" is "powerful for feminist reflection precisely because it critiques the distorted power structures of human society."[49] However, she also points out that diverse cultural contexts require different conceptions of gender justice and strategies for addressing it: "Women in Afghanistan and Bangladesh . . . have a profoundly different understanding of individual rights and citizenship than do Western women. Consequently, those who advocate for gender justice at the level of institutional or constitutional rights touch the lives of women in these societies very little."[50] Stewart finds in the Old Testament a model for cultivating multiple perspectives on justice and also sees it as challenging Western feminist conceptions that justice should be centered on achieving equality and impartiality. Instead "justice in the Hebrew Bible . . . celebrates God's concern for human life" and seeks "to promote wholeness and flourishing."[51] With this focus it "attends to human particularity rather than to the abstraction of political or gendered classes."[52] While justice in the Old Testament aims at human flourishing for all, that may not look the same for women in significantly different cultural contexts.

Dick Boer reveals his interpretive interest in his subtitle *Attempting a*

---

ed. Bernd Janowski, Stuttgarter Bibelstudien 200 (Stuttgart: Katholisches Bibelwerk, 2005), 41–72, translation ours.

46. Ibid., 47–50; see also Marie-Theres Wacker, "'Religionsgeschichte Israels' oder 'Theologie des Alten Testaments'–(k)eine Alternative? Anmerkungen aus feministisch-exegetischer Sicht," *Jahrbuch für Biblische Theologie* 10 (1995): 142–46. Wacker observes how some interpreters have connected the "mirrors" belonging to these women (Ex. 38:8) with pagan practices. She suggests an alternative view that the mirrors were simply the women's personal possessions, which they sacrificially gave to make the bronze basin. In this understanding, the verse conveys "the active participation of all, the men as well as the women, in the construction of the sanctuary . . . and with this an inclusive perception of the community of Israel" (p. 147, translation ours).

47. Fischer, "Zwischen Kahlschlag, Durchforstung und neuer Pflanzung," 62, translation ours.

48. Ibid.

49. Anne W. Stewart, "Woman Wisdom and Her Friends: A Feminist Biblical Theology of Justice," in *After Exegesis*, 107.

50. Ibid., 106.

51. Ibid., 107.

52. Ibid.

Biblical Theology in the Service of Liberation. As a Dutch theologian who ministered in East Germany before the collapse of the Berlin Wall, Boer takes his point of departure from a Dutch labor song that calls for "delivery from slavery," which he sees as aptly summarizing the central concern of the Torah (see Ex. 20:2).[53] Throughout his work he seeks to show how the biblical text supports a program of socialist revolution. For example, he compares ancient Egypt to present-day capitalist societies, saying, "Are we not familiar with a society, in its various guises, that robs people of their means of production: from the slave-holding society to the capitalist mode of production?"[54]

In light of his experience in a failed socialist state, Boer recognizes the problem that liberation movements can often take on the tyrannical nature of the society they are trying to overthrow. Distinguishing between "ideal Israel" and "real Israel," he connects the real Israel exemplified in the dark period of the judges and the oppressive practices of the monarchy with the failure of ideals found in the socialist movement.[55] Nevertheless, he finds hope in the prophetic promises of a messianic king who "uses his power to empower the people to become a society without domination."[56] He then discusses how these promises are fulfilled in Jesus, who "embodies limitless solidarity," providing the foundation for "a Christian aesthetic of resistance."[57]

POINTS OF TENSION

Extent to Which the Bible Is Critiqued or Deconstructed

A significant point of tension for postmodern Old Testament theologies concerns the extent to which they seek to critique or deconstruct biblical texts. Trible observes that whereas some feminist scholars "denounce Scripture as hopelessly misogynous [prejudiced against women]," others operate from a more positive perspective on the Bible and focus on highlighting texts that are liberating for women.[58] This tension between affirmation and critique is found not just in feminist works but throughout the category of postmodern Old Testament theology. Wu affirms the authority of the biblical text, interpreted in light of the author's original intent, and seeks merely to reshape or expand traditional interpretations by pointing out their inherent

---

53. Dick Boer, *Deliverance from Slavery: Attempting a Biblical Theology in the Service of Liberation*, trans. Rebecca Pohl (Leiden, Brill: 2015), 1.
54. Ibid., 42.
55. Ibid., 167, 210–26.
56. Ibid., 217.
57. Ibid., 229, 270.
58. Trible, "Five Loaves and Two Fishes," 286.

cultural limitations.[59] In a similar fashion, Heffelfinger declares that "holding the biblical text as revelatory, I find myself more willing to conclude that contemporary theories are insufficient than to reach the same conclusion about the biblical text."[60]

Andiñach wrestles with the ethical problem of the conquest narratives, particularly in light of the history of Native Americans being violently wrested from their land by European settlers, sometimes with biblical justification. However, despite his concern "that the Scriptures never again be used to justify oppression and dispossession,"[61] he does not reject the conquest narratives or follow the leading of other scholars who read them from the perspective of the Canaanites.[62] Instead he seeks to understand them in light of Israel's history, contending that they reflect the later reality of the continual threats Israel faced concerning its land, which culminated in the nation's exile. Therefore he suggests that these texts "can be understood as a literary revenge" upon Israel's more recent enemies written centuries after the time period they describe.[63] He also points out that the biblical narratives depict the Israelites as continuing to live with Canaanites throughout their existence in the land.[64]

Likewise, Brueggemann avoids critiquing the biblical text despite what he sees as a somewhat problematic portrayal of YHWH, which "allows a play of violence, on occasion, that cannot be contained in any sense of justice."[65] He describes the tendency to reject violent texts as "a contemporary form of Marcionism, in which we simply choose the 'best parts' of the text as reliable."[66] Even with its difficulties, Brueggemann finds the Old Testament's construal of the world to be more compelling than the "military consumerism" dominating modern Western society.[67] In his view, the Western metanarrative authorizes individuals to autonomously pursue their own happiness by

---

59. Wu, "Biblical Theology from a Chinese Perspective," 1.

60. Heffelfinger, "Embodiment in Isaiah 51–52 and Psalm 62," 64.

61. Andiñach, *El Dios que está*, 161, translation ours.

62. On this type of reading, see Robert Allen Warrior, "Canaanites, Cowboys, and Indians: Deliverance, Conquest, and Liberation Theology Today," *Christianity and Crisis* 49 (1989): 261–65; Andrea Smith, "Decolonizing Theology," *Union Seminary Quarterly Review* 59 (2005): 63–78; Nur Masalha, "Reading the Bible with the Eyes of the Canaanites: Neo-Zionism, Political Theology and the Land Traditions of the Bible (1967 to Gaza 2009)," *Holy Land Studies* 8 (2009): 55–108.

63. Andiñach, *El Dios que está*, 161, translation ours; similarly, O'Connor, "Stammering toward the Unsayable," 309. O'Connor reads the violent stories of Genesis as trauma literature that serves the "urgent, immediate purpose of helping Judah survive the near destruction of the nation [at the time of the exile] by insisting that God is there for them, even as God eludes definition."

64. Andiñach, *El Dios que está*, 162.

65. Brueggemann, *Theology of the Old Testament*, 250.

66. Brueggemann refers here to the second-century CE heretic Marcion, who rejected the Old Testament, arguing that it presented a different God than did the New Testament ("*Theology of the Old Testament: Testimony, Dispute, Advocacy* Revisited," 30).

67. Idem, *Theology of the Old Testament*, 718–21.

obtaining and consuming resources, using force when necessary. By contrast, he sees the Old Testament as presenting a world stamped with the "staggering sovereignty and inexplicable fidelity" of YHWH, who generously gives gifts and makes and keeps promises, allowing for "hope beyond every explanatory option."[68] This world overturns power structures and invites authentic and assertive dialogue with YHWH, while also creating a community of *genuine neighborliness.*"[69]

Addressing texts that portray violence against women, Fischer argues not that modern interpreters should reject them but instead that they should interpret these difficult texts from "the hermeneutical center" of "the God who wills abundant life."[70] The God who liberates his people from slavery in Egypt and who protects the foreigner, widow, and orphan is a God who is "partial on behalf of the oppressed."[71] For Fischer, the oppressed include those who experience any form of gender injustice. After all, "the dominance of the male gender over the female does not conform to the divine order of creation" but instead reflects "the order of the fallen creation."[72] Working from this perspective, Fischer suggests that highlighting texts about the suffering of women can be liberating, as it exposes injustice and grants "the victim a voice."[73]

Walsh goes much farther, arguing that "our versions of God suffer distortion" and that "the Bible, because it is written with human hands, has some of these human distortions in it."[74] She sees such distortion in the book of Job, which in her view portrays God as giving in to Satan's dares (as did Eve in the garden of Eden) and exercising his omnipotence in a bullying manner.[75] Ultimately, Walsh contends that "the theophany in Job [chaps. 38–41], in effect, deconstructs *itself,* forcing Job and his readers to seek some more real presence of the divine. . . . It offers in parable a critique of an omnipotent God. It exposes the limiting idol of God as all-controlling creator, hovering over creatures to manage each and every last detail, *except* the broken heart of his faithful servant, Job."[76]

---

68. Ibid., 719.

69. Ibid., 720, italics original.

70. Fischer, "Zwischen Kahlschlag, Durchforstung und neuer Pflanzung," 71, translation ours.

71. Ibid., 63, translation ours.

72. Ibid., translation ours.

73. Ibid., 71, translation ours.

74. Walsh, *Chasing Mystery,* 107; see also Rogerson, *Theology of the Old Testament,* 41. Rogerson says, with regard to the more violent biblical narratives, that the biblical writers' "understanding of the divine was imperfect and corrupted by too ready an attempt to create God in their own image, and to attribute to him ingratitude and obtuseness."

75. Walsh, *Chasing Mystery,* 90.

76. Ibid., 91, italics original; see also idem, "The Wisdom in Rupture: Brueggemann's Notion of Countertestimony for Postmodern Biblical Theology," in *Biblical Theology: Past, Present, and Future,* ed. Carey Walsh and Mark W. Elliott (Eugene, OR: Cascade, 2016), 167–76.

Leo Perdue also calls for critique of the biblical text: "When the Bible presents views that are sexist, racist, homophobic, militaristic, vicious, and neocolonial, in a word, inhumane and thus opposed to the well-being of creation and creatures, then these must be strongly opposed."[77] In a similar fashion, Wonil Kim advocates for an approach in which "non-life-giving, destructive theologies [within the Old Testament] can be boldly exposed and challenged, even corrected, by life-giving, constructive theologies also found in the Hebrew Bible / Old Testament."[78] For example, he argues that Old Testament theologians should critique theologies grounded in "conquest, patriarchy, [and] domination of nature" and espouse instead theologies founded on "liberation, equality, [and] stewardship of nature."[79]

Divergent Interpretive Methods and Conclusions

Another point of tension concerns the use of divergent interpretive methods, which can lead to competing conclusions. In *The Collapse of History* and the follow-up volume *Reconstructing Old Testament Theology*, Perdue describes how history (particularly historical-critical study) has ceased to be the dominant paradigm for doing Old Testament theology. He therefore outlines a number of newer interpretive methods and emphases,[80] though most of these have not yet been extensively applied to producing Old Testament (or biblical) theology.

Nevertheless, even among the postmodern Old Testament theologies surveyed here, a variety of methods are used—sometimes even within the same work—and these differing methods can lead to widely divergent conclusions. For example, Rogerson adopts a historical-critical understanding of the law of jubilee (Leviticus 25), which declares that every fifty years the Israelites are to free their slaves and return land that has been purchased to its original owner. Rogerson sees this law as deriving from the problems of the "dispossessions of small landowners and the enslavement of free men and women that occurred in post-exilic Judah."[81] Therefore he contends that Israel's theological

---

77. Leo G. Perdue, *Reconstructing Old Testament Theology: After the Collapse of History*, Overtures to Biblical Theology (Minneapolis: Fortress, 2005), 351.

78. Wonil Kim, "Beyond Dialogue: Toward a Dialectical Model of Theology of the Hebrew Scripture / Old Testament," in *Methodological Studies*, 113.

79. Ibid., 121.

80. Perdue covers recent efforts to focus on creation and myth, as well as canonical and literary approaches, narrative theology, social-anthropological approaches, theology of imagination, postmodern theology, Jewish biblical theology, feminist theologies, Latin American and African American theologies of liberation, and postcolonial theology (Leo G. Perdue, *The Collapse of History: Reconstructing Old Testament Theology*, Overtures to Biblical Theology [Minneapolis: Fortress, 1994]; idem, *Reconstructing Old Testament Theology*).

81. Rogerson, *Theology of the Old Testament*, 130.

reflection on property developed "from the importance of private property to the gradual realization that this was a major cause of social injustice, and thus to attempts to argue that all property belonged to Yhwh."[82]

Jesurathnam also views the jubilee through a historical-critical lens and understands it as a product of the postexilic period. Connecting the time period of the jubilee with the length of the exile (which he counts from 587–538 BCE), he contends that "the year of returnees from exile would then be the fiftieth year. During this time a total freedom of the community should be restored and a redistribution of the land and wealth had to be implemented."[83] However, unlike Rogerson, Jesurathnam gives the bulk of his discussion to applying the law to his own context. After citing numerous statistics about poverty and landlessness in India, particularly among the Dalits, he concludes that according to the biblical text, "God is the owner of the land given to the human beings as a gift and thus human greed and unnecessary want cannot be justified."[84]

Brueggemann and Boer offer a more text-centered approach to the jubilee, rather than a historical-critical reading. They focus on the connection between the jubilee and the exodus and understand the law as central to the organization of Israel's society. Brueggemann sees the jubilee as part of YHWH's program to create an "Exodus community" in his image.[85] Boer presents a similar interpretation, though using terminology that derives from his Marxist ideology. He describes the jubilee as "the climax of the revolution prescribed by the Torah," which serves as "the material foundation for the Kingdom of Freedom" by giving everyone a share in the means of production.[86] He views the release of debts and freeing of slaves every seven years, along with the jubilee, as "a preventative measure that pre-empts the danger of the project 'Israel' turning back into an 'Egypt,' . . . a 'Land of Oppression.'"[87] Therefore, for Brueggemann and Boer, the law of jubilee cannot be divorced from the exodus narrative and read merely in light of the socioeconomic problems of the postexilic period.

A survey of how some of the scholars in this category treat the book of Job also illustrates the major differences in theological conclusions that result from the use of diverse interpretive methods. For example, is the God of

---

82. Ibid., 132; O'Brien also strongly argues for the importance of historical-critical readings ("Biblical Theology in Context[s]," 60–67).

83. Jesurathnam, *Old Testament Theology*, 89.

84. Ibid., 96.

85. Brueggemann, *Theology of the Old Testament*, 189.

86. Boer, *Deliverance from Slavery*, 165.

87. Ibid.

the whirlwind in Job 38–41 "an idol,"[88] or is he idol-breaking[89]—"a divine counterimage associated not with death but with life"?[90] Is God portrayed as a "hectoring Captain of Fate,"[91] or do the divine speeches indicate "that he is profoundly 'present' in creation but that his presence has little to do with reward and punishment"?[92] Espousing the latter view, Carleen Mandolfo compares Job 38–41 to post-Holocaust scholar Melissa Raphael's description of God's presence in the Nazi death camps "in the women who were simply present . . . with the suffering of the other."[93] Finally, does Job receive "a reassurance that his life at the public and moral level has not been in vain,"[94] or does he encounter "a God in whose presence the issues of moral calculus of Job and his friends appear unworthy and trivial" so that Job is "[no] longer interested in the question"?[95] Divergent interpretive methods entail different sets of assumptions and questions, which at times lead to incompatible conclusions.

Criteria for Evaluating the Legitimacy of Theological Conclusions

A final point of tension concerns criteria for evaluating the legitimacy of theological conclusions. Since postmodern Old Testament theologies yield such a broad range of conclusions, some means of evaluation seems necessary. However, an unrestrained postmodernism offers no means for assessing the value of a particular Old Testament theology. As we noted earlier, in its more extreme forms, postmodernism denies the possibility of any objective truth.[96] Each community has its own "truths," and there is no basis for intercommunal dialogue or any check against a self-interested theology.[97] While the works

---

88. Walsh, *Chasing Mystery*, 90.

89. See Brueggemann, *Theology of the Old Testament*, 391. Brueggemann contends that the picture of God that Job and his friends previously held was "precisely one of the images prohibited by the terrible God of Sinai" and suggests that in his response "the God of the whirlwind refuses the domestication to which Israel was intensely tempted."

90. Wilhelm Schwendemann, "God's Answer to Job," in *Transgressors: Toward a Feminist Biblical Theology*, ed. Claudia Janssen, Ute Ochtendung, and Beate Wehn, trans. Linda M. Maloney (Collegeville, MN: Liturgical, 2002), 158.

91. Walsh, *Chasing Mystery*, 90; see also McEntire, *Portraits of a Mature God*, 165. McEntire sees the aim of the book as "a reassertion of divine freedom" and asks, "If Israel's God does not operate by a predictable, reliable system of justice, then what keeps the divine behavior from becoming entirely capricious?"

92. Carleen Mandolfo, "Job and the Hidden Face of God: A Feminist Biblical Theology of Divine Judgment," in *After Exegesis*, 57. Schwendemann contends that "what is truly astonishing in [38:8–11] is how lovingly God approaches both the chaos and the creation itself, caring for the created universe as if it were a tiny infant" ("God's Answer to Job," 159).

93. Mandolfo, "Job and the Hidden Face of God," 47.

94. Rogerson, *Theology of the Old Testament*, 170.

95. Brueggemann, *Theology of the Old Testament*, 391.

96. See p. 128.

97. See Perdue, *Reconstructing Old Testament Theology*, 3. Later Perdue notes that "in its quest to reject

surveyed in this chapter avoid such radical postmodernism, most do little to establish a common basis for dialoguing across party lines or determining how to evaluate postmodern theologies of different stripes.

Nevertheless, various criteria can be gleaned from a survey of these authors. For some, the biblical text itself provides constraints. Brueggemann seems to view faithfulness to the full range of Israel's testimony about God as a primary criterion for evaluating an Old Testament theology. He is concerned that "church theology as commonly practiced is characteristically reductionist concerning the Bible" and contends that "it is the work of biblical theology to counter the reductionism and to bear resilient witness to those texts and their interpretations that do not 'fit.'"[98] An example of this can be seen in his discussion of YHWH's "fierceness"—his "potential for extraordinary destructiveness."[99] In response to the potential objection that he has overemphasized texts that are "rather marginal to the total witness of Israel," Brueggemann says that he aims "only to give full notice to those texts most often submerged in theological exposition."[100]

Yet as noted earlier, other works are more open to critiquing the views of the Old Testament according to how well they cohere to certain external norms.[101] Most notably, texts that seem to portray God as violent or that advocate human violence or domination are often rejected as not conforming to the interpreter's religious and ethical ideals. For example, considering the problem of biblical texts that are patriarchal, Trible declares that "modern believers are commanded to choose life over death. Within this dialectic movement, feminism might claim the entire Bible as authoritative, though not necessarily prescriptive," requiring a redefinition of the Bible's authority.[102]

Perdue offers the most substantial reflection on criteria for evaluation, arguing that a good biblical theology should address historical concerns and cultural and economic realities (both in the ancient text and in contemporary society), as well as the theology that emerges from considering the biblical text in light of these factors.[103] He sees historical study as necessary in allowing interpreters to achieve sufficient distance from the biblical text so that they do

authoritarianism, postmodernism ironically has opened wide the gate to this same evil. Postmodernism allows authoritarianism to enter and provide the basis on which to deprecate all human values and any human groups it so chooses" (p. 345).

98. Brueggemann, *Theology of the Old Testament*, 107.

99. Ibid., 275.

100. Ibid., 276.

101. See pp. 139–41.

102. Trible, "Five Loaves and Two Fishes," 294.

103. Perdue, *Reconstructing Old Testament Theology*, 13; see also Bird, "God of the Fathers Encounters Feminism," 148–50.

not simply read their own culture and ideas into it. However, once they have achieved that critical distance, they may then move into a "second naïveté," where they enter into the world of the biblical text, "leading to the engagement of life and faith."[104] Perdue emphasizes that the use of critical reason is essential throughout this process. Also, in an effort to avoid domineering interpretations, he contends that another criterion for Old Testament theology should be how well it coheres with the experience of oppressed people groups.[105]

Jesurathnam similarly calls for "two listenings of the Bible," one that is "Hebraic and Jewish" (historical), and a second that seeks to "interpret and appropriate the biblical message to [the interpreter's] own struggles and sufferings."[106] He also advocates for an Old Testament theology that aims to produce "a just and equal society" and "build up communities of love, caring and sharing,"[107] and his particular interest in the Dalits resembles Perdue's concern for a theology that takes the oppressed into account.

TEST CASE: EXODUS

Postmodern Old Testament theologies use the book of Exodus in a wide variety of ways, reflecting their considerable differences in method and interest. From a feminist perspective, Trible points out that the story of the exodus is put in motion by a handful of women, who have often gone unnoticed: "Two midwives, a Hebrew mother, a sister, the daughter of Pharaoh, and her maidens fill these passages. The midwives, given the names Shiphrah and Puah, defy the mighty Pharaoh, who has no name. The mother and sister work together to save their baby son and brother. The daughter of Pharaoh identifies with them rather than with her father. This portrait breaks filial allegiance, crosses class lines, and transcends racial and political differences. A collage of women unites for salvation; with them the Exodus originates."[108]

Interpreting Exodus with an eye toward Chinese culture, Wu emphasizes the family dimensions of the exodus narrative, pointing out that God designates Israel as his "firstborn son" (Ex. 4:22–23). This relationship generates family responsibilities—God "adopts them in order to bear his name among the nations."[109] To enable them to fulfill these responsibilities, he gives them

---

104. Perdue, *Reconstructing Old Testament Theology*, 344. The phrase "second naïveté" is associated especially with the work of Paul Ricoeur.

105. Ibid., 343–45; see also Wittenberg, "Old Testament Theology, for Whom?" 230–31.

106. Jesurathnam, *Old Testament Theology*, 4–5.

107. Ibid., 74.

108. Trible, "Five Loaves and Two Fishes," 290.

109. Wu, "Biblical Theology from a Chinese Perspective," 18.

his law, which is intended to help them "learn righteousness and a sense of shame," but ultimately they betray their father.[110]

With a focus on narrative readings, McEntire examines the characterization of God in the Sinai narrative, contending,

> It is difficult to escape the problematic theological conclusion that the divine being is acquiring a new sense of self-awareness here. This being has destroyed most of the earth once [Genesis 6–9] and two entire cities another time [Genesis 19], and has twice attacked and injured or nearly killed a specifically chosen human partner [Gen. 32:22–32; Ex. 4:24–26]. God seems aware of the danger in [Ex.] 19:23 and succeeds in keeping an appropriate distance from the people, if regretfully. . . . This deity is far too dangerous and unpredictable for direct contact with ordinary human beings.[111]

Boer understands the exodus narrative as reflecting the situation of third-century BCE Egypt, where he believes it received its final form. Read from that much later context, "the name 'Egypt' turns into a kind of metaphor," which "now refers to the whole sequence of empires that succeeded one another in this region and cornered the people of Israel. All of these empires are subsumed under this one house of bondage, from which Israel is delivered."[112] In Boer's view, this metaphorical reading of Egypt allows the exodus to serve as a paradigm for all people who are oppressed. He sees further support for this in the prophetic call for Israel to be a "light to the nations" (Isa. 42:6 NRSV), contending that Israel's role is to "let the light of the Kingdom of Freedom, Equality and Solidarity shine for all" in order to bring about "world revolution."[113]

Brueggemann similarly applies the exodus narrative to the contemporary world: "The God of Israel is a relentless opponent of human oppression, even when oppression is undertaken and sponsored by what appear to be legitimated powers. Thus Yahweh functions . . . as a delegitimator of failed social institutions and as a legitimator of revolutionary human agents."[114] In light of the atrocities of the twentieth century, Brueggemann expresses some doubt about the enduring power of the exodus narrative, but he sees figures

---

110. Ibid.
111. McEntire, *Portraits of a Mature God*, 69.
112. Boer, *Deliverance from Slavery*, 44.
113. Ibid., 52.
114. Brueggemann, *Theology of the Old Testament*, 180.

like Martin Luther King Jr. and Nelson Mandela as offering some hope that it may continue to spark movements of liberation.[115] Elsewhere Brueggemann considers the impact of the exodus not just on humanity but on all of creation, arguing that it "has the effect of 'righting' creation. . . . The outcome of the exodus is that by this miracle of deliverance, creation can function again as a fruitful system of life, a function that has been disrupted by the environmental destructiveness of Pharaoh's regime."[116]

Rogerson draws on the distinction that social anthropologist Claude Lévi-Strauss made between "hot" and "cold" societies. Cold societies seek to maintain traditional structures, whereas hot societies allow historical factors to bring about transformation.[117] Applying this conceptual scheme to the biblical text, Rogerson attempts to distinguish between hot histories, which challenge readers "to look critically at their situation with a view to changing and improving it," and cold histories, which uphold the status quo.[118] Examining the narratives of Israel complaining about the lack of food and water in the wilderness (Exodus 16–17), Rogerson identifies them as hot narratives, which raise a number of unanswered questions: "Why do people who have been delivered from slavery feel resentful rather than grateful? How can people who have seen miracles performed on their behalf still doubt that divine power is on their side? Why is it that God persists in identifying himself with a people that is so obviously unfit for such attention?"[119] Ultimately, he concludes that "the remarkable thing about the Old Testament is the persistence of its visions of a better humanity and a better world," despite all evidence to the contrary.[120]

---

115. Ibid., 181.
116. Idem, *Old Testament Theology*, 166.
117. Rogerson, *Theology of the Old Testament*, 25–26.
118. Ibid., 29.
119. Ibid., 34–35.
120. Ibid., 39.

CONCLUSION

The world of Old Testament theology is full of riches and well able to reward those who study it, but as seen in the previous pages of this book, it exhibits a bewildering and disorienting diversity. We have attempted to provide some measure of order to the chaos by drawing a map that identifies seven approaches (mountain peaks), grouped into three parts (regions). In this chapter, we first summarize these approaches and then outline some other sources of Old Testament theology and consider the future of the discipline. We conclude with an invitation for you to begin your own journey into the field of Old Testament theology.

SUMMARY

To help you focus in on the common features and points of tension for each approach to Old Testament theology and make it easier to compare them, we have included the definition of each approach here.

Part 1: History

Old Testament Theology Grounded in Biblical (Hi)story: Old Testament theology that is grounded in biblical (hi)story focuses on retelling Old Testament history, views the Old Testament as story, understands the whole Bible as one story, and sees it as *the* story that shapes us. Points of tension among scholars who adopt this approach include how the story is outlined, how the nonnarrative literature is incorporated, and what role the New Testament plays in interpreting the Old.

Historical-Critical Old Testament Theology: Historical-critical Old Testament theologies employ historical-critical reconstructions as the foundation for their Old Testament theology and read the Old Testament descriptively. Points of tension include debate about whether to call their work Old Testament theology or history of Israelite religion, which historical-critical reconstructions they use and the degree of historicity they see in the text, and the role of the New Testament in their work.

Part 2: Theme

Multiplex Thematic Old Testament Theology: Old Testament theologies that adopt a multiplex thematic approach are structured around multiple themes, draw connections to the New Testament, and reflect a concern for the church. Points of tension for multiplex thematic theologies include the source of the themes, which themes are emphasized, and which interpretive methods are used.

Old Testament Theology Focused around a Central Theme: Old Testament theologies focused around a central theme assume that the Old Testament has a center, emphasize the unity of the Old and New Testaments, and are prescriptive. Points of tension for theologies in this category include the identity of that center, the incorporation of nonnarrative literature, and the role of historical-critical methods.

Part 3: Context

Canonical Old Testament Theology: Canonical Old Testament theologies focus on the final canonical form of the biblical text, interpret texts in light of their broader Old Testament context, read the Old Testament as Christian Scripture, and see Old Testament theology as prescriptive. Points of tension among proponents of this approach include which canon is followed, the significance of the history of interpretation, and the role of historical-critical methods.

Jewish Biblical Theology: Jewish biblical theology follows the extent and order of the Jewish canon, emphasizes diversity, and focuses on topics of importance for Jews. The points of tension for Jewish biblical theology include the question of its existence, the role of postbiblical Jewish material, and the influence of the Holocaust on biblical theology.

Postmodern Old Testament Theology: Postmodern Old Testament theologies emphasize diverse perspectives within the Old Testament, reflect on the context of the interpreter, embrace subjective experience, and are attentive to interpretive interests and power dynamics. Points of tension for those who take this approach include the extent to which the biblical text is critiqued or deconstructed, the use of divergent interpretive methods leading to competing conclusions, and the criteria that are adopted for evaluating the legitimacy of theological conclusions.

THE BROADER WORLD OF OLD TESTAMENT THEOLOGY

The dominant mode of Old Testament theology has been to produce large volumes that cover the theology of the entire Old Testament. However, Old

Testament and biblical theology have also been done extensively on a smaller scale.[1] In this conclusion we provide only a brief survey of these other types of sources of biblical theology, but our online annotated bibliography *(https://zondervanacademic.com/OTTheoBibliography)* offers a further glimpse of some of the riches available in these areas.

Thematic Studies and Theologies of Individual Biblical Books

One of the most common places where biblical theology appears outside of the more comprehensive works has been in smaller books, essays, and journal articles focusing on particular themes. The authors do not claim that these themes are the center of the Old Testament or the Bible but see them as prominent enough that investigation rewards the research. Many of these thematic studies are found in stand-alone books, such as the collection of essays in *Central Themes in Biblical Theology*, edited by Scott Hafemann and Paul House.[2] However, several series are also devoted to this type of work, including:

- New Studies in Biblical Theology
- Overtures to Biblical Theology
- Studies in Old Testament Biblical Theology
- Biblical Theology for Life
- Essential Studies in Biblical Theology

Various dictionaries, such as the *New Dictionary of Biblical Theology*, also present biblical-theological summaries of particular themes as well as of individual books of the Bible.[3] A valuable online source for biblical theology is the Bible Project, whose stated aim is "to help people experience the Bible as a unified story that leads to Jesus."[4] Toward that end, they offer videos, a blog, and a podcast examining the theology of biblical books and themes.

---

1. For a discussion of this phenomenon, see James Barr, *The Concept of Biblical Theology: An Old Testament Perspective* (Minneapolis: Fortress, 1999), 52–61.

2. Scott J. Hafemann and Paul R. House, eds., *Central Themes in Biblical Theology: Mapping Unity in Diversity* (Grand Rapids: Baker Academic, 2007).

3. T. Desmond Alexander, Brian S. Rosner, D. A. Carson, and Graeme Goldsworthy, eds., *New Dictionary of Biblical Theology* (Downers Grove, IL: InterVarsity, 2000). Other examples include Walter A. Elwell, ed., *Evangelical Dictionary of Biblical Theology*, Baker Reference Library (Grand Rapids: Baker, 1996), which is also available online: *www.biblestudytools.com/dictionaries/bakers-evangelical-dictionary*; and from a Catholic perspective, Xavier Léon-Dufour, ed., *Dictionary of Biblical Theology*, 2nd ed. (Frederick, MD: Word Among Us, 1995).

4. The Bible Project, *https://bibleproject.com/*, accessed 16 January 2020.

Word studies are sometimes rich with implications for biblical theology as well and may be found in sources like the *New International Dictionary of Old Testament Theology and Exegesis*.[5]

Another natural place to find biblical theology is in commentaries, which seek to present the message of a biblical book. Some series that often contain biblical-theological reflection include:

- Apollos Old (or New) Testament Commentary
- Belief: A Theological Commentary on the Bible
- Biblical Theology for Christian Proclamation
- The Two Horizons Old (or New) Testament Commentary
- Interpretation: A Bible Commentary for Teaching and Preaching
- The New American Commentary
- The NIV Application Commentary
- The Story of God Bible Commentary

Zondervan has even recently published a biblical theology study Bible, which seeks to provide the reader with insights from biblical theology on the same page as the biblical text.[6]

Theological Introductions to the Old Testament

Another common source of Old Testament theology is in introductions and summaries of the Old Testament. While generally written for Old Testament survey classes and not explicitly designed as Old Testament theologies, they frequently include theology as part of their overview of the Old Testament. In particular, the line between Old Testament theologies and self-described "theological introductions" to the Old Testament is quite fuzzy. Many examples of these could be provided, but we will briefly survey two of them here.[7] The multiauthored *Theological Introduction to the Old Testament* gives significant attention to asking theological questions.[8] With the exception of a chapter on wisdom included at the end, the book is arranged

---

5. Willem A. VanGemeren, ed., *New International Dictionary of Old Testament Theology and Exegesis*, 5 vols. (Grand Rapids: Zondervan, 1997).

6. D. A. Carson, ed., *NIV Biblical Theology Study Bible: Follow God's Redemptive Plan as It Unfolds throughout Scripture* (Grand Rapids: Zondervan, 2018).

7. For some other examples, see Richard S. Hess, *The Old Testament: A Historical, Theological, and Critical Introduction* (Grand Rapids: Baker Academic, 2016); Mark W. Hamilton, *A Theological Introduction to the Old Testament* (Oxford: Oxford Univ. Press, 2018).

8. Bruce C. Birch, Walter Brueggemann, Terence E. Fretheim, and David L. Petersen, *A Theological Introduction to the Old Testament*, 2nd ed. (Nashville: Abingdon, 2005).

chronologically, based on a historical-critical reconstruction.[9] Each chapter begins with a survey of the time period and the basic critical conclusions regarding the books in view, before moving on to theological reflections. Another example is the multiauthored *Biblical-Theological Introduction to the Old Testament*, which operates from the premises that "Jesus is the theological center of the Old Testament" and that the kingdom of God is "the thematic framework for the Bible."[10] Each chapter looks at background issues, structure and outline, and message and theology, while also drawing connections to the New Testament.

Metastudies of Old Testament Theology

Finally, because of both the complexity of defining Old Testament theology and the diversity of works in the field, many scholars have offered metastudies, which discuss various aspects of the discipline's history and methods. For those who desire a deeper study of Old Testament theology as a field, works like the following provide a rich source of data about these issues.

- James Barr, *The Concept of Biblical Theology*
- Scott J. Hafemann, ed., *Biblical Theology: Retrospect and Prospect*
- Gerhard Hasel, *Old Testament Theology: Basic Issues in the Current Debate*
- Edward W. Klink III and Darian R. Lockett, *Understanding Biblical Theology*
- James K. Mead, *Biblical Theology: Issues, Methods, and Themes*
- Ben C. Ollenburger, ed., *Old Testament Theology: Flowering and Future*
- Carey Walsh and Mark W. Elliot, eds., *Biblical Theology: Past, Present, and Future*

THE FUTURE OF OLD TESTAMENT THEOLOGY

As should be clear by this point in the book, Old Testament theology is a flourishing field. We do not know what will happen in the future, but we anticipate that all of the categories we have noted will continue to grow, though likely at uneven rates. Perhaps the most significant area of expansion in the coming years will be in postmodern Old Testament theologies, rooted

---

9. For example, Deuteronomy is included at the end of the monarchy.

10. Miles V. Van Pelt, ed., *A Biblical-Theological Introduction to the Old Testament: The Gospel Promised* (Wheaton, IL: Crossway, 2016), 25, 28.

in particular interpretive contexts. As H. Wheeler Robinson noted in 1946, Old Testament theology "will have to be rewritten in each generation, for each has different needs and each will interpret the past in its own characteristic way."[11] In our global age, we are increasingly aware that Old Testament theology must also be written from within different interpretive communities, since they each have their own unique needs and perspectives.

For this reason, we expect to see more works by female, minority, and majority-world authors over the next few decades. As we were writing this book, we quickly realized that the vast majority of work in the field of Old Testament theology was by white men. As Phyllis Trible said in 1989, the "guardians of the discipline [of biblical theology] have fit a standard profile. They have been white Christian males of European or North American extraction, educated in seminaries, divinity schools, or theological faculties."[12] Unfortunately, change has been slow in the decades since then. We searched extensively to find the entries in our bibliography by women and people of color, most of which are essays rather than full-scale theologies.[13] In a survey of Old Testament theology in Africa, Bungishabaku Katho says that no African scholar has produced an Old Testament theology that compares with those written in Europe and the United States,[14] and private communication with scholars working in Latin America and Asia confirm that non-Western scholars have rarely written biblical theologies.

A variety of reasons could be proposed for this lack. First, the guild of Old Testament scholars in general is dominated by white men. Phyllis Bird points out that only recently have a significant number of women begun participating in the guild,[15] and the same could be said for people of color.

---

11. H. Wheeler Robinson, *Inspiration and Revelation in the Old Testament* (Oxford: Clarendon, 1946), 282, though he also contended that Old Testament theology would be marked by some consistency, having "its inevitable poles around which all else turns. Over against each other are God and man, and all that lies between can be conceived as belonging to the Kingdom—the active kingly rule—of God."

12. Phyllis Trible, "Five Loaves and Two Fishes: Feminist Hermeneutics and Biblical Theology," *Theological Studies* 50 (1989): 285.

13. The few full-scale theologies are primarily in the postmodern category (see chap. 7). For two thematic studies, see Puttagunta Satyavani, *Seeing the Face of God: Exploring an Old Testament Theme* (Carlisle, UK: Langham, 2014); Jacqueline E. Lapsley, "A Theology of Creation—Critical and Christian," in *Methodological Studies*, vol. 1 of *Theology of the Hebrew Bible*, ed. Marvin A. Sweeney, Resources for Biblical Study 92 (Atlanta: Society of Biblical Literature, 2019), 141–52.

14. Bungishabaku Katho, "Faire la théologie de l'Ancien Testament en Afrique aujourd'hui: Défis et perspective," *Old Testament Essays* 23 (2010): 84–85.

15. Phyllis A. Bird, "The God of the Fathers Encounters Feminism: Overture for a Feminist Old Testament Theology," in *Methods*, vol. 3 of *Feminist Interpretation of the Hebrew Bible in Retrospect*, ed. Susanne Scholz, Recent Research in Biblical Studies 9 (Sheffield: Sheffield Phoenix, 2016), 141. While many earlier women engaged in biblical interpretation (see Marion Ann Taylor and Agnes Choi, eds., *Handbook of Women Biblical Interpreters: A Historical and Biographical Guide* [Grand Rapids: Baker Academic, 2012]), the academic field of biblical studies was often not open to them.

Second, the kind of comprehensive biblical theology that has been published in the past does not always resonate with such scholars. Jacqueline Lapsley and Patricia Tull deem comprehensive approaches to be "totalizing" and contend that feminist interpreters often avoid them, "since they have tended to reflect androcentric [male-centered] bias."[16] Finally, female, minority, and majority-world scholars might also have other priorities. Bird observes that many female interpreters have been engaged in developing feminist hermeneutics or exploring neglected female characters in the biblical text.[17] Similarly, the attention of majority-world and minority scholars has often been focused on developing new interpretive methods and writing contextual commentaries.[18]

Addressing these issues is difficult. James Spencer contends that "finding ways to integrate the experiences and concerns of the global church into the field of Old Testament theology is one of the greatest challenges facing a predominantly Western academy."[19] Given that female, minority, and majority-world scholars are still relative newcomers to the scholarly guild, hopefully, the work that they are doing in biblical interpretation will in time provide the exegetical foundations for new paths to the peaks in the mountain range of Old Testament theology. However, the mere passage of time may not be enough; it is also important to intentionally seek their involvement in the discipline.

---

16. Jacqueline E. Lapsley and Patricia K. Tull, "Introduction: Wisdom Rebuilds Her House," in *After Exegesis: Feminist Biblical Theology: Essays in Honor of Carol A. Newsom*, ed. Patricia K. Tull and Jacqueline E. Lapsley (Waco, TX: Baylor Univ. Press, 2015), 6.

17. Bird, "God of the Fathers Encounters Feminism," 141–42. Bird also notes that the assumption of the Old Testament's authority within the discipline can be troubling for some women. For essays on feminist hermeneutics, see Linda Day and Carolyn Pressler, eds., *Engaging the Bible in a Gendered World: An Introduction to Feminist Biblical Interpretation in Honor of Katharine Doob Sakenfeld* (Louisville: Westminster John Knox, 2006). For a feminist commentary that gives significant attention to female characters, see Carol A. Newsom, Sharon H. Ringe, and Jacqueline E. Lapsley, eds., *Women's Bible Commentary*, 3rd ed. (Louisville: Westminster John Knox, 2012).

18. Katho, "Faire la théologie de l'Ancien Testament en Afrique aujourd'hui," 84–85. For examples of these kinds of studies, see David Tuesday Adamo, ed., *Biblical Interpretation in African Perspective* (Lanham, MD: Univ. Press of America, 2006); Hugh R. Page Jr., ed., *The Africana Bible: Reading Israel's Scriptures from Africa and the African Diaspora* (Minneapolis: Fortress, 2010); Esau McCaulley, *Reading while Black: African American Biblical Interpretation as an Exercise in Hope* (Downers Grove, IL: IVP Academic, 2020); Lily Fetalsana-Apura, *A Filipino Resistance Reading of Joshua 1:1–9*, International Voices in Biblical Studies 9 (Atlanta: Society of Biblical Literature, 2019); Jione Havea and Peter H. W. Lau, eds., *Reading Ruth in Asia*, International Voices in Biblical Studies 7 (Atlanta: Society of Biblical Literature, 2015); Mary F. Foskett and Jeffrey Kah-Jin Kuan, eds., *Ways of Being, Ways of Reading: Asian American Biblical Interpretation* (St. Louis: Chalice, 2006); Elsa Tamez, *When the Horizons Close: Rereading Ecclesiastes*, trans. Margaret Wilde (Maryknoll, NY: Orbis, 2000); Francisco Lozada Jr. and Fernando F. Segovia, eds., *Latino/a Biblical Hermeneutics: Problematics, Objectives, Strategies*, Semeia Studies 68 (Atlanta: Society of Biblical Literature, 2014).

19. James Spencer, "Old Testament Theology for a Multi-Ethnic Church," in Bryan C. Babcock, James Spencer, and Russell L. Meek, *Trajectories: A Gospel-Centered Introduction to Old Testament Theology* (Eugene, OR: Pickwick, 2018), 220.

There have been some encouraging signs of progress in this regard. At a practical level, some of the societies dedicated to biblical scholarship (e.g., the Society of Biblical Literature, the Institute for Biblical Research, and the Evangelical Theological Society) have sought ways to incorporate women and people of color more fully through such means as travel scholarships and events designed to cultivate connections. Similarly, publishers have sought to publish material from these scholars, both in series explicitly designed for the purpose—such as the International Voices in Biblical Studies from the Society of Biblical Literature Press—and in more general publications. In addition, some publishers are attempting to improve access to research material for majority-world scholars through such means as open access publishing, both for academic journals (such as *Biblica* and *Old Testament Essays*) and book series (including Ancient Near Eastern Monographs, International Voices in Biblical Studies, and Orbis Biblicus et Orientalis).[20] Hopefully, the coming years will see further efforts to support the work of women and people of color, particularly in the area of Old Testament theology.

Since every attempt to capture the theology of the Old Testament is partial and constrained by the perspective of the interpreter, we look forward to seeing further contributions to the field by a wide variety of scholars—female and male, Western and majority-world—using each of the approaches we have outlined and possibly some new ones. While we as readers will not always agree with the assumptions and conclusions of scholars working in this field, each Old Testament theology has something to teach us if we are open to listening. As John Goldingay observes, "Many starting points, structures, and foci can illuminate the landscape of the OT; a multiplicity of approaches will lead to a multiplicity of insights."[21]

We also expect to see more efforts to communicate Old Testament theology to an audience that is increasingly dependent on digital information. Those who see Old Testament theology as prescriptive for the church today will need to find ways to bridge the growing gap between academic study of the Old Testament and the average churchgoer. Spencer notes that for a long period of church history, most Christians were unable to read the Bible for themselves because of limited access to manuscripts and the lack of literacy in

---

20. One promising endeavor by the Society of Biblical Literature is the International Cooperation Initiative, which offers resources at a reduced rate from a variety of publishers "for persons in countries with a per capita GDP that is substantially lower than the average per capita GDP of the United States and the European Union" ("Online Books," Society of Biblical Literature, *www.sbl-site.org/publications/onlinebooks.aspx*, accessed 30 January 2020).

21. John Goldingay, *Theological Diversity and the Authority of the Old Testament* (Grand Rapids: Eerdmans, 1987), 115; see also Robert L. Foster, "The Christian Canon and the Future of Biblical Theology," *Horizons in Biblical Theology* 37 (2015): 5–6.

biblical languages. Suggesting that the church may again be moving in that direction, as both biblical literacy and deep, reflective reading practices are on the decline, he exhorts Old Testament theologians "to cultivate a viable, influential presence in the new [digital] media space while continuing to call the church back to deep reading of the Scriptures in print."[22] While organizations like the Bible Project have already begun to address this issue, we hope that the coming years will produce substantial growth in digital presentations of Old Testament theology.

INVITATION TO A JOURNEY INTO OLD TESTAMENT THEOLOGY

Having mapped out the terrain of recent approaches to Old Testament theology and briefly considered its future, we would like to conclude by issuing an invitation for you to begin your own journey up to one (or more) of the peaks in the mountain range. We have offered brief snapshots of the views from the mountain peaks, but they are no substitute for the experience of sitting atop a mountain and savoring the breathtaking vistas yourself! But which path should you take? Many of you will be reading this book as part of a class, and your professor will have already chosen an Old Testament theology for you to explore. For those of you who have the choice, we suggest that you should first determine which approach most deeply resonates with you and then select one of the paths found in this book that leads to that peak. Our online annotated bibliography can also assist you in finding a suitable path. Once you have read a work in one category, then you may want to choose something from a different category (preferably one that feels foreign to you) to provide you with a different vantage point, offering a new set of vistas.

If you are studying or teaching through an Old Testament book, then it would be more helpful to read a biblical theology of that book or a broader Old Testament theology that includes particular attention to that book. If you are interested in a specific theme in the Old Testament, then look for a biblical-theological treatment of that theme in one of the series we listed, or find an Old Testament theology that highlights that theme. Whichever path you choose, take your time and soak in the views!

As you embark on your journey, we also encourage you to think about how you can read the Old Testament theologically for yourself. An overarching question that can guide a theological reading of the Old Testament is, what

---

22. James Spencer, "Old Testament Theology and the Digital Age," in *Trajectories*, 235.

does this passage convey about God and his relationship to the world? But following the approaches we have outlined in this book, you may also want to consider some further questions.

- Where does this passage fit into the story of God's dealings with Israel and the cosmos? (See chap. 1: "Old Testament Theology Grounded in Biblical [Hi]story.")
- What can I learn about the history behind the text (especially the situation of its author or redactors) and the ancient Near Eastern context, and how might that affect theological conclusions derived from the text? (See chap. 2: "Historical-Critical Old Testament Theology.")
- What significant themes are found in this passage, and how are those themes developed throughout the Bible? (See chap. 3: "Multiplex Thematic Old Testament Theology.")
- Do I find any suggestions for a central theme of the Old Testament compelling? If so, how does this passage tie into that theme? (See chap. 4: "Old Testament Theology Focused around a Central Theme.")
- How does reading this passage in light of the larger biblical canon affect my understanding of it? In particular, how does this passage relate to the New Testament? (See chap. 5: "Canonical Old Testament Theology.")
- How might a Jewish reader understand this passage, and how might that inform or challenge a Christian interpretation? (See chap. 6: "Jewish Biblical Theology.")
- How is the theological understanding reflected in this passage challenged or qualified by other passages that suggest different views? How does my sociocultural and theological location affect my reading of the passage, and how does my engagement with the passage speak to my situation? What can I learn by reading this passage in community with other people who have different backgrounds? (See chap. 7: "Postmodern Old Testament Theology.")

In conclusion, we leave you with one final exhortation. As we noted earlier, the Jewish canon ends with the book of Chronicles,[23] which retells Israel's history from Adam to the end of the exile in order to provide hope and guidance for the postexilic community of Jews. Second Chronicles concludes with the decree of the Persian king Cyrus, who permitted any exiled Jews who

---

23. See table 5.2 on p. 102.

wished to do so to return to their land and rebuild their temple. This was their chance to reenter their promised land—their Eden—where God could dwell in their midst in his holy temple as he did before the exile. Then they could once again "go up [*'alah*] to the mountain of YHWH" to meet with him "in his holy place" (Ps. 24:3, translation ours).

The final verse of 2 Chronicles culminates with an invitation for exiled Jews to journey up to the promised land, the dwelling place of God: "Whoever is among you of all his people, may the LORD his God be with him. Let him go up [*'alah*]" (2 Chron. 36:23 ESV). These final words of the Hebrew Bible are also our words of blessing and exhortation to those among you of all God's people who hear this invitation to journey through the rugged terrain of Old Testament theology. Our hope is that you will meet with God at the top of a mountain as you experience the awe-inspiring beauty of the Old Testament in all its depth and complexity. May YHWH your God be with you on the trek, and may you go up!

SUMMARY OF APPROACHES

Approach	Common Features	Points of Tension
OT Theology Grounded in Biblical (Hi)story	1. Focus on Retelling Old Testament History 2. The Old Testament as Story 3. The Whole Bible as One Story 4. The Bible as the Story That Shapes Us	1. How the Story Is Outlined 2. Incorporation of Nonnarrative Literature 3. Role of the New Testament in Interpreting the Old
Historical-Critical OT Theology	1. Historical-Critical Reconstruction as the Foundation of Old Testament Theology 2. Primarily Descriptive	1. Old Testament Theology versus History of Israelite Religion 2. Historical-Critical Reconstructions and Degree of Historicity 3. Role of the New Testament
Multiplex Thematic OT Theology	1. Structured around Multiple Themes 2. Connection to the New Testament 3. Concern for the Church	1. Source of the Themes 2. Themes Emphasized 3. Interpretive Methods Used
OT Theology Focused around a Central Theme	1. Assumption of a Center 2. Unity of the Old and New Testaments 3. Prescriptive	1. The Identity of the Center 2. Incorporation of Nonnarrative Literature 3. Role of Historical-Critical Methods
Canonical OT Theology	1. Focus on the Final Canonical Form 2. Interpreting Texts in Light of Their Broader Old Testament Context 3. Reading the Old Testament as Christian Scripture 4. Prescriptive	1. Which Canon? 2. The Significance of the History of Interpretation 3. The Role of Historical-Critical Methods

(cont.)

Approach	Common Features	Points of Tension
Jewish Biblical Theology	1. Extent and Order of the Jewish Canon 2. Emphasis on Diversity 3. Topics of Importance for Jews	1. The Question of Its Existence 2. Role of Postbiblical Jewish Material 3. The Influence of the Holocaust on Biblical Theology
Postmodern OT Theology	1. Emphasis on Diverse Perspectives within the Old Testament 2. Reflection on the Interpreter's Context 3. Embrace of Subjective Experience 4. Attentiveness to Interpretive Issues and Power Dynamics	1. Extent to Which the Bible Is Critiqued or Deconstructed 2. Divergent Interpretive Methods and Conclusions 3. Criteria for Evaluating the Legitimacy of Theological Conclusions

SUBJECT INDEX

Aaron, 31, 41, 105

Abihu, 105

Abraham (Abram), 16–17, 19, 23, 25, 30, 70, 94, 109, 126, 132

Absalom, 17

Adam, 17, 24, 29–30, 65, 71, 97, 158

Ahab, 41

allegory, 49, 84, 116

ancient Near East
  legal collections of, 70–71
  religion of, 32, 50, 68–69, 71–72, 96
  role in Old Testament theology, 32, 40–41, 51, 68–69, 122, 158

angel, 18, 23, 65–66, 130

anger (divine), 57, 96, 123–26, 130

anti-Semitism, 40, 48, 76, 96, 120–21, 124

antisupernaturalism, 35–36, 108. *See also* miracles

Apocrypha, 77, 101–2

archaeology, 6–7, 15–16, 33, 39, 43, 46

ark of the covenant, 85

Assyria, 37, 51

atonement, 19, 59

authority
  of the Bible, 37–38, 59, 64, 77, 91, 93, 100–101, 108, 112, 138–39, 144, 155
  of postbiblical material, 104–6, 122–23
  rejection of (*see* critique of the Bible)
  See also church

authors (biblical)
  divine, 18, 29, 126
  New Testament, 97, 111
  Old Testament, 5, 17–18, 29, 64, 95, 105, 113, 120, 126, 135, 140, 158
  See also composition of the Old Testament; redactors

Baal, 17. *See also* ancient Near East: religion of

Babylon, 22–23, 37, 64, 72. *See also* exile, Babylonian

Bathsheba, 17

biblical theology movement, 6–7

blessing, 26–27, 31, 57–58, 70, 84, 118–19

Cain, 17, 57

Canaan, 45–46, 88, 95, 116–17, 139. *See also* conquest

canon
  canonical Old Testament Theology, 46, 55, 68, 80–81, 91–110, 128, 141
  Catholic (*see* Apocrypha)
  effect on biblical theology, 102, 105–6, 112–13, 134, 158
  Jewish (Hebrew) canon, 102–4, 112–13, 158
  Protestant (Greek) canon, 102–3, 112

Catholic, Roman, 102, 105, 134, 151. *See also* Apocrypha

center of Old Testament theology
  rejection of, 6, 25, 56–58, 114–15
  use of, 3, 29, 73–88, 98, 117, 135, 140, 153, 158

Christ. *See* Jesus; Messiah

church
  in biblical narrative, 26
  canon of (*see* canon)
  contemporary, 15, 22, 155
  early, 4, 104, 110, 126 (*see also* historical-cultural background: of interpretation)
  role of, 25, 30
  theology for, 4–5, 13, 16, 60–62, 99–101, 104, 116, 156–57
  theology of, 2, 4, 21, 95, 105–6, 116, 123, 144

church (cont.)
  use of the Old Testament in, 1, 21, 49
    (*see also* prescriptive readings)
compassion, 57, 62, 87, 96
composition of the Old Testament
  Daniel, 36
  Isaiah, 36, 48–49, 94–95
  Torah, 35–36, 44–47, 50, 69–70, 86, 93,
    106–7, 126
conquest (of Canaan), 23, 116–17, 139. *See
  also* Canaan
context of the interpreter, 3, 5, 116–19,
  131–32, 158
Copenhagen school, 41, 47
covenant
  Abrahamic, 24, 26, 57, 70, 78–79, 132
  Davidic, 24, 26, 67, 78–80, 95, 113–14,
    126–27
  of grace, 24
  Mosaic, xii, 23–27, 70–72, 78–79, 81,
    84–85, 87, 114, 126–27
  new, 24, 26, 78, 97
  Noahic, 19, 24, 26, 78
  as theme, 6, 24–27, 59, 67, 76, 78–79,
    87, 105
  of works, 24
creation, care for, 22, 58, 100
cosmos, 61, 99, 126, 141, 143
  in ancient Near East, 69
  new, 19, 23–26, 82
  original, 20, 30–32, 57–58, 65–66, 69,
    84, 88, 97, 102, 112
  restoration of, 24, 32, 59, 94, 127, 147
  as stage in biblical story, 23, 25–26, 34,
    67, 75
  theology of, 28, 57–59, 65–67, 69,
    77–78, 81, 83–84, 94, 97–98, 100,
    115, 119, 126, 130, 140
criticism
  cognitive environment, 68–69
  historical (*see* historical criticism)
  redaction, xi, 45–46, 108
  source, xi, 2, 44–45, 86, 114
  tradition-historical, 45
critique of the Bible, 38–39, 123–26,
  138–41
curse, 27, 57–58, 84

David, 17, 19, 27, 46, 80, 94–95, 104, 113
day of YHWH, 83
death-of-God theology, 124
Deborah, 137
descriptive readings, 3, 37–44, 77, 99, 122,
  134
Deuteronomist source, 44, 69
Deuteronomistic history, 79. *See also*
  historical books
dialogical biblical theology, 113–14, 116, 123
diversity, 3, 5, 15, 55, 65–67, 75, 81,
  83–84, 113–14, 120–21, 129–32, 158
divine name. *See* name

economics, 61, 135–36, 138, 141–42, 144
Eden, 17, 24, 28, 30, 32, 57, 82, 88, 94,
  140, 159
Egypt
  God's defeat of, 31–32, 83, 88, 107
  as a metaphor, 109, 146
  as an oppressive empire, 3, 59, 71–72,
    83, 88, 107, 138, 140, 142, 146
  See also exodus
election, 30, 60, 65–67, 77, 79, 81
Elijah, 17–18
Elisha, 18
Elohist source, 44, 69–70
eschatology, 23, 59, 116
Esther (person), 126
ethics, 38, 40, 67, 77, 83, 87, 100, 116, 119–20,
  139, 144
Eve, 17, 24, 29–30, 71
event. *See* revelation: as event
evil (problem of), 61–63, 123–26
exegesis, 2, 48, 58, 60–61, 104–6, 121, 131
exile
  Babylonian, 25, 34, 36, 41, 59, 109, 125,
    142
  See also sin-exile-restoration pattern
exodus
  of church, 22
  effect on biblical theology, 78–79, 85,
    117, 125, 134
  historicity of, 45, 47, 51, 86, 106–7, 146
  as Israel's foundational event, 31, 50–51,
    107, 109
  second, 109–10

test cases, 9, 31–32, 50–51, 70–72,
    86–88, 109–10, 126–27, 145–47
    as type, 6, 31, 71, 109–10
    See also Egypt; salvation
Ezekiel (prophet), 64

faith
    rule of, 4, 105
    as theme, 16, 30, 46, 51, 62–63, 76–77,
        81–82, 117, 129–30, 134, 145
faithfulness (divine), 57, 67, 125–26, 130
fall, 23–26, 29, 63, 65, 75
fear of YHWH, 28, 70, 83
feminist biblical theology, 132–34,
    136–40, 144–45, 154–56
forgiveness, 62, 96
free will, 17. *See also* responsibility

Germany, Nazi, 6, 48, 115–16, 143
glory (divine), xii, 46, 58, 68, 79–80,
    83–85, 87–88, 110, 130
gods. *See* ancient Near East: religion of;
    angel; idolatry
golden calf, 41, 88
grace, 24, 30, 57, 67, 78, 96, 115
guidance, 22, 109

Habakkuk (prophet), 23
Hannah, 104
Hebrew
    Adonai, 2
    'alah, 159
    'almah, 98
    arm, word for, 133
    Elohim, 44
    history of language, 35
    mal'ak, 18,
    nephesh, 68
    Shema, 95
    tannin, 31
    Torah, 66 (*see also* Torah)
    Yahweh/YHWH, 2, 44
Hexateuch, 44–46, 117
Hezekiah, 98
historical books, 27, 103, 107. *See also*
    Deuteronomistic history

historical criticism
    centrality of, 34–37
    description of, 33–37, 44–47
    effect on biblical theology, 5, 33–51, 117,
        122
    rejection of, 15–16, 86, 107–9
    sources of (*see* Yahwist source; Elohist
        source; Deuteronomist source; Priestly
        source)
    use of, 3, 33–51, 69–70, 85–86, 91,
        106–7, 117
    See also criticism
historical-cultural background, 15, 50–51,
    103, 128, 158
    of biblical theology, 4–7, 153
    of interpretation, 42–43, 104–6,
        113–14, 121–23, 126, 136
    of Israelite religion, 38–43, 50–51, 121
    redemptive, 14, 16, 20, 22–24, 48, 102
    See also ancient Near East; archaeology
historicity, 7, 15–16, 33–37, 41, 44–47, 72,
    85–86, 108
history
    effect on Old Testament theology,
        13–51, 112–13 (*see also* narrative)
    See also revelation
holiness
    of God, 80–81, 94, 105
    of Israel, 26, 30, 70, 87, 93–95, 105
    of Scripture, 91, 121
    of tabernacle/temple, 59, 159
holocaust (Shoah), 96, 123–26, 143
honor/shame, 132, 146
hope, 62, 66, 102, 104, 135, 138, 140

ideology. *See* interpretive interests
idolatry, 58, 61, 71, 83, 101, 114, 130,
    140, 143. *See also* ancient Near East:
    religion of
image of God, 22, 59, 61, 83, 119
imperialism, 50–51, 135
interpretive interests, 136–38
intertextuality, 4, 94–96, 113, 125. *See also*
    New Testament; historical-cultural
    background: of interpretation
Isaiah (prophet), 36, 49, 98, 125

Jacob, 94, 109
Jerusalem
    as capital city, 17, 37, 49, 60, 94, 133
    destruction of, 37, 85, 125, 134
    God's presence in, 30, 82, 84
    modern-day, xii, 118
    New, 30, 109
    tradition, 114, 126
Jesus
    as center of the Bible, 19, 29, 82, 96, 98,
        120, 153
    coming of, 6, 25–26, 28–29
    fulfillment of the Old Testament in, 4,
        19–20, 23–24, 30, 48, 67, 98, 109–10,
        118, 127, 132, 138, 151
    identity of, 80, 123
    reading the Old Testament backward in
        light of, 29–30, 58–59, 96–99
    words of, 60–61, 106
    work of, 19–20, 29–31, 59, 62, 76, 83,
        99, 102, 118
    See also canon; New Testament
Jewish biblical theology, xi, 3, 111–27, 141,
    150, 158
Jezebel, 17, 41
Job (person), 58, 62, 135, 140, 143
John the Baptist, 110
Joseph, 94
Joshua, 47, 117
Josiah, 22, 35–36
jubilee, 83, 141–42
judges, 25, 36, 137–38
judgment
    final, 22, 59–60
    of individuals, 38, 79–80, 84–85, 96,
        104–5
    of Israel, 22, 88, 109, 124–26
    of nations, 32, 64, 72, 79–80, 83, 87–88
    as theme, 67
justice
    of God, 32, 57, 80, 88, 91, 146
    lack of, 22–23, 32, 117–19, 124–26, 130,
        135, 138–43
    retributive, 135
    social, 32, 51, 57, 62, 71, 87, 119, 135,
        137, 140, 142, 145–47

king
    foreign, 31, 32, 37, 51, 70, 158
    God as, 21–22, 24–26, 28, 31–32, 66,
        124, 132
    humanity as, 22, 69
    Israel's, 17, 23, 27, 31, 35, 66, 78, 80, 95,
        98, 104, 138
    See also Messiah; kingdom: of God
kingdom
    of Freedom, 142, 146
    of God as a theme, 24–25, 30, 67,
        78–80, 82, 84, 87, 132, 135, 153–54
    of God versus human kingdoms, 18, 26,
        31, 80
    Northern, 18, 37, 44, 114
    of priests, 31, 70, 87
    Southern, 44, 114

lament, 125, 130
land, promised, 22, 25–26, 32, 45, 70, 80,
    87, 113, 115–19, 123, 139, 142, 159.
    See also jubilee; return from exile
law. See Torah
liberation theology, 118, 124, 137–38,
    141–42, 146–47
Lot, 17, 95
love
    divine, 22, 26, 31, 57, 68, 71, 79, 96,
        124–26, 143
    human, 22, 95, 100–101, 145

Manasseh, 125
manna, 110
map, 7–10, 149, 157
marriage, 30, 71, 80
mercy, 80, 88, 100, 105, 124–26
Messiah, 29, 68, 81, 98, 105, 126, 138. See
    also Jesus; New Testament
metanarrative, 20–21, 24, 63, 75, 139–40
metaphor (divine), 80, 100, 124, 130, 132,
    137, 145–46
methods of interpretation, 2–3, 68–70, 91,
    111, 141–43, 145, 153, 155. See also
    criticism; historical criticism
midrash, 121–23
minority interpretation, 8, 83, 133–38,
    154–56

miracles, 18, 20, 30, 35, 147. *See also* antisupernaturalism

Mishna, 121

mission, 25, 60, 68, 70, 77, 83, 87, 135, 146

monotheism, 49, 65, 66, 95

Moses
authorship by, 35
in cover image, xi–xii, 9
deliverance through, 31–32, 51, 87, 110
historicity of, 72, 85–86
life of, 51, 114, 123
as prophet, 117
relationship with God, 88, 125–26
revelation through, 23, 126
as type, 6, 110
See also Torah

multiplex thematic Old Testament theology, 26, 55–73, 82, 158

Nadab, 105

name (divine), 2, 23, 44, 49–50, 58, 64–66, 80, 87–88, 125, 130, 145

narrative
artistry, 17
cultural, 20, 128
genre, 7, 9, 27, 35, 72, 74, 83–84, 94, 108 (*see also* historical books)
readings, 13–32, 68, 146
structure of the Bible, 18–19, 23–31, 68, 75, 80, 82, 130–32, 151, 158
theology, 16, 141
See also revelation: as story

nations
relationship to God, 57, 64, 68, 72, 81, 95, 119, 145
relationship to Israel, 6–7, 65–66, 68, 70, 94, 118–19, 145–46
theology of, 22–23, 61, 66, 130
See also Assyria; Babylon; Egypt; Persia; Tyre

Nazi Germany, 6, 48, 115–16, 143

new creation. *See* creation

New Testament
in biblical theology, 1, 8, 19, 23, 25–26
connections with the Old Testament, 28, 30, 43, 48–49, 58–60, 76, 96, 109–10, 112, 116, 120, 153, 158

discontinuity with the Old Testament, 59–60, 115
as fulfillment of the Old Testament, 4, 28, 97
independence of the Old Testament from, 3, 28, 39, 42, 49–50, 59–60, 76–77, 97, 112–13, 120
interpreting the Old Testament in light of, 28–30, 97–99, 123, 127
Old Testament as foundation for, 4, 19
rejection of, 112
unity with the Old Testament, 3, 6, 18–20, 41–42, 58–59, 74, 76, 80, 96–99, 120, 151
witness of, 101, 125, 139
See also canon; Jesus

Noah, 17, 19–20, 24, 26, 78

offspring, 29, 70

original sin. *See* sin

Palestinians, 117–19

Passover, 19, 72, 107, 109

patriarchs, 16, 22, 25, 45, 47, 69–70, 78, 85, 87, 109. *See also* Abraham; Jacob

peace, 118, 141

Pentateuch, 2, 35, 44, 69, 79, 84–85, 93, 102–3, 107, 116–17, 126, 138

Persia, 37, 41, 158

Pharaoh
hardening of heart, 17, 72
as oppressive ruler, 22, 31–32, 51, 107, 109, 145, 147
See also Egypt

plagues, 17, 31–32, 71

popular religion. *See* historical-cultural background: of Israelite religion

postbiblical interpretation. *See* historical-cultural background: of interpretation

postmodernism, 20–21, 105, 128–47

praise. *See* worship

prayer, 58, 62, 67, 110, 116, 124

prescriptive readings, 3, 20–23, 38–39, 41–42, 44, 60–62, 77–78, 99–101, 156. *See also* authority; canon; New Testament

presence (divine)
experience of, 15, 58, 66, 81–82, 94, 143
lack of, 17, 62, 82, 123–26, 134, 140

presence (divine) (cont.)
  reflection of, 70
  as theme, 26, 30, 56, 84, 87–88
  See also sanctuary
Priestly source, 44, 47, 69–70, 115
priests
  in Israel, 6, 57–59, 78, 81, 84, 93, 115
  kingdom of, 31, 70, 87
promise
  Abrahamic, 25–26, 57, 70, 87
  Davidic, 114
  end-time restoration, 58
  messianic, 29, 98, 138
  Mosaic, 87
  as theme, 10, 48, 62, 67, 70, 76, 79,
    81–84, 97, 117, 127, 140
  See also land, promised
promised land. *See* land, promised
prophecy
  in biblical story, 25–26
  ex eventu, 36
  as revelation, 23, 67, 102, 109
prophet, 23, 30, 36, 49, 78, 112, 117, 135
prophetic books, 27, 36, 68, 79, 81, 83–84,
    94, 102–3, 107
prophetic messages, 18, 20, 22, 57–58, 64,
    74, 98, 116, 130, 138, 146
Protestant, 101–4, 112, 123, 134
Protoevangelium, 29
psalms (genre), 27, 116, 125

rabbinic interpretation. *See* historical-
    cultural background: of interpretation
Rachel, 137
reception history. *See* historical-cultural
    background: of interpretation
redaction criticism. *See* criticism
redactors, 18, 44–45, 108–9, 158
redemption. *See* salvation
redemptive history. *See* history
repentance, 64, 125
responsibility (human), 22, 115, 125–26,
    132, 145
return from exile, 25, 27, 94, 109, 113, 142,
    158–59
revelation
  as event, 13, 16

Mosaic, 23, 32, 50, 67, 85, 87–88, 107,
    117, 126
  redemptive, 22–23, 29, 85
  as story, 13, 16–18
  as theme, 23, 26, 64–67, 84, 126
  See also authority; history
righteousness, 29, 57, 80, 102, 124–26, 146

Sabbath, 32, 61, 71, 82, 85, 110, 115
sacrifice, 19, 26, 57, 59
salvation
  from covenant disorder, 59
  in the exodus, 22, 59, 86–88, 145
  exodus as paradigm for, 31, 50–51,
    71–72, 87, 109, 124, 138, 140, 146–47
  by humans, 63, 115, 145
  of individuals, 18, 20, 57, 62, 85, 109,
    125, 132
  of Israel, 16, 22, 37, 59, 88, 127, 133
  through Jesus, 24, 29, 59, 71, 76, 87, 99,
    109–10, 138
  restoration of creation (*see* creation)
  as stage in biblical story, 23–26, 75
  as theme, 24, 57, 58–59, 63, 67, 80,
    82–84, 94–95
  See also historical-cultural background:
    redemptive; sin-exile-restoration
    pattern
sanctuary
  as God's dwelling place, 30–32, 60,
    80–82, 88, 159
  land of Israel as, 32, 70–71
  Old Testament theology as, 9
  tabernacle, 30, 32, 59, 88, 94, 110, 116, 137
  temple, 30–31, 35, 60, 66, 78, 85, 113,
    115–16, 159
Sarah, 94, 109
Satan, 26, 28–29, 60, 97–98, 109, 140
Saul, 17
sensus plenior, 29
serpent. *See* snake
servant (in Isaiah), 19–20, 68, 95
sexuality, 85, 100, 141
sin
  against God, 25, 30, 57–58, 71, 88, 109, 124
  original, 60, 65
  against others, 57

as theme, 59, 61, 66, 105, 125
See also atonement; forgiveness;
judgment
sin-exile-restoration pattern, 26–27, 31
Sinai
Israel at, 45, 70, 87–88
Moses on, xi, 9
revelation at, 9, 28, 50, 66–67, 71, 88,
107–8, 126, 143, 146
tradition, 86, 116
See also covenant: Mosaic; Torah
slaves
in Egypt, 31–32, 59, 70–72, 83, 138,
140, 147
freedom for, 60–61, 138, 141–42
of gods, 69, 71
snake, 28–29, 31, 97
sociology, 39, 119
Solomon, 23, 27, 85
sovereignty (divine)
over Egypt, 17, 31–32, 51, 71, 107
as theme, 17, 64, 108, 123–26, 130, 140, 147
Spirit of God, 18, 30, 60, 68, 99, 119
story. *See* revelation: as story; narrative
subjective experience, 116–19, 133–35, 145
suffering, 19, 59, 61–63, 66, 98, 102,
123–26, 133, 135, 140, 143, 145
systematic theology, 2, 5, 14–15, 23, 28,
36, 38, 41, 56, 63–64, 97, 105–6, 119

tabernacle. *See* sanctuary
Talmud, 105, 121–22
Tanak, 102–3, 109, 112–13, 117, 122
Targum, 105
temple. *See* sanctuary
theological interpretation of Scripture, 2,
91–92, 98, 101, 105
theophany, xii, 23, 28, 42, 87, 101, 107,
140, 154
Torah
book of the law, 35

Christian understanding of, 115, 126–27
as foundation for the Old Testament,
78–79, 107
genre, 28, 94, 106–9, 113–14, 116, 126,
134, 141–42
Jewish understanding of, 115–16, 121,
126
life generated by, 32, 71, 87, 107, 113,
119, 142, 146
relationship to covenant, 27, 59, 66,
70–71, 78–79, 87, 114
as theme, 24, 66–67, 70, 94–95, 115–16,
132
See also Pentateuch; revelation: Mosaic
tower of Babel, 17, 25
Trinity, 30, 59, 64, 95
typology, 6, 31, 49, 71, 116
Tyre, 64

unity of the Old Testament, 3, 18, 73–75,
78, 114

violence, 32, 38, 95, 139–40, 117, 139–40,
144, 146

wilderness wanderings, 23, 25, 110, 125,
134, 147
wisdom
biblical, 61, 66, 81, 84–85, 100, 102,
109–10, 119, 152
books, 27–28, 83–85, 135
as revelation, 67, 84, 117
worship, xi, 35, 45, 57–58, 61–62, 66,
70–71, 77, 88, 100, 109, 134. *See also*
prayer

Yahwist source, 44, 46–47, 69–70, 86, 93

Zion. *See* Jerusalem
Zionism, 117–18
Zipporah, 137

AUTHOR INDEX

Adamo, David Tuesday, 155
Albertz, Rainer, 34, 38, 40, 43, 50–51
Albright, William, 6
Alexander, T. Desmond, 14, 21–23, 26, 30–31, 151
Allen, Leslie C., 55–58, 61, 65–67, 71–72
Anderson, Bernhard W., 73, 76–77, 79
Anderson, Gary A., 92, 102, 105–6, 110
Andiñach, Pablo R., 129, 131, 133–34, 139
Ateek, Naim Stifan, 117–18
Babcock, Bryan C., 55–56, 65–66, 155
Ballard, H. Wayne, 55, 65–68, 71
Barr, James, 7, 34, 39, 41–42, 49, 107–8, 121, 151, 153
Bartholomew, Craig G., 14, 16, 21, 24–28, 32
Barton, John, 34, 37–38, 42, 46
Bauks, Michaela, 55, 60, 64–67, 69, 72
Beale, G. K., 4
Beckwith, Roger, 102
Ben Zvi, Ehud, 111, 120–21
Berding, Kenneth, 4
Berthelot, Katell, 116
Birch, Bruce C., 152
Bird, Phyllis A., 7, 134, 136, 144, 154–55
Block, Daniel I., xii, 115
Blumenthal, David R., 124
Boda, Mark J., 2–3, 92–93, 96, 99–100, 103, 106
Boer, Dick, 129, 137–38, 142, 146
Bray, Gerald, 4
Brendsel, Daniel J., 4
Brettler, Marc Zvi, 113
Brown, Jeannine K., 15, 27
Brueggemann, Walter, 5, 116, 120, 129–30, 136, 139–40, 142–44, 146–47, 152
Carr, David M., 80, 83

Carson, D. A., 4, 151–52
Chester, Tim, 14, 18, 25, 29, 32
Childs, Brevard S., 7, 91–94, 96–104, 106–8, 120
Chisholm, Robert B., Jr., 19–20, 28
Choi, Agnes, 154
Claassens, L. Juliana M., 130, 132
Cline, Robert, 14–15, 18–19, 23, 26–27
Collins, John J., 34, 37, 42, 74
David, Joseph E., 116
Day, Linda, 155
Dempster, Stephen G., 73, 80, 84, 88, 113
Dozeman, Thomas B., 47
Dumbrell, William J., 73, 78, 87
Duvall, J. Scott, 14, 73, 75–76, 82, 86, 88
Eichrodt, Walther, 5–6, 73–74, 76, 78, 83–85, 87, 120, 122
Eissfeldt, Otto, 5
Elliott, Mark W., 153
Ellis, Peter F., 46
Elwell, Walter A., 151
Emerson, Matthew Y., 14, 18, 23, 26
Fackenheim, Emil L., 125
Feldmeier, Reinhard, 55, 57–58, 60, 63, 65–67, 69, 71
Fetalsana-Apura, Lily, 155
Fischer, Georg, 46
Fischer, Irmtraud, 129, 136–37, 140
Fishbane, Michael, 4, 113, 119
Foskett, Mary F., 155
Foster, Robert L., 156
Fowl, Stephen E., 91
Frankel, David, 119
Frei, Hans W., 16
Fretheim, Terence E., 152
Frymer-Kensky, Tikva, 122–23
Gabler, Johann P., 5

Gaventa, Beverly Roberts, 15
Gentry, Peter J., 14–15, 17, 24, 26–27
Gerstenberger, Erhard, 34, 37–38, 40, 47, 49, 51, 120
Gertz, Jan Christian, 47
Gese, Hartmut, 34, 48–49
Gesundheit, Shimon, 111, 117, 122
Gignilliat, Mark S., 33
Goheen, Michael W., 14, 16, 21, 24–28, 32
Goldberg, Michael, 21
Goldingay, John, 14–17, 19, 21–22, 25–28, 31–32, 55, 58, 61, 64–68, 71, 156
Goldsworthy, Graeme, 14, 18, 22–24, 27, 29–30, 151
Goshen-Gottstein, M. H., 111, 113, 116–18, 122
Greenberg, Moshe, 117
Greenstein, Edward, 106
Grindheim, Sigurd, 92, 96, 98, 106
Grisanti, Michael A., 35
Gunneweg, Antonius H. J., 34, 43, 49
Hafemann, Scott J., 55, 58, 63, 65–66, 71, 151, 153
Hamilton, James M., Jr., 73, 75–77, 83–88
Hamilton, Mark W., 152
Hasel, Gerhard F., xi, 4, 7, 10, 55–56, 65, 153
Havea, Jione, 155
Hayes, John H., 4
Hays, J. Daniel, 14, 73, 75–76, 82, 86, 88
Heffelfinger, Katie M., 133, 139
Herrmann, Wolframm, 34, 43, 49, 51
Hess, Richard S., 152
Hirshman, Marc, 116
House, H. Wayne, 117
House, Paul R., 92–95, 100–101, 103, 106, 108, 151
Janowski, Bernd, 82
Jeon, Jeong Koo, 14–15, 24, 26–27, 29–30
Jeremias, Jörg, 34, 37, 43, 49, 51
Jesurathnam, Kondasingu, 129, 132–33, 135, 142, 145
Justin Martyr, 105
Kaiser, Otto, 73, 77–79, 84, 86
Kaiser, Walter C., Jr., 10, 73, 76, 82–84, 86–87
Kalimi, Isaac, 40, 112, 115, 119, 121, 124

Kasher, Asa, 114, 123
Katho, Bungishabaku, 83, 154–55
Keel, Othmar, 38, 43
Kelle, Brad E., 47
Kessler, John, 74, 77, 81, 84
Keyser, B. Donald, 55, 65–68, 71
Kim, Wonil, 141
Kinlaw, Dennis F., 56, 62, 65–66
Klink, Edward W. III, 2, 8, 10, 13, 33, 92, 153
Knauf, Ernst Axel, 39
Knierim, Rolf P., 74–76, 80
Köhler, Ludwig, 56, 60, 62–63, 65–69
Kuan, Jeffrey Kah-Jin, 155
Lapsley, Jacqueline E., 129–33, 154–55
Lau, Peter H. W., 155
Lawrence, Michael, 14, 19, 21, 26
Lemche, Niels Peter, 34, 41, 47
Léon-Dufour, Xavier, 151
Levenson, Jon D., 112, 114, 120–21, 124, 126–27
Levinson, Bernard M., 48, 116
Lévi-Strauss, Claude, 147
Linafelt, Tod, 125
Lockett, Darian R., xii, 2, 8, 10, 13, 33, 92, 153
Loden, Lisa, 118
Long, Burke O., 130
Longgar, William Kenny, 135
Lozado, Francisco, Jr., 155
Lunde, Jonathan, 4
Lyotard, Jean-François, 20
Mandolfo, Carleen, 143
Martens, Elmer A., 74, 80, 87
Masalha, Nur, 139
McCaulley, Esau, 155
McDermott, Gerald R., 117
McEntire, Mark, 129–31, 133, 143, 146
Mead, James K., 4–5, 10, 153
Meek, Russell L., 55–56, 59, 62, 65–67
Merrill, Eugene H., 74, 79, 84
Moberly, R. W. L., 92, 95, 98, 101, 104, 110
Monmonier, Mark, 9
Moore, Megan Bishop, 47
Munayer, Salim J., 118
Murphy, Roland E., 34–35, 41
Newsom, Carol A., 155

Niehaus, Jeffrey J., 14–15, 17–18, 24, 26–27, 30
O'Brien, Julia M., 131, 133, 142
O'Connor, Kathleen M., 134, 139
Ollenburger, Ben C., 4, 8, 153
Olson, Dennis T., 130
Oswalt, John N., 56, 62, 65–66
Ouro, Roberto 80–81
Page, Hugh R., Jr., 155
Pate, C. Marvin, 14, 17, 26–27, 31
Perdue, Leo G., 7, 16, 39, 111, 121, 124, 129, 141, 143–45
Petersen, David L., 152
Pressler, Carolyn, 155
Preuss, Horst Dietrich, 74, 76–77, 81, 86–87
Provan, Iain, 56, 61–63, 65–66
Prussner, Frederick C., 4
Pseudo-Dionysius, 106
Pury, Albert de, 39
Rad, Gerhard von, 5–6, 34, 36, 44–46, 48–50, 85, 107, 115–16, 120, 122
Raheb, Mitri, 118
Rashbam, 105
Rashi, 105
Ratheiser, Gershom M. H., 4, 112, 116, 120
Rendtorff, Rolf, 92, 96, 99, 103–4, 107, 109, 113
Reventlow, Henning Graf, 10
Richards, E. Randolph, 14
Richter, Sandra, 14, 19–21, 24, 26, 27, 31
Ricoeur, Paul, 131, 145
Ringe, Sharon H., 155
Roark, Nick, 14–15, 18–19, 23, 26–27
Roberts, Vaughn, 14–15, 19, 22, 25, 27, 32
Robinson, H. Wheeler, 154
Rogerson, John W., 129, 140–43, 147
Rom-Shiloni, Dalit, 112, 122
Rosner, Brian S., 151
Routledge, Robin, 56–57, 60, 64–68, 70–71
Rubenstein, Richard L., 124
Sailhamer, John H., 92, 94, 96, 99, 103–4, 108–9, 113
Sanders, James A., 91
Satyavani, Puttagunta, 154
Schaper, Joachim, 43
Schmid, Konrad, 34, 37–39, 41, 47, 49, 51
Schreiner, Thomas R., 74–75, 79–80
Schultz, Richard, xii, 99, 108

Schwendemann, Wilhelm, 143
Scobie, Charles H. H., 92, 94, 97–100, 103–4, 108, 110
Segovia, Fernando F., 155
Seitz, Christopher R., 92–94, 104, 107
Shimon, Zvi, 115
Smend, Rudolf, 80
Smith, Andrea, 139
Smith, James K. A., 20
Smith, Ralph L., 56, 59, 63, 65–68
Sommer, Benjamin D., 2, 42, 112–16, 120–21, 123, 126
Soulen, R. Kendall, 99
Spencer, James, 55–56, 58, 65–66, 71–72, 155–57
Spieckermann, Hermann, 55, 57–58, 60, 63, 65–67, 69, 71
Stalder, Will, 118
Steuernagel, Valdir, 135
Stewart, Anne W., 137
Strawn, Brent A., 41
Sundermeier, Theo, 43
Sweeney, Marvin A., 103, 112–13, 115, 120, 123–26
Tamez, Elsa, 155
Taylor, Marion Ann, 154
Terrien, Samuel, 74, 76, 82, 84–85, 87
Thompson, Thomas L., 40–41
Treier, Daniel J., 91, 105
Trible, Phyllis, 129, 136, 138, 144–45, 154
Tsevat, Matitiahu, 112, 121
Tucker, W. Dennis Jr., 14
Tull, Patricia K., 129, 131–33, 155
Vang, Preben, 14,
VanGemeren, Willem A., 152
Vanhoozer, Kevin J., 91, 105
Van Pelt, Miles V., 153
Vos, Geerhardus, 14–16, 23, 26–27
Vriezen, Th. C., 74, 80, 84
Wacker, Marie-Theres, 137
Walsh, Carey, 129–30, 134, 140, 143, 153
Waltke, Bruce K., 80, 92, 95, 101, 106, 108–9, 116
Walton, John H., 56, 59, 64–71, 82
Warrior, Robert Allen, 139
Watson, Francis, 92, 98–99, 105, 107–8
Wellhausen, Julius, 44, 47, 85, 107, 115

Wellum, Stephen J., 14–15, 17, 24, 26–27
Williams, Michael, 14–16, 18, 23–24,
    26–27, 29–31
Witherington, Ben, III, 92–93, 97,
    100–101, 106
Witte, Markus, 47
Wittenberg, Gunther H., 132–33, 135, 145
Wright, Christopher J. H., 9–10, 74,
    76–77, 83, 87, 116

Wright, G. Ernest, 7, 13–17, 19, 25
Wright, N. T., 21
Wu, Jackson, 129, 132, 138–39, 145
Youngblood, Ronald, 56, 61, 65–67, 71
Yu, Charles, 80, 92, 95, 101, 106, 108–9,
    116
Zevit, Ziony, 111–12, 121, 124
Zimmerli, Walther, 56, 60, 64–67, 69–70
Zuck, Roy B., 14, 19, 28

SCRIPTURE INDEX

Genesis

book of 17, 27, 44, 47,
51, 69–70, 97,
102–3, 117, 139
1. . . . . 29–30, 69
1–3. . . . . 17, 24, 30
1:2 30
1:21 28
1:22 57
1:26 22
1:26–28 . . . . 58, 79
1:28 . . . . 31, 57, 67
2. . . . . 30, 130
2:3 57
3. . . . . 64, 98, 130
3–11. 65
3:1 28
3:8 57
3:14–19 57
3:15 . . . . 24, 29
3:17 57
4:11–16 57
4:11 57
5. 17
6–7 130
6–9 146
8–9 131
11. 17
12. 17
12:1–9 95
12:2 70
12:3 57
12:10–20 109
13. 62
14:14 35
17:7–8 78
17:8 70
19. . . . . 95, 146

Exodus

book of . . . . . .xii, 9, 22, 31,
50–51, 70–71, 83,
86–88, 102–3, 106,
109, 126, 145
1–15. 126
2:1–10 51
2:16 137
3. . . . . 50, 87–88
4:21 72
4:22–23 . . . . 32, 145
4:24–26 146
5:22–6:8 . . . . 80, 87
6. 87
6:7 70
8:15, 32 72
9:12 72
10:1 72
14:16 32
15. 109
15:12 32
15:17 32
16. 110
16–17. 147
16:4 110
17:1–7 110
19. 87
19–24. 70
19–40 . . . . 87, 126
19:5–6 95
19:6 . . . . 70, 87
19:23 146
20–23 87
29:6 137
31–32. 109
32:22–32 146
39. 94

Exodus

20:2 . . . . 72, 138
20:5 105
20:5–6 96
20:8 85
20:24 58
22:25–27 62
32–34 88
32. 88
34:6 57
34:6–7 . . . . 4, 88, 96
34:10–35 88
38:8 137

Leviticus

book of 93–94, 102–3
10:1–3 105
25. 141
26:12 78–79

Numbers

book of. 102–3
4:20 110
6:22–27 58
11:10 57
12:1–15 94
14:18 96

Deuteronomy

book of. . . . 27, 35–36, 44,
79, 102–3, 115, 153
3:11 35
6:4 95–96
6:13–15 57
7:9–10 105
8:2–5 110
8:3 95
13. 38
15. 61

26:5–9 . . . . 45, 50
30:15 62
32:4 57
34 35
34:8 117
34:9–12 . . . . 108, 117

Joshua
book of 44, 46,
102–3, 117
1:1 117
1:1–9 108
1:8 117
24:2–13 . . . . 47, 50
24:14 71

Judges
book of 36, 102–4
4:4–5 137
18 35
19 95
20–21 95

Ruth
book of 102–4
3:11 104

1 Samuel
book of 102–4
2:22 137
15:11 57
16:1–13 46

2 Samuel
book of 102–3
7:7–17 95
11:4 94
15:25 110
16 17

1 Kings
book of . . 18, 36, 79, 102–3
8:23 96
19:2 18
19:11–12 61

2 Kings
book of 18, 36, 47, 79,
102–3

2:9 18
22:8 35
24:3 125

1 Chronicles
book of 79, 102–3, 112, 158
23:13 58

2 Chronicles
book of . . 102–3, 112, 158
30:9 96
33 125
36:23 159

Ezra
book of . . . 79, 102–3, 131
1 109

Nehemiah
book of . . . 79, 102–3, 131
1:5 57
9:17 96
9:32 96

Esther
book of . . . 27, 102–3, 131

Job
book of 84, 102–3, 125,
140, 142
1:10 58
1:21 58
38:11 20
38–41 . . . . 140, 143

Psalms
book of . . . 1, 27–28, 57, 65,
84, 102–3, 107,
113, 116
1 . . . . 108, 116
7:1 62
8 98–99
8:6 99
16:5 62
24:3 159
24:5 57
37:7, 34 62
46 60

48 60
69:1–4 62
74:2 50
74:13 31
78 109
78:21 57
86:15 96
103:8 96
104:1–2 xii
105 109
106 109
111:4 96
115:3–8 58
115:12–18 58
135 109
136 109
145:8 96
148 61
150 116

Proverbs
book of 1, 85, 102–4
31:10 104

Ecclesiastes
book of 65, 102–3, 129

Song of Songs
book of . . 27, 83–84, 102–4
6:8–9 95

Isaiah
book of 68, 102–3, 125
1:1 36
1–39 49
6:9–10 125
7:14 98
10:12–19 57
11:9 62
26:20 57
40–55 . . . . . 36, 48–49, 94
40:3 110
42:1–9 19
42:6 146
42:14 137
43:14–21 109
49:1–13 19
50:4–11 19

51:9 133
51:9–52:12 133
52:7 133
52:11 133
52:13–53:12 19
56–66 36
65:23 58

Jeremiah
book of 68, 102–3
7:9 94
7:21–23 79
18:1–12 64

Lamentations
book of 102–3, 125

Ezekiel
book of 68, 102–3
9–10 30
16:42 57
26–28 64
40–48 30

Daniel
book of 36, 102–3, 131
7:1 36
7–12 36

Hosea
book of 102–3
2:19 57
4:2 94
8:13 109
9:3 109
11 109

Joel
2:13 96

Amos
book of 124
2:4–16 57

Jonah
4:2 96

Micah
4:3 62
6:2–8 109
6:8 62

Habakkuk
2:5–14 22

Zephaniah
3:8 57

Zechariah
8:13 58

Malachi
book of 102–3
3:10 58
4:4–6 108

Matthew
1:23 98
3:16 30
4:4 110
6:11 110
6:24 61
8:23–27 20
16:18 60
27:51 59

Mark
1:3 110
7:13 106

Luke
1:34 98
9:30–31 110

John
1:1–3 . . . . 30, 59
1:14 . . . . 59, 110
6:30–59 110

Romans
book of 6, 132
1:21 58
1:22–23 58
3 115
3:1 60

5:12 65
7 115
8:19–23 59
8:29 59
9:4–5 79

1 Corinthians
3:9 77
5:7 109
10:4 110
15:25–27 99
15:49 59

2 Corinthians
4:4 59

Galatians
book of 19, 132
3 115
4:26–28 60

Ephesians
5:5 58
5:22–23 30

Colossians
1:15 59
3:5 58

Hebrews
book of 98–99
2:5–9 98
4:12 . . . . xii, 3
9–10 19
10:20 59
12:29 28

James
3:9–10 59

Revelation
book of 19, 30
17–18 22
20–22 30
21 59
21–22 20
21:3 30